SWAMP POP

SWAMP POP

Cajun and Creole Rhythm and Blues

Shane K. Bernard

University Press of Mississippi Jackson

The paper in this book meets the guidelines for permanence and durability of the
Committee on Production Guidelines for Book Longevity of the Council on
Library Resources.

Library of Congress Cataloging-in-Publication Data

Bernard, Shane K.
    Swamp pop : Cajun and Creole rhythm and blues / Shane K. Bernard.
        p.   cm. — (American made music series)
    Includes bibliographical references (p.   ), discographies, and index.
    ISBN 0-87805-875-3 (cloth : alk. paper). — ISBN 0-87805-876-1 (paper : alk. paper)
    1. Swamp pop music—History and criticism.   I. Title.   II. Series.
    ML3539.B47   1996
    781.64—dc20   95-53231
                                                                       CIP
                                                                       MN

British Library Cataloging-in-Publication data available

To K.T.B.

Almost inaudible now, the radio swung into a bilingual song by Cajun singer Rod Bernard and his friend Jack Clement. It was about a modern Cajun girl at the fais do-do, a Cajun-style Saturday night hoedown. The English version went:

> *She don't like to ride in my pirogue,*
> *Don't even know how to cook gumbo.*
> *She upsets her Cajun papa*
> *When she does the Twist at the fais do-do.*

So even the Cajuns are nervous about remaining themselves. But I think they will survive.

—Bern Keating, *National Geographic*, 1966

CONTENTS

ACKNOWLEDGMENTS

I wish to thank professors Carl Brasseaux, Barry Ancelet, and Jim Dormon of the University of Southwestern Louisiana for sharing their knowledge of South Louisiana's culture and history; editors JoAnne Prichard and Anne Stascavage of the University Press of Mississippi and musicologist David Evans of the University of Memphis for their guidance; music writers John Broven, Bill Millar, and Larry Benicewicz for offering advice and source material despite the long distances; my fellow student Julia Girouard for co-researching "Colinda"; musicians Charles Adcock and Ricky Rees for critiquing my opinions on music and for contributing to interviews; and especially musicologist Anne K. Simpson of the University of Southwestern Louisiana for assistance with musical analysis and transcriptions. In addition, I wish to thank the swamp pop musicians, songwriters, producers, and promoters who granted my requests for interviews, particularly Johnnie Allan for sharing his insights into swamp pop, helping to locate other interviewees, and allowing me access to his personal archives; and my father, Rod Bernard, for helping to arrange interviews, especially with a few reluctant interviewees.

I wish to acknowledge the following songwriters and publishers of song lyrics that appear in the text.

"Alligator Bayou" (E. Futch) La Lou Music BMI ℗ 1970. Reprinted by permission.

"The Back Door" (D. L. Menard) Flat Town Music BMI ℗ 1975. Reprinted by permission.

"Before I Grow Too Old" (Domino, Bartholomew, Guidry) EMI Unart Catalog, Inc. BMI ℗ 1960

"Breaking Up Is Hard to Do" (G. Bourgeois, H. Meaux) Songs of PolyGram International, Inc. BMI ℗ 1959

"Cajun Man" (Guidry, Guillot) Flat Town Music BMI ℗ 1966. Reprinted by permission.

"Cajun Rap Song" (M. Ducote, K. LaBorde, D. Normand) Flat Town Music BMI ℗ 1988. Reprinted by permission.

"Colinda" (anonymous) traditional Cajun folk song

"Done Most Everything" (Bobby Charles Guidry, C. C. Adcock) Marsh Island Music/Island Music Ltd. Admin. by Songs of PolyGram International, Inc. BMI © 1989

"Fais Do Do (Fay Doe Doe)" (Jack Clement, Rod Bernard) Copyright © 1962 Songs of PolyGram International, Inc. Used by permission. All rights reserved.

"Hippy-Ti-Yo" (Arr. M. Smith) Hip Hill Music BMI ℗ 1958. Reprinted by permission.

"I'm Leaving It Up to You" (D. Terry, Jr., Don F. Harris) Venice Music BMI ℗ 1963

"Later Alligator" (R. Guidry) Arc Music BMI ℗ 1956

"Let's Do the Cajun Twist" (Bourque, Norris) Flat Town Music BMI ℗ 1962. Reprinted by permission.

"Little Cajun Girl" (L. Martin, G. Rodrigue) Flat Town Music BMI ℗ 1961. Reprinted by permission.

"Lonely Days, Lonely Nights" (J. Guillot) Flat Town Music BMI ℗ 1959

"Mathilda" (Thierry, Khoury) Combine Music BMI ℗ 1959

"Mon chère bébé créole" (as sung by Dennis McGee) traditional Cajun/Creole folk song

"Opelousas Sostan" (B. Graeff, V. Palmer) Flat Town Music BMI ℗ 1971. Reprinted by permission.

"Pardon Mr. Gordon" (Bernard, Soileau) Jamil Music BMI ℗ 1958

"Please Accept My Love" (C. Garlow) Ft. Knox/Trio Music BMI ℗ 1958

"Promised Land" (Chuck Berry) Arc Music BMI ℗ 1964

"Recorded in England" (E. Hughes, R. Bernard) La Lou Music BMI ℗ 1966

"Slop and Stroll Jolie Blonde" (E. Shuler) TEK Music Publishing BMI ℗ 1960

"South to Louisiana" ["North to Alaska"] (Johnny Horton, Tillman B. Franks) © 1960 Twentieth Century Music Corp. © Renewed 1988 EMI Robbins Catalog, Inc. All rights controlled by EMI Robbins Catalog, Inc. (Publishing) and Warner Bros. Publications, Inc. (Print). All rights reserved. Reprinted by permission.

"Sweet Dreams" (Don Gibson) Acuff-Rose BMI ℗ 1963

"This Should Go On Forever" (J. Miller, B. Jolivette) Jamil Music BMI ℗ 1959

"I'm Twisted" (writer and publisher unknown)

"Your Picture" (R. Guidry) Arc Music BMI ℗ 1961

Some case studies appeared previously in a different form in *Now Dig This* (UK) and *Goldmine* music magazines.

FOREWORD

An Overview of South Louisiana's Cultural Development

South Louisiana arguably represents North America's greatest musical wellspring. In this century alone, cosmopolitan New Orleans has given the world jazz and has contributed immeasurably to the rise of rhythm and blues and rock 'n' roll, producing a seemingly endless list of internationally famed musicians. The musical contributions of rural south Louisiana—often obscured by the achievements of more visible performers from the neighboring metropolitan center—have been no less impressive. The region's French-speaking parishes, now commonly called Acadiana, spawned three very distinctive musical genres that also have enjoyed international popularity: Cajun, zydeco, and swamp pop music.

The decades-long coexistence of these genres in such a small geographical area belies the region's cultural diversity and complexity, which are enduring legacies of the bayou country's early development. South Louisiana's polyglot population constitutes what is widely recognized to be the most complex rural society in the United States. This society was forged in the frontier setting of the Attakapas and Opelousas posts, where natives of three continents were brought together by the fortunes of war.

At the time of the first transatlantic contacts, the Attakapas and Opelousas regions, initially encompassing all of southwestern Louisiana, were a sparsely populated area, a result (according to oral tradition) of efforts by neighboring native American tribes to exterminate the reputedly cannibalistic indigenous Attakapas. Despite overtures from tribesmen who were anxious to acquire iron implements, the Attakapas' unsavory reputation discouraged significant European expansion into the area until the 1760s. Beginning in that decade, successive waves of Europeans, native Frenchmen, and Acadian exiles established their homes along the region's major watercourses. African slaves accompanied some of these pioneers, particularly the European-born former French military officers who constituted the nucleus of the frontier elite.

This French frontier elite met with a difficult decision after France's loss in the Seven Years' War. Generally second or third sons barred from inheritance of estates by their birth order, these former officers had been given the opportunity, at the time of the colonial garrison's general discharge of September 15, 1763, to accept large land grants along the Louisiana frontier in lieu of reassignment to another part of the French empire. After accepting the proffered land, these former officers, like their counterparts who settled along the Mississippi, attempted to recreate upon the banks of Bayou Teche their vision of feudalistic France—with themselves as the local aristocracy.

The world view of these would-be aristocrats brought them into direct conflict with that of the groups they attempted to cast in the role of a colonial peasantry: recently discharged enlisted men from Fort Toulouse (in what is now Alabama) and the Acadian exiles. Despite their radically different backgrounds, the former enlisted men and the Acadians had much in common. The ancestors of both groups had come primarily from the Poitou province of France. Both sprang from peasant stock and had spent sufficient time along the North American frontier to cast off their ancestors' social and economic shackles and to develop not only a group identity, but a fierce sense of individualism. Both groups also shared a common language, customs, religion, and values.

In addition, both groups had endured misfortunes at the hands of the British. The members of the Fort Toulouse garrison, for example, had been forced to relocate because of the British occupation of Alabama in 1764, and their evacuation of the post had been complicated by the resistance of the local Alabama Indians with whom some of the enlisted men were allied by marriage. The hardships encountered by the Alabama immigrants, however, paled by comparison with those endured by the Acadians following their expulsion from Nova Scotia in 1755. By the 1750s British authorities had come to view the colony's Acadian population as a potential threat to Nova Scotia's internal security. Hence, in 1755 approximately six thousand Acadian settlers were removed forcibly from the Bay of Fundy Basin by British soldiers, placed on waiting ships, and then dispersed throughout the thirteen British seaboard colonies. Arriving shortly after the onset of hostilities between French and British forces along the Appalachian Mountains, the exiles were accorded a frigid reception by their reluctant hosts, who, like the Nova Scotian administrators, viewed the Acadians as a potential fifth column. The Acadians thus endured prolonged physical and economic hardship, neglect, and abuse at the hands of the British government and colonists.

Acadians who escaped the first wave of deportation fared even worse. Some six thousand to twelve thousand Acadians sought refuge at Cape Breton Island, Prince Edward Island, and in what is now New Brunswick after the onset of the 1755 deportations. Some of these refugees organized themselves into paramilitary resistance forces, but most of the refugees simply sought to avoid seizure and deportation. Harassed by the British navy in their new settlements along the northern coast of New Brunswick, hundreds of refugees succumbed to malnutrition and disease.

No longer willing to endure the staggering toll in human misery, members of the Acadian resistance surrendered to British authorities in Nova Scotia in late 1758. The British took these Acadians and their families to detention centers in Halifax, where they remained for the duration of the French and Indian War.

At the end of the conflict the Acadians imprisoned at Halifax capitalized upon a clause in the 1763 Treaty of Paris allowing the exiles an eighteen-month grace period in which to relocate upon French soil. Most of the surviving members of the Acadian resistance movement, under the leadership of Joseph Broussard *dit* Beausoleil, pooled their financial resources, chartered a ship, and traveled to New Orleans via Santo Domingo. The Acadians, who reached the colonial capital in February 1765, found the colony in the midst of a beef shortage. Having had extensive experience raising cattle in Canada, the Acadians were permitted by Louisiana's colonial government to travel to Bayou Teche, where they were expected to raise cattle on shares for retired French military officer Antoine Bernard d'Auterive. The agreement with d'Auterive soon dissolved and the Acadians established their own ranches.

The exiles quickly adapted to their new surroundings, and through their industriousness, pragmatism, and frugality, achieved their pre-dispersal standard of living within ten years of their arrival in Louisiana. The peasant values that formed the basis of the Acadians' success in Louisiana also served as a source of friction with the region's elite. Clashes between French Creole pretension and Acadian egalitarianism inevitably resulted from the groups' conflicting world views and served to reinforce the social, cultural, and economic barriers separating the groups; the clashes also served to forge a permanent ascribed association between the Acadians—popularly called Cajuns by the mid-nineteenth century—and poverty.

   This stereotype became so pervasive in Louisiana following the Civil War
that poor French speakers of non-Acadian backgrounds were universally regarded as Cajun by the beginning of the twentieth century. This ascriptive
association resulted in large part from the virtual collapse of south Louisiana's
economy in the wake of the Civil War. Indeed, a majority of white antebellum
freeholders were reduced to tenantry by 1880. The economic homogenization
of the white population caused a corresponding transformation of cultural mark-
ers. As economic distinctions between diverse immigrants disappeared, and as
the resulting intercultural exchanges between tenants of different backgrounds
increased, cultural blending occurred, producing not only a new identity for
the members of this group, but also a new, synthetic culture. By 1900 persons
with such distinctly non-Acadian surnames as Romero (Spanish), Hoffpauir
(German), McGee (Scots-Irish), and François (nineteenth-century French immi-
grant) were generally considered Cajuns because of their poverty and inevitable
intermarriage with French-speaking members of the Cajun community. No
area of French south Louisiana was immune from this trend. In fact, when the
area in which the Fort Toulouse refugees settled after 1764 seceded from St.
Landry Parish in 1910, the region was officially designated Evangeline Parish
(after Longfellow's poem, based loosely on the Acadian exile) because of the
population's presumed but nonexistent Acadian heritage.

   South Louisiana's French melting pot was profoundly influenced by the area's
African-American community. The Creoles of color, generally descendants
of black slaves and white planters, were particularly influential in the area's
cultural development. Though a tiny minority of Louisiana's African-American
community, the French-speaking Creoles of color nevertheless exercised a
degree of influence that far outstripped their demographic significance. As
with the Cajuns, the Creoles of color, who were universally free and generally
prosperous before the Civil War, endured a precipitous fall into tenantry in the
late nineteenth century.

   As a result of their tumbling economic fortunes, many Creoles of color
found themselves occupying the same economic niche as liberated slaves and
their descendants, from whom the Creoles had attempted to distance themselves for decades. As their self-imposed walls of insularity crumbled, the Creoles began to interact with other blacks to a far greater extent than during the
early post–Civil War period. Because most blacks in the plantation areas were
English-speaking and Protestant, the Creoles of color gravitated toward the
French-speaking black minority, with whom they shared a common religion,

Roman Catholicism. In the early twentieth century, intermarriage between members of the two groups, though limited, led to the creation of a new group, the members of which, in the late 1980s and early '90s, would come to identify themselves as black Creoles.

These French-speaking blacks (both black Creoles and Creoles of color) interacted daily with Cajuns, often working shoulder-to-shoulder with them in the cotton fields of the southwestern Louisiana prairie country. This daily inter-action and the resulting cross-cultural "pollination" gave birth to the two com-modities for which the region is most widely known: its cooking and its music.

The process of interethnic borrowing that gave birth to these cultural institu-tions also engendered swamp pop music. Like its predecessors, swamp pop was born during a period of significant social change. From the 1890s until the 1960s Cajuns were besieged by forces of Anglo-American intolerance. Fired by the progressivism of the age, the state government mandated compulsory education in 1916 and compulsory education in English in 1921. In the 1930s, '40, '50s and early '60s, co-opted members of the Cajun elite, who constituted a large percentage of the teaching faculties of south Louisiana's white public schools, ruthlessly attempted to stamp out Cajun French while denigrating Cajun culture as a whole. Creoles of color and black Creoles experienced a similar movement of enforced Americanization.

Young Cajun and Creole musicians were deeply affected by this atmosphere and sought a departure from the music of their elders. Generally born between 1935 and 1945, when more mainstream sounds like western swing and bluegrass threatened to overwhelm traditional south Louisiana sounds, swamp pop musi-cians, as teenagers, would produce a new musical style that reflected more ac-curately the realities of their changing world. In the 1950s and '60s, swamp pop songs and musicians enjoyed a degree of popularity unprecedented in the bayou country's rich musical tradition. For forty years swamp pop music has retained a large and devoted following in south Louisiana. This enduring loyalty attests to the continuing cultural and social relevance of the genre, which effectively mirrors the cultural blending that forged the region's distinctive ethnic groups.

Carl A. Brasseaux
Lafayette, Louisiana

SWAMP POP

LOUISIANA SATURDAY NIGHT: AN INTRODUCTION

Steering down the asphalt ribbon called Highway 190, you accelerate through the subtropical night across the flat prairie between Opelousas and Eunice, eager for an evening of rough-hewn south Louisiana music. Which nightclub to check out? you wonder. The Step Inn Club or the Green Lantern in Lawtell? The Purple Peacock in Eunice? Maybe the Jungle Lounge or the Rendezvous to the north at Ville Platte?

A flicker of neon catches your eye. Slowing to a crawl you pull into the graveled lot of one of the oldest, perhaps the largest, certainly the most legendary swamp pop nightspot: the Southern Club, on the outskirts of Opelousas. You enter the vast, smoky, dimly lit structure, cross a dance floor of swirling couples and glance at the familiar figures mingling around the bandstand: Johnnie Allan, Warren Storm, Rod Bernard, Tommy McLain, Clint West, Bobby Charles. A motley group, one performer might wear sneakers, worn-out blue jeans, and perhaps an old letter jacket; another, two-toned suedes, pleated slacks, a fancy dress coat, and a flashy tie studded with musical notes. Most share an interest in pomade and wild pompadours, but some prefer the simple flattop.

Allan takes the stage as a guitarist bangs out a random riff, a drummer stomps his bass pedal, and a mike screeches momentarily. The singer gives a quick nod and the band breaks into the opening strains of a typically gut-wrenching south Louisiana ballad. Eyes shut tightly, his face contorted as though in pain, Allan belts: "LONELY DAYS AND—*LONELY NIGHTS, DEAR* . . . I CRY MYSELF TO *SLEE—EEP!*"

You've just observed swamp pop in its natural habitat.

As the son of swamp pop pioneer Rod Bernard, I grew up around swamp pop artists and the music they created, but afforded the genre little attention

Earliest known photo of Rod Bernard and the Twisters, taken at the Southern Club, Opelousas, La., circa February 1957. Left to right: Mike Genovese, Charles Boudreaux, Rod Bernard (with guitar), Willie Harmon, and Charles Lyman. (Photo courtesy of Rebecca Boudreaux Duhon)

during my childhood. I vaguely recall the Shondells (my father's group, not Tommy James's) in their flashy, late '60s-style sports coats and narrow ties, waving goodbye as they left for a "dancejob" at some local nightspot. I remember Warren Storm and Cypress rehearsing in my family's usually tranquil living room, cables, monitors and mike stands strewn between the TV and couch, the drum set standing near the fireplace. And I recall my father's only appearance at the New Orleans Jazz and Heritage Festival, where he introduced me to his old friend, ailing zydeco legend Clifton Chenier.

I also remember a troupe of a dozen or so Englishmen appearing at my family's doorstep in 1979, quizzing my father about his early musical career, taking countless snapshots, and guzzling huge quantities of beer. I didn't know what the commotion was about and at the time I didn't care; I found our visitors' strange accents far more interesting and wanted only to continue kicking around my soccer ball with them in the backyard. Among those visitors, however, was music writer John Broven, who first introduced me (and the rest of south Louisiana) to the term *swamp pop*.

Still, I remained only passively interested in the genre until I tired of the Top 40 a few years later and sought refuge in the rockabilly sounds of artists like Elvis, Carl Perkins, Jerry Lee Lewis, and Roy Orbison. Rummaging through my father's record collection in search of vintage Sun issues, I discovered a variety of early swamp pop releases by family friends like Johnnie Allan, Tommy McLain, and Warren Storm—and I also unearthed dozens of my father's own recordings on the Carl, Jin, Hallway, La Louisianne, and Arbee labels. I curiously placed those fragile 45s on my turntable and to my delight found the same raw, unpolished qualities I admired so much in rockabilly. The sound was different, but I was hooked.

As my admiration grew for swamp pop, however, I became increasingly concerned about whether it could survive and about how it was perceived by other music enthusiasts. Of course my father's contributions to the genre made my concerns all the more personal. Working on a master's degree in American history at the time, I accepted Professor Carl A. Brasseaux's advice to adopt swamp pop as the subject of my thesis, which I eventually entitled "Twistin' at the Fais Do-Do: The Roots of South Louisiana's Swamp Pop Music." This volume draws considerably on that thesis. Due to the paucity of books on swamp pop music and artists (this study constitutes the first book dedicated solely to the genre) my research relied heavily on often hard-to-find collectors' and music magazines like *Now Dig This* (England), *Big Beat of the Fifties* (Australia), *American Music Magazine* (Sweden) and the more accessible *Goldmine* (USA). However, unlike most historians, who usually are confined to examining their subjects' musty literary remains, I actually was able to consult most of my subjects in person, as nearly all resided within a fifty-mile radius of my Lafayette home. Yet tracking down a long-retired swamp popper like King Karl challenged my resolve. (I finally found him one night sitting in his Toyota pickup truck at the Evangeline Maid Bakery near downtown, where he served irregularly as a security guard.) And although his former musical partner was easier to contact (I spotted his name in the Lafayette area phone book) finding his house on the prairies of rural St. Landry Parish proved more difficult. In the end, however, my efforts yielded over thirty hours of audiotaped interviews with nearly every major swamp pop pioneer.

But what, exactly, is *swamp pop*? The swamp pop sound is typified by highly emotional vocals, simple, unaffected (and occasionally bilingual) lyrics, tripleting honky-tonk pianos, bellowing sax sections, and a strong rhythm and blues backbeat. Upbeat compositions often possess the bouncy rhythms of Cajun and black Creole two-steps, and their lyrics frequently convey the local color and *joie de vivre* that pervades south Louisiana. Swamp popper Gene King's 1961 recording "Little Cajun Girl" exhibits these characteristics, coupling vivid, folksy lyrics with the animated beat of a traditional two-step:

> Hey little Cajun girl, let's go,
> *Allons au village.*
> We'll eat some *fricassé*
> And drink that *bon café.*
> Hey little Cajun girl, let's go,
> *Allons au village.*

Slow, usually melancholic swamp pop ballads, however—with their heavy, "triplety" feel, undulating bass lines, climactic turnarounds, and dramatic breaks—exhibit the heartbroken, what's-the-use-of-living laments common to many traditional Cajun and black Creole compositions, born generations ago of widespread poverty, hard living, and the loneliness of a largely rural existence. These qualities are illustrated notably in the swamp pop anthem "Mathilda," recorded in 1958 by black Creole swamp poppers Cookie and the Cupcakes:

> Mathilda I'll cry and cry for you,
> Yes, no matter what you do.
> Yes, I'll cry and cry in vain.
> I want my baby back again.[1]

Classics of the swamp pop genre include Dale and Grace's "I'm Leaving It Up to You" (1963), Johnny Preston's "Running Bear" (1959), Freddy Fender's "Before the Next Teardrop Falls" (1974), Phil Phillips's "Sea of Love" (1959) and Jimmy Clanton's "Just a Dream" (1958), all Top Ten national hits. Three of these recordings—"Running Bear," "I'm Leaving It Up to You" and "Before the Next Teardrop Falls"—reached number one on the national charts. In fact, over twenty swamp pop recordings have broken into the *Billboard Hot 100* since 1958. But in south Louisiana—the birthplace of swamp pop—fans and artists regard as even more essential to the basic swamp pop repertoire numerous songs that are less popular nationally. These standards include such regional hits as Clint West's "Big Blue Diamonds" (1965), Tommy McLain's "Sweet Dreams" (1966), Randy and the Rockets' "Let's Do the Cajun Twist" (1962), T. K. Hulin's "Graduation Night" (1964), Rufus Jagneaux's "Opelousas Sostan" (1971), and Johnnie Allan's "South to Louisiana" (1962).[2]

From obscure south Louisiana origins swamp pop went on to exert an influence on popular music both in the U.S. and abroad. Notable swamp

Johnny Preston (at the microphone) with his guitarist, Johnny Piggot, circa 1959. (Photo courtesy of the Johnnie Allan Collection)

pop–inspired tunes include Bill Haley and the Comets' cover (rerecording) of "Later Alligator," the Rolling Stones' version of Barbara Lynn's "You'll Lose a Good Thing," the Honeydrippers' rendition of "Sea of Love," and the Beatles' original composition "Oh! Darling," which exudes the triplet rhythmic quality and emotionalism typical of swamp pop ballads. Recently the swamp pop sound appeared in country and western hits like T. Graham Brown's "I Tell It Like It Used to Be," Mark Collie's "Shame Shame Shame Shame," and Billy Joe Royal's "Burned Like a Rocket."

The makers of swamp pop music describe the genre in various terms. One might refer to it as white rhythm and blues; another as a combination of rock 'n' roll and country and western music; and yet another as rockabilly with a strong blues element. A few swamp pop musicians deny the genre possesses any distinctive qualities, insisting it resembles music hailing from anywhere in the U.S. Others, however, refer to swamp pop as a blend of many influences arising in a specific geographic region, a view embraced by this study. Specifically, I consider swamp pop to be a rhythm and blues hybrid that is influenced mainly by New Orleans rhythm and blues, country and western, and Cajun and black Creole music, and that is indigenous to southeast Texas and the Acadiana region of south Louisiana. (Acadiana embraces a twenty-two parish area of south Louisiana officially recognized by the state legislature for its sizable Cajun population.)

Unlike its Cajun and zydeco sister genres, which divide along racial lines and depend strongly on folk instrumentation and francophone lyrics, swamp pop is a biracial genre that relies primarily on English lyrics and 1950s rhythm and blues instrumentation. No contrast exists between swamp pop performed by Cajuns and that performed by black Creoles: The sounds are one and the same. In fact, so convincingly did Cajun swamp poppers mimic their black Creole counterparts—whom Cajuns tended to regard as superior artists, and who originated the genre shortly before Cajuns adopted and contributed to its developing sound—that many radio listeners and record consumers mistakenly regarded the Cajun swamp poppers as black performers.

Swamp pop first appeared in its south Louisiana homeland in the early 1950s, though its pioneers made no conscious effort to create a new, distinct musical sound. A product of increasingly rapid Americanization in rural and small-town south Louisiana, swamp pop represents the natural result of colliding cultural elements—Cajun and Creole, black and white, French and English, rural and urban, folk and mainstream—that coalesced on the prairies of southwestern Louisiana to create a harmonious whole. In this way swamp pop's birth parallels the rise of other 1950s regional genres like New Orleans rhythm and blues and Memphis rockabilly.

Although a closer relative to New Orleans rhythm and blues, swamp pop shares many qualities with its distant Tennessee cousin. Swamp poppers and rockabillies, for instance, drew heavily on their local cultures for inspiration and source material, and exhibited their peculiar dialects and inflections both in song and everyday speech. Both also hailed largely from working-class families residing in rural and small-town settings, and as musical innovators fused black and white sounds to create new musical genres that initially defied categorization. And unlike New Orleans performers, who frequently relied on studio musicians during recording sessions, swamp poppers and rockabillies usually recorded with their own groups, offering listeners a rough, homespun quality often absent from the somewhat more refined and complex New Orleans rhythm and blues recordings.[3]

Swamp pop filled a musical void in Acadiana where no local, distinct, youth-oriented pop idiom existed prior to its advent, though its sister genres, Cajun and zydeco, in varying degrees drew on the rhythm and blues sound, which had drifted into the region via radio, records, and big-city traveling bands. (A few mainstream rhythm and blues artists, however, did operate locally in Acadiana during the 1950s, among them Good Rockin' Bob, Classie Ballou, Jay Nelson, and Leroy Washington, but their styles failed to command the attention of local or national audiences and did not contribute directly to the advent of a distinctly regional sound.) By 1952—two years before Elvis helped to launch rock 'n' roll by cutting "That's All Right" in Memphis's Sun Studio, and three years before Bill Haley and the Comets' "Rock Around the Clock" impacted American pop culture—the diverse, exotic ingredients required for the genesis of swamp pop already had converged to create this distinct rhythm and blues subgenre. (*Rhythm and blues* is essentially an umbrella term for a variety of related but distinct musical styles encompassing virtually all black popular music from the late 1940s through the '60s except modern jazz and gospel.)[4]

Although often misunderstood and even ignored by many enthusiasts of south Louisiana's ethnic music, swamp pop deserves recognition and preservation as the region's third major indigenous genre, along with Cajun and zydeco—not only because it once thrived in the region and even attracted a national audience, but because it descends from traditional Cajun and black Creole sources. Most swamp poppers grew up immersed in Cajun and black Creole culture and music, and as children also absorbed the strains of country and western music, which had appeared in the region by the mid-1930s; but it was the appearance of big-city rhythm and blues on the Cajun and black Creole prairies that acted as the catalyst for swamp pop's creation during the early 1950s. Although swamp pop is primarily a local rhythm and blues idiom, it bears the imprint of its ethnic roots and thus should be viewed *not* as an aberration of traditional music (as some maintain) but, like Cajun and zydeco, as a positive expression of the entire Cajun and black Creole experience. Information gathered from over fifty interviews with swamp pop musicians, songwriters, producers, and promoters supports this interpretation.

The subject of south Louisiana, however, seems to invite inaccuracy among writers, including music writers, many of whom frequently misuse terms like *Cajun* and *Creole* and often incorrectly portray New Orleans as the center

Van Broussard performing at Dutch Town High School, Dutch Town (Ascension Parrish), La., 1957. (Photo courtesy of Jimmy Rogers/CSP Records)

of Cajun and rural black Creole culture. Although it supports a large urban black Creole population, New Orleans bears no legitimate claim to rural black Creole culture or to Cajun culture. In fact, only 1 percent of Orleans Parish residents (compared to 50 percent of residents in the central Acadiana parish of Vermilion) list *Cajun* or *Acadian* as their primary ethnic identification; parishes immediately abutting metropolitan New Orleans report similarly low Cajun populations—less than 7 percent. Many writers also imperil the accuracy of their research by using hip-sounding hyperbole. Describing south Louisiana music as "that cricket-chirpin', frog-croaking, spanish-moss drippin' sound," for instance, reveals little or nothing to the reader. This study of south Louisiana's swamp pop music attempts to avoid such weaknesses and tries to place swamp pop in its proper cultural perspective.[5]

Although many sources define *Cajuns* as "Louisianians who descend from French-speaking Acadians," increasing numbers of scholars offer a more complex, more comprehensive view, ascribing the character of present-day Cajuns to a dynamic and continual process of ethnic interaction. While most early pre-expulsion Acadians hailed from the Centre-Ouest provinces of France, others descended from families of Spanish, Irish, Scottish, English, Basque, and even native American origins. After their expulsion from Nova Scotia in 1755, exiled Acadians in Louisiana again intermarried with other ethnic groups, particularly with French, Spanish, English, German, and later Anglo-American settlers, as well as with native Americans. In addition, Cajuns borrowed much of their culture from their black Creole neighbors. This cross-cultural blending in Acadia and south Louisiana transformed many diverse ethnic groups into a single new ethnic group: the Cajuns. Thus, present-day Cajuns derive not merely from French-speaking Acadians, but from a variety of ethnic groups over which Acadian culture appears to have predominated (at least until this century, when Cajuns experienced a widespread process of Americanization).[6]

The meaning of *Creole* is even more complex than that of *Cajun* because historically many types of Creoles have existed, a fact often overlooked by those delving into south Louisiana music. The term *Creole* actually was coined by Spanish and Portuguese settlers in the New World and originally referred to anyone of Old World ancestry born in the colonial New World. By the antebellum period, however, the term was applied commonly to anyone born in Louisiana, regardless of language, social status, or ethnic origin (except native Americans). Thus, white Louisianians—including those of full or mixed Spanish, French, German, English, and even Cajun extract—technically qualified as Creoles.

Louisianians of African descent also identify themselves as Creoles and over the last half century have come virtually to monopolize the term. In fact, today two distinct but related African-derived groups utilize the term jointly, namely, *black Creoles* and *Creoles of color*, both primarily of Catholic, francophone descent, yet distinguishable from one another by subtle ethnic and cultural differences. Creoles of color, for instance, tend to possess lighter complexions and choose to segregate themselves from black Creole society (and vice versa), perpetuating a longstanding enmity between the two related ethnic groups. Recently, however, Creoles of color and black Creoles inaugurated a new era of cooperation aimed at self-preservation, and in general both groups today refer to themselves simply as Creoles (although for clarity's sake this study usually refers to all Creoles of African descent as *black Creoles* to avoid confusion with white Creole groups). Incidentally, the oft-used phrase *black Cajun*—employed by a small number of black Creoles before the recent surge in their ethnic pride, and still utilized by outsiders unaware of accepted ethnic labels—is a misnomer, as the word *Cajun* generally denotes a person of white ancestry. In fact, many black Creoles take offense at being dubbed Cajuns, if only because the term appears to deny the existence of a distinct black Creole culture.[7]

Although Cajuns and black Creoles possess separate, well-defined cultures, they do share a degree of common cultural and linguistic traits, borrowing from one another through the process of acculturation. This shared heritage exhibits itself most clearly in the indigenous music of south Louisiana. Cajun and black Creole music developed side-by-side and cross-cultural borrowing occurred frequently, the early 1930s duet recordings of Cajun musician Dennis McGee and black Creole accordionist Amédé Ardoin illustrating this practice. But these genres borrowed from numerous other sources; as folklorist Barry Jean Ancelet notes about an early McGee recording, "the singer, whose name reflects Irish roots and whose facial features reflect American Indian origins, describes the loneliness of a cowboy's life in French to the tune of a European mazurka clearly influenced by the blues." Traditional Cajun and black Creole music helped in turn to engender south Louisiana's third major indigenous genre: swamp pop, a combination of rhythm and blues, country and western, and Cajun and black Creole music.[8]

A few other matters of interpretation also demand attention. For instance, the term *south Louisiana* often is applied in the text as a "catch-all" phrase to describe both the Acadiana region *and* a small portion of southeast Texas. In fact, swamp pop hails almost exclusively from these two adjoining regions. Without exception, however, southeast Texas swamp pop artists are Cajuns or black Creoles whose parents migrated across the Sabine River around World War II to labor in the Beaumont–Port Arthur region's oil- and defense-related plants. These transplanted Cajuns and black Creoles maintained strong familial and cultural links to south Louisiana, inspiring some to refer jokingly to their adopted home as "Cajun Lapland" (where Cajun country laps over into southeast Texas).[9]

I regard Cajun music as both accordion- and string-based music (though less influential Cajun folk ballads, performed a capella, persist to the present); and I regard black Creole music as zydeco and its precursors, such as *juré* (described as "Louisiana French shouts accompanied only by improvised percussion . . . and vocal counterpoints") and *la-la* and *pic-nic* music (both denoting post–World

War II accordion-based dance music shortly before its evolution into modern zydeco around the early 1950s).[10]

In the endnotes I usually cite the most readily available sources for recordings (preferably on compact disc) rather than original, often hard-to-find sources (outmoded 45 rpm singles, for instance—although a discography of 45s appears in the swamp pop timeline at the back of this volume). Original releases are cited only when more accessible sources cannot be located.

Finally, I chose the subjects of my case studies because they typify so well the swamp popper experience: All were young Cajun and black Creole musicians who were heavily influenced by the francophone cultures and music of south Louisiana and southeast Texas and who unwittingly helped to create a new indigenous musical genre carrying the mark of their ethnic heritage. All subjects checked their studies for accuracy and completeness at least once, except for Huey "Cookie" Thierry. Thierry's study was inspected by his manager, Ernest Jacobs, who discussed the work with Thierry and other early members of their musical group.

WHO NAMED IT SWAMP POP AND WHAT IS IT?

Swamp pop goes by many different names: *swamp bop, swamp rock, Cajun rock, Cajun pop, bayou rock 'n' roll, bayou boogie, bayou beat,* even *the Gulf Coast sound.* The terms *south Louisiana music* and *south Louisiana rock 'n' roll,* however, appear more frequently, as does the more generic *swamp music,* usually encompassing both *swamp pop* and *swamp blues*—the latter of which actually hails from beyond Acadiana (mainly from around Baton Rouge) and is related to swamp pop only insofar as many swamp bluesmen (like Slim Harpo, Lightnin' Slim, and Silas Hogan) recorded in Crowley, where they were backed in the studio by local swamp poppers. But among fans and artists the most popular name by far is *swamp pop music* or simply *swamp pop.* From this term derives the more recent coinage *swamp popper* (or, less commonly, *swamp popster*), which refers to a performer of the genre; it also can refer to a song or even an enthusiast of the genre. Despite its wide currency, much confusion surrounds the origin and meaning of the term *swamp pop.* While its performers concern themselves mainly with performing, serious swamp pop enthusiasts continue to debate the question, "What is swamp pop?"[1]

Surprisingly, the term *swamp pop* originated not in south Louisiana nor even in the United States, but in England, where young music enthusiasts stumbled on the imported sound shortly after its American inception. As author of the first extensive study of swamp pop music, John Broven of Newick, East Sussex, often is cited as the term's inventor. Broven, however, attributes the term to his compatriot, music writer Bill Millar of Dartford, Kent, who confesses in a 1978 issue of the English music magazine *New Kommotion,* "All these years I've been into blues, soul, doowop and swamp-pop, especially swamp-pop . . . . When the entire school was fixated by Presley's Neapolitan balladry, I'd be monopolizing the communal Dansette with 'This Should Go On Forever,' 'I'm a Fool to Care,' or 'Breaking Up Is Hard to Do,' revelling in the secret loveliness of it all. Where those records actually came from was anybody's guess, but now we know better."[2]

Millar states he probably coined the term *swamp pop* in the late 1960s, observing that he refers to swamp popper Warren Storm's "straight from the swamps appeal" in a 1969 article in the English music magazine *Shout.* Millar in turn traces his inspiration for this phrase to the American music trade magazine *Billboard,* which applied a similar phrase (probably around 1960) to Baton Rouge bluesman Lightnin' Slim. He desired a more concise phrase, however, and coined *swamp pop,* a term he used informally until the appearance of his ground-breaking article "Swamp Pop-Music [*sic*] from Cajun Country." Published in 1971 in the English pop music weekly *Record Mirror,* the article contains the earliest known use of the term *swamp pop.* The phrase, however, appears only in the heading, which leads Millar to suggest that a "sub-editor" borrowed the term offhandedly for the article. But this, he adds, is unlikely: "I've no way of remembering how I coined the phrase (if it was actually down to me)," he writes, "[but] . . . I think I was calling it 'swamp pop' for years before I was writing about it."[3]

Millar's invention gradually caught on with other English music writers, among them John Broven, who acquired a taste for the peculiar sounds of south Louisiana in grammar school, the English equivalent to American high school. Around 1957 or 1958 he befriended fellow music enthusiast Mike Leadbitter, called by Broven a "forgotten hero" of music writing. (Leadbitter died prematurely in 1974.) Encouraging each other's interests, they zealously compiled discographies and corresponded with American producers, particularly south Louisiana producers. Echoing Millar, Broven recalls in his *South to Louisiana: The Music of the Cajun Bayous*: "Together we began delving into the uncharted mysteries of the South Louisiana music scene. And what treasures we found! Until then I had been blissfully unaware of the bayou origins of rock 'n' roll classics in my record collection like 'This Should Go On Forever' by Rod Bernard, . . . 'Sea of Love' by Phil Phillips, and 'I'm a Fool to Care' by Joe Barry."[4]

Around 1960 or 1961 Broven and friend Leadbitter pieced together enough clues to realize that many of their favorite recording artists hailed from south Louisiana. By this time Broven had entered the banking industry, but in his spare time he continued to gather information on the unusual music from overseas. In addition, Broven wrote for and edited the English music magazine *Blues Unlimited.* Leadbitter cofounded this publication in 1963 and contributed

Warren Storm at the Rainbow Club, Kaplan, La., 1958. (Photo courtesy of the Johnnie Allan Collection)

a regular column entitled "Cajun Corner." He also conducted several fact-finding tours of south Louisiana during the late 1960s and early '70s. In his wake followed other English music writers, including Broven.[5]

Broven's travels in the 1970s and early '80s resulted in the publication of two important books: *Rhythm and Blues in New Orleans* (published in Europe as *Walking to New Orleans: The Rhythm and Blues of New Orleans*) and *South to Louisiana,* the first musical study to recognize and afford equal attention to south Louisiana's three major indigenous genres—Cajun, zydeco, and swamp pop. During his research Broven avoided use of the local terms *south Louisiana music* and *south Louisiana rock 'n' roll,* regarding both as cumbersome and the latter as "loosely and often incorrectly applied" because *rock 'n' roll* suggests "fast, beatty music all the time." Broven also objected to the term because "for [those of] us who lived through the era, classic rock 'n' roll lasted from 1956 to 1959. After that the music became *rock. Swamp pop* has lasted far longer than 1959, so *south Louisiana rock 'n' roll* is not strictly correct on this basis." His decision to use the term *swamp pop* in his interviews and in his published works (which are more readily available in the U.S. than those of other English music writers) accounts largely for its current popularity in south Louisiana.[6]

In fact, *swamp pop* quickly became the term of preference among swamp pop fans and artists, finding particularly strong support in performer Johnnie Allan, widely hailed as the "ambassador of swamp pop" because of his efforts to promote and preserve the genre both in the U.S. and abroad. A few swamp poppers, however—such as Rod Bernard and Roy Perkins—detest the term for various reasons. Although aware of the term, others, like Bobby Charles, express indifference regarding the swamp pop label. "Somebody told me I was a swamp pop musician," he recalls, "I said 'Oh, *really?*' I mean, I didn't know what the hell they were talking about . . . I just thought it was people who lived in the swamp who had a pop record, I don't know! . . . [But] if you got to name your children, I guess you have to give it a name, too!"[7]

Nevertheless, *swamp pop* continues to gain usage in its homeland and abroad. American music writers like New Orleanians Jeff Hannusch (also known as "Almost Slim," formerly of New Orleans' *Wavelength* magazine and author of *I Hear You Knockin': The Sound of New Orleans Rhythm and Blues*) and Rick Olivier (or "Rico," also formerly of *Wavelength*) employ the term freely in their works, as does Baltimore-based music writer Larry Benicewicz, who contributes numerous swamp pop-related articles to the *Newsletter of the Baltimore Blues Society* (also called *Bluesrag*) and the slick *Blues Life Journal* of Vienna, Austria. Lending greater validity to the term *swamp pop,* folklorist Barry Jean Ancelet of the University of Southwestern Louisiana employs the term in his academic publications, as does music historian Mirek Kocandrle of Boston's Berklee College of Music, who lists swamp pop as a distinct genre in his *History of Rock and Roll: A Selective Discography.* Belgian musicologist Robert Sacré of the University of Liège employs *swamp pop* in his book *Musiques cajun, créole et zydeco,* and French music writer Bernard Boyat uses the term in his articles on south Louisiana music. The term also appears in the massive *Guinness Encyclopedia of Popular Music* and in English music writer Charlie Gillett's *Sound of the City: The Rise of Rock 'n' Roll,* early editions of which described the genre as "bayou blues" and "cajun." (It remains to be seen whether an increasingly notable trend among some music writers to apply *swamp pop* to practically any pop-oriented sound even remotely associable with south Louisiana will help to promote or dilute authentic swamp pop music.)[8]

Despite the term's widespread use, the question remains: What is swamp pop? Music writers frequently cite two competing views, the most popular of

A Paul Harris photo of Johnnie Allan (far left) with British swamp pop enthusiasts/music writers (left to right) Charlie Gillett, Bill Millar, Ray Topping, and John Broven at a London pub, June 10, 1981. (Photo courtesy of Paul Harris)

which derives from New Orleans rhythm and blues performer Mac Rebennack, better known as "Dr. John." This view holds that swamp pop consists only of slow ballads with E flat–B flat chord progressions. A glance at the original source of this definition, however—the liner notes of Rebennack's 1972 *Gumbo* album—reveals that the performer makes no reference to *swamp pop* nor attempts to define any musical genre. Rather, he merely describes one of the album's tracks, a cover of New Orleans rhythm and blues artist Earl King's "Those Lonely Lonely Nights," as "a classic south Louisiana two-chord (E-flat B-flat) slow ballad"—a far cry from declaring all swamp pop songs slow ballads. Based on misquoted data, this alleged view of swamp pop must be dismissed as groundless. A second, more obscure view, however, issues from acclaimed swamp pop saxophonist Harry Simoneaux. His clever, highly quotable definition—"half Domino and half fais do-do"—correctly implies the important roles of New Orleans rhythm and blues (Fats *Domino*) and traditional Cajun music (*fais do-do*) on swamp pop's development. Inevitably, his witticism neglects several other vital influences, such as country and western and black Creole music.[9]

The issue of *swamp pop*'s meaning actually turns upon several points of debate, such as what cultural forces created and influenced swamp pop and whether swamp pop constitutes a rock 'n' roll or rhythm and blues idiom. The most controversial issue, however, concerns the ballad/rocker question: Does swamp pop consist only of slow, usually melancholic ballads like Cookie and the Cupcakes' "Mathilda," Rod Bernard's "This Should Go On Forever" and Tommy McLain's "Sweet Dreams," or does it also include more upbeat rockers like Johnnie Allan's "Promised Land," Randy and the Rockets' "Let's Do the Cajun Twist" and Lil' Bob and the Lollipops' "I Got Loaded"? Music writers tend to fall into one of two camps, backing either a broad or narrow interpretation of *swamp pop*. (This parallels a similar debate among rockabilly enthusiasts, many of whom regard that genre as consisting only of bluesy rockers, despite the recording of more country-influenced ballads like Elvis's "I Forgot to Remember to Forget," Carl Perkins's "Sure to Fall" and Jerry Lee Lewis's "Crazy Arms.")

Swamp pop music often evokes comparisons to gumbo, a traditional south Louisiana dish containing a diversity of ingredients and based on a blend of influences. Broven's description of swamp pop confirms the validity of the comparison: he characterizes it as a mixture of Cajun emotionalism, hillbilly (country and western) melodies, and New Orleans–style rhythm and blues instrumentation stressing the guitar, piano, and saxophone. Jeff Hannusch calls it a "hybrid" musical style combining Cajun music and New Orleans rhythm and blues. Larry Benicewicz concurs, identifying in swamp pop a blend of rhythm and blues (particularly from New Orleans) and the "inherent melancholia" of Cajun music. New Orleans writer Macon Fry calls swamp pop "a blend of New Orleans R&B, Country, and Gulf Coast Blues with a Cajun French accent." Washington, D.C., music writer Joe Sasfy describes it as a fusion of Cajun music, country, and Domino-style rock 'n' roll. And Bill Millar notes that "the influences [lie] as much in the intensity of early Elvis and the black music of Fats Domino as the French-Cajun style of Joseph Falcon." Comparing it to "Mama's best clean-out-the-icebox-gumbo," Rick Olivier offers a colorful, comprehensive description of swamp pop (and aptly notes the influence of popular black artists from beyond Louisiana, who, though eclipsed by New Orleans rhythm and blues performers, also impacted the developing genre): "Take Fats Domino's piano triplets, some of Hank Williams' pathos, take the joyous spirit, happy harmonies, and incessant beat of good [Cajun or zydeco] chanky-chank, take some Jimmy

Reed funk and a little of B. B.'s blues, take the simple but brilliant compositions of Cookie Thierry or Bobby Charles, the great vocals of Phil Phillips or Rod Bernard, mix this up with the powerful playing of the area's best musicians and you get a twenty-five-year-old recipe for real south Louisiana rock 'n' roll called swamp pop."[10]

Despite the similarity of these descriptions, a few divergent opinions are apparent: Olivier, for instance, views the contribution of Cajun music as essentially upbeat, while Benicewicz sees it as melancholic. Of course, Cajun music exhibits a wide spectrum of emotions; compare, for instance, Dennis McGee's mournful "O malheureuse" to his festive "Happy One-Step," or Doc Guidry's tearful "La valse d'amitié" to his lively rendition of "Colinda." Nevertheless, it is significant that these writers identify intense emotionalism as Cajun music's chief contribution to swamp pop music. And if this is the primary gift of Cajun music to swamp pop, so it is also of black Creole music, an equally emotional genre influencing swamp pop not only through Cajun swamp poppers—who were extremely familiar with zydeco and its precursors—but also through the handful of dynamic, talented black Creole swamp poppers, most of whom grew up listening to and even performing traditional black Creole music.[11]

Another matter of contention, however, regards the idiomatic character of swamp pop: is it rock 'n' roll, or is it rhythm and blues? The genre evidently originated in the early 1950s among black Creoles playing a distinctive rhythm and blues style (a sort of proto–swamp pop) in largely rural and small-town south Louisiana nightclubs. Cajuns shortly adopted the sounds pioneered by their black Creole neighbors, adding stronger Cajun and country and western elements. (This musical process parallels what occurred throughout the South in the 1950s, when white, often teenage Southerners embraced the rhythm and blues music developed by young black Southerners.) Besides these few minor alterations, swamp pop changed little after its adoption by Cajun swamp poppers; in fact, its stability seems to stem from the Cajuns' desire to imitate their black Creole counterparts. Swamp pop's resistance to change accounts for its retention of uniquely '50s melodies, vocal styles, and instrumentation, and this conservatism in part explains the genre's decline in popularity and near extinction during the mid-to-late 1960s, when most swamp pop artists refused to embrace the "Mersey sound" of the British Invasion and declined to participate in the subsequent "rock" explosion.

Swamp poppers' devotion to the genre's rhythm and blues roots suggests swamp pop remains essentially a rhythm and blues hybrid. In his article "Rock!

It's Still Rhythm and Blues," music scholar Lawrence Redd, however, claims that "for nearly three decades now, rock has been regarded by many as separate and apart from rhythm 'n' blues, but references to the music in the early fifties indicate that the two terms were used interchangeably. It was in early 1957 that the first suggestion of a distinction between the musics appeared in print [in *Billboard*, but] . . . no rationale was offered to explain how and when rock became a 'distinct idiom.'"[12]

Redd contends that major American record companies, hoping to remove negative racial connotations from popular youth-oriented music, conspired to split rock 'n' roll and rhythm and blues into separate genres. Stressing the artificiality of the split, Redd insists that in reality the genres remained united, a view strongly applicable at least to swamp pop music. The tradition of interethnic borrowing between Cajun and black Creole musicians (for example, the biracial McGee-Ardoin recordings of the early 1930s, featuring a Cajun fiddler and a black Creole accordionist) may have helped to preserve the natural union of rhythm and blues and rock 'n' roll in south Louisiana long after their forced segregation in other regions. So the terms *rock 'n' roll* and *rhythm and blues* both apply to swamp pop, as the genre is simultaneously rock 'n' roll and rhythm and blues. (For clarity's sake, however, this study most often employs the term *rhythm and blues* rather than *rock 'n' roll*.)[13]

The most problematic issue, however, remains the ballad/rocker question, and over this matter pioneer swamp pop writers Bill Millar and John Broven square off politely. Other writers tend to support one of their rival views. One could argue that Millar's narrow interpretation—that swamp pop consists only of slow, usually melancholic ballads—holds precedence because he invented the term *swamp pop*. But Millar has altered his concept of the genre during the past twenty-five years, shifting from an extremely broad to an inversely narrow interpretation. In his 1971 article "Swamp Pop-Music from Cajun Country," for example, Millar not only identifies as swamp pop the tell-tale ballads (Phil Phillips's "Sea of Love," Joe Barry's "I'm a Fool to Care," Cookie and the Cupcakes' "Got You on My Mind") but also several upbeat songs, including Rod Bernard's rockabilly-ish "Pardon Mr. Gordon" and Cleveland Crochet's accordion-driven "Sugar Bee." Millar even cites as swamp pop a few upbeat songs from far beyond south Louisiana, and seems to regard as being within the genre's realm covers of "Jambalaya" by Jimmy C. Newman and Fats Domino (as well as the original by Hank Williams, Sr.). Millar now dismisses the 1971 *Record Mirror* article as "naive," however, asserting, "For me swamp pop describes *ballads,* i.e., the big hits of . . . [Rod Bernard], Joe Barry, Dale & Grace, Jivin' Gene, etc. Of course, these and other South Louisiana artists sang up-tempo songs and when they did they sang rock 'n' roll (not especially distinctive from rock 'n' roll anywhere else in the U.S.A.). I know that's not quite true, but what I'm trying to say is that there is a certain ballad sound that can be identified with South Louisiana."[14]

On the other hand, Broven advocates a broad interpretation of *swamp pop,* encompassing ballads and rockers. "The musical sound [of swamp pop]," he comments in *South to Louisiana,* "centered on gentle, melodic ballads cast within a narrow format . . . . But the up-tempo rock 'n' roll outings were still an essential part of any swamp-pop repertoire." Broven repeats elsewhere that "Swamp-pop music consists of fast and slow songs." He thus alludes to Johnnie Allan's cover of the Chuck Berry rocker "Promised Land" as "an intriguing swamp-pop adaptation of an R&B song, enlivened by the Cajun accordion sound." Likewise, he considers the Ace (UK) label *Rod Bernard* album, containing ballads and rockers, as "swamp pop at its *varied* infectious best" (emphasis added). Following this example, Jeff Hannusch extends the boundaries of swamp pop even farther, noting that the boisterous "Cajun Rap Song" by the south Louisiana group Cypress City "proves that swamp pop can be influenced by most any style of music—even rap."[15]

In the end, a broad interpretation seems most natural because all of swamp pop's major influences—Cajun, black Creole, rhythm and blues, and country and western music—contain slow and fast, melancholy and joyful compositions. Indeed, nothing in the term *swamp pop* inherently suggests a narrow definition. *Swamp* merely refers to the music's geographic origin (and somewhat misleadingly, as the region primarily consists of prairies, marshes, and river country). And *pop* merely suggests pop music—or, rather, *popular music,* a general term that covers a variety of genres and applies to music reflecting the average taste and intelligence of a people. More specifically, however, *pop* refers to "the melodic side of rock . . . which strives for memorable tunes and clear sentiments . . . [and] also connotes accessibility, disposability and other low-culture values." Weighing the merits and shortcomings of these diverse and sometimes irreconcilable views on swamp pop music, and on rock 'n' roll and rhythm and blues in general, I offer my own definition of *swamp pop:*

> A rhythm and blues hybrid indigenous to southeast Texas and the Acadiana region of south Louisiana, and influenced mainly by New Orleans rhythm and blues, country and western, and Cajun and black Creole music.

This definition embraces the broad interpretation of *swamp pop* and recognizes the rather obvious influences of New Orleans rhythm and blues and country and western music. It also acknowledges the often subtle yet nonetheless vital role of Cajun and black Creole music.[16]

Regarding the geographic limits imposed by the definition: Although some transplanted Cajuns and black Creoles live beyond south Louisiana and southeast Texas (having departed their traditional homelands in sizable numbers since around World War II), the great majority of Cajuns and black Creoles—and the great majority of swamp pop artists—reside in southeast Texas and the Acadiana region of south Louisiana. The vital elements restricting swamp pop to these specific regions are Cajun and black Creole culture and music: the genre emerged and thrived only where these forces dominated the local cultural landscape. Indeed, an adequate understanding of swamp pop music requires an examination of Cajun and black Creole history and culture, influences overlooked or at least downplayed by past inquiries into the genre.

THE SOUND OF SWAMP POP

Classically trained listeners may discern in the swamp pop sound—particularly in its ballad form—a limited melodic range and a lack of dynamic nuance. These compositional qualities, however, are common to most popular musical genres, including rhythm and blues, rock, blues, gospel, and country and western music. But even within the context of popular music, swamp pop impresses with its sameness of harmony and structure. Despite formulaic qualities, swamp pop compositions often lend themselves to variation, improvisation, added measures, breaks (dramatic pauses), rides (solos), and other interpretive devices, possibly stemming from the informal musical education of swamp pop artists, who rely almost exclusively on their "play-by-ear" abilities rather than on "constraining" musical notation. Swamp pop's ingenuity lies less in its structure or harmony (which often resemble those of more mainstream rhythm and blues idioms) than in its remarkably intense emotionalism.

The genre appears to have borrowed this peculiar intensity from traditional Cajun and black Creole music, which, while they capture a wide range of emotions, excel at conveying pathos and despair. Renowned Cajun fiddler Dewey Balfa explains, "In Cajun music you can hear the lonesome sound and the hurt . . . just like the blues sound of the black man is a sound of deep hurt, deep sorrow. The Acadians had it very tough from Nova Scotia down to Louisiana, and when they did get to Louisiana they had a hard time. And sometimes I feel that the Cajun sounds are of the loneliness and hardship they had back then." This tendency emerges even in the earliest Cajun recordings, such as Dennis McGee's "Mon chère bébé créole" (1929):

'Gardez donc malheureuse!	Look, unhappy one!
Tu m'abandonnes pour toujours, malheureuse!	You leave me forever, unhappy one!
Ah yé yaille! Je suis après m'en aller, c'est pour mourir.	Oh it hurts! I'm going away to die.

Within the collective swamp pop repertoire this emotionalism is perhaps best exemplified by black Creole artist Clarence Garlow's classic swamp pop composition "Please Accept My Love," first popularized by Goldband artist Jimmy Wilson (1958):

> If you let me be your slave,
> Your love I'll cherish to my grave.
> If you should die before I do,
> I'll end my life to be with you.

(It is perhaps with some sense of humor, however, that Garlow begins his fervent devotional with the admission "I don't even know your name / But I love you just the same.")[1]

This pervasive feeling is conveyed both through swamp pop's instrumentation (the conversant sax, piano, and guitar are particularly apt communicators, as is the powerful, almost primitive beat) and through its ardent but simple lyrics and vocal delivery. Both slow and upbeat swamp pop compositions exhibit highly impassioned lyrics (only a handful of swamp pop instrumentals exist), which often document the workaday trials of Cajuns and black Creoles. The most common theme by far among swamp pop compositions is *love:* love lost, love coveted, and—in seemingly fewer instances—love attained.

Swamp pop song titles reflect this preoccupation: "Sea of Love," "Secret of Love," "Cradle of Love," "Our Love," "Our Teenage Love," "I Love You," "I'll Never Love Again," "Shelly's Winter Love," "Love of the Bayou," "Lover's Blues," "Lost Love," "Lovin' Cajun Style," "Do You Love Me So." Other titles also reflect the genre's obsession with this emotion: "Got You on My Mind," "Try to Find Another Man," "Lord I Need Somebody Bad Tonight," "Breaking Up Is Hard to Do." The objects of love occasionally lend their names to song titles: "Mathilda," "Belinda," "Candy Ann," "Cheryl Ann," "Colinda," "Irene," "Cindy Lou," "Shirley Jean," "Genevieve." Swamp pop's simplicity extends beyond its subject matter and lyricism, however, to its basic chord structures, which usually consist of only a two- or three-chord harmonic pattern—a sameness alleviated by subtle melodic or rhythmic interpretations in the vocal line. Swamp pop ballads, for instance, consist almost always of one or two eight-bar phrases. Swamp pop rockers, on the other hand, consist more often of twelve- or sixteen-bar phrases.

Both swamp pop ballads and rockers use simple harmonic progressions. In fact, harmonic background can be as basic as the utilization of only I (tonic) and V (dominant) chords; I, IV (subdominant) and V. A blues element is apparent in tunes concluding on I^7 chords. Frequently, however, tunes end in a fadeout before the final cadence. More often than rockers, swamp pop ballads include before the second verse one or two extra measures or an instrumental or vocal break. A melodic filler called the turnaround (prominent, for instance, in "Mathilda" and "Lonely Days, Lonely Nights") sometimes appears between phrases, often ending with a break in which the vocal part is dramatically suspended while the instruments carry on the rhythm (though in some cases the musicians also pause for one or two beats). In triplet pattern the turnaround's harmonic progression is simply I–IV, I.

Turnaround

The tempo for ballads generally falls within a metronomic range of 60 to 80 quarter note beats per minute; for rockers, 138 to 208. Determined in most cases by a singer's vocal range, key preference varies greatly among artists, save for a general inclination toward the key of B flat when performing more upbeat compositions. Key and tempo rarely change within a swamp pop performance; tempo certainly never shifts suddenly, although it sometimes accelerates gradually during a performance (a characteristic common to the black folk music tradition). Rhythmic intricacies exist only in the artists' interpretations, not as basic compositional ideas, although rhythmic changes also may occur between A and B sections. Most songs include instrumental introductions, though occasionally a vocalist begins with unaccompanied pickups, joined by the band on the next downbeat. The range of the vocal part remains within a tenth, rarely straying beyond an octave. Regarding form, swamp pop songs either are strophic (verses with identical music) or binary (i.e., AB, ABA, or AABA, presenting two melodies).[2]

Instrumentation among swamp pop groups usually includes the upright piano (or, nowadays, the electric keyboard), lead guitar, rhythm guitar, electric bass, and percussion trap sets. More traditional Cajun and black Creole instruments—namely, the accordion, fiddle, and *frottoir* (rubboard)—occasionally are utilized, especially in swamp pop rockers. In the rare absence of drums, the piano and bass carry the rhythm. The harmonica appears less frequently, as do a variety of improvised percussion instruments, including guitar backs, cardboard boxes, or—as in the case of Johnnie Allan's "South to Louisiana" (1962)—coconut shells, alternative sources of percussion being a trademark of prolific swamp pop producer J. D. Miller.[3]

For comparison the following chart lists chord progressions for several representative swamp pop ballads. It reveals that many of the ballads feature the AABA structure consisting of four eight-bar phrases. The chart also shows the range of harmonic variation within an eight-bar section and indicates that the primary chords, I, IV, and V (tonic, subdominant and dominant) can occur in any measure—although IV never appears in the final eighth measure. If II or II[7] is used, it always leads to V. The blues progression of I to III[7] to IV in "Big Blue Diamonds" and the flatted VI chord in "Lonely Days, Lonely Nights" represent notable harmonic variations.

A triplet figure supplies the underlying rhythm of Cookie and the Cupcakes' "Mathilda" (1958), the quintessential swamp pop recording. After an introduction pronounced breaks occur at the close of each eight-measure phrase. A guitar solo occurs midway through the performance, and no new melodic or harmonic material is introduced. Although most swamp pop ballads begin on the tonic chord (I), "Mathilda" starts on the subdominant (IV). The figure below shows the bass guitar's treatment of the triplet pattern, reinforced by the piano's left hand. This pattern follows the song's chord changes. (For ease of reading and comparison, this and other examples appear in the key of G, although this may not be a given composition's original key.)[4]

Mathilda

In "Mathilda" and King Karl and Guitar Gable's similar "Irene" (1956) the piano's right hand simply executes chords, reinforcing the triplet rhythm. In

"Mathilda"	IV	IV	I	I	V	V	I/IV	I	
"Irene"	I	I	V	V	V	V	I	I	
"This Should Go On Forever" (AABA)									
(A section)	IV	IV	I	I	V	IV	I/IV	I	
(B section)	IV	IV	I	I	II⁷	II⁷	V/II⁷	V⁷	
"Breaking Up Is Hard to Do"	I	I	V	V	V	IV	V	V	
"Lonely Days, Lonely Nights" (AABA)									
(A section)	I	I	V	V	V	IV	I/IV	I	
(B section)	IV	IV	I	I	II	II	V/♭	VI	V/break
"Big Blue Diamonds" (AA'BA)									
(A section)	I	III⁷	IV	IV	I	I	V	V	
(A' section)	I	III⁷	IV	IV	I	V	I/IV	I⁷	
(B section)	IV	IV	I	I	II⁷	II⁷	V	V	
"Sweet Dreams" (2 alternating sections)									
(A section)	I	II⁷	V	V	I	II⁷	V	V	
(B section)	I	IV	I	V	I/IV	I/V	I/IV	I/V	
"Before I Grow Too Old"	I	IV	V	I	I	IV	V	I	
"Your Picture"	I	I	V	V	V	V	I	break	
"I'm Leaving It Up to You" (AABA)									
(A section)	V	V	I	I	V	V	I/IV	I	
(B section)	IV	IV	I	I	II	II	V	V	

addition, breaks occur in "Irene" at intervals coinciding with those in "Mathilda." Both of these strophic compositions have only an A section. The exclusive use in "Irene" of I and V chords (except a single IV chord appearing in the instrumental interlude) produces a repetitious harmony due largely to the prolonged V chord. The configuration played by the bass guitar and saxophone within each measure corresponds closely to that in "Mathilda."

Irene

The tune of "Irene" is embellished slightly with flatted sevenths, a sound characteristic of blues and black spirituals.[5]

Rod Bernard's "This Should Go On Forever" (1958) begins with an introduction of one augmented V chord, rolled and sustained. Typical of many popular ballads, its tune adheres to an AABA form with breaks after each eight-measure phrase. Configuration of the bass line varies somewhat from the simpler ones in "Irene" and "Mathilda," and the musicians achieve additional variation in the B section by using a quarter and eighth note bass pattern.

This Should Go On Forever (A)

B section:

This Should Go On Forever (B)

Lyrically, Bernard's recording (the song was composed and originally recorded by black Creole swamp popper King Karl) ranks among the genre's more risqué contributions owing largely to the impious lyrics "If it's *sin* to really love you, then *a sinner I will be*." Inoffensive in south Louisiana's subtropical moral climate, these lyrics proved troublesome in more rigid Anglo-America, prompting famed dance program emcee Dick Clark to ask Bernard to rerecord the song for his spring 1959 "American Bandstand" appearances; complying, the swamp popper altered the song's sultry lyrics to the sanitized "If it's *wrong* to really love you, then *wrong I'll always be*."[6]

Jivin' Gene on tour, backed by Rod Bernard's Twisters, with J. V. Terracina on saxophone, circa 1960. (Photo courtesy of the Johnnie Allan Collection)

Punctuated by breaks, Jivin' Gene's "Breaking Up Is Hard to Do" (1959)—not to be confused with the 1962 Neil Sedaka hit—features tremolos on piano and forceful chordal triplets. It contains no B section, but avoids redundancy through the use of different lyrics for repeated A sections. The bass pattern, following a simple harmonic progression, is altered rhythmically.[7]

Breaking Up Is Hard To Do

Gene's lyrics exemplify the simple, unaffected feeling common to the swamp pop ballad. With its rudimentary rhyme scheme and gushing adolescent sentiments, the song might have originated in a high school student's diary:

Breaking up is hard to do.
Breaking up is sad and blue.
Making up is the thing to do.
Don't you know what I say is true?[8]

Adhering to the AABA form, Johnnie Allan's "Lonely Days, Lonely Nights" (1958) exhibits a turnaround prior to the B section and a break before the final A section. The A section's bass pattern, supplied in turn by electric bass, guitar, and saxophone, is actually a variation on the "Irene"/"Mathilda" patterns.[9]

Lonely Days, Lonely Nights (A)

The pattern transforms in the B section to:

Lonely Days, Lonely Nights (B)

Clint West's "Big Blue Diamonds" (1965), inspired by rhythm and blues artist Little Willie John's 1962 version, follows an AA'BA form and has neither introduction nor breaks. A III^7 (mediant) chord appears in the second measure, and the song's chord progressions are more complex than those in most other swamp pop ballads. In addition, its bass line is less well defined than those in other ballads of the genre—a feature possibly resulting from the song's relatively late recording, when less bluesy, more pop-oriented sounds dominated the airwaves and jukeboxes. The A section is adapted from a standard eight-bar blues progression. The B section's chord progression, however, resembles those of "This Should Go On Forever" and "Lonely Days, Lonely Nights."[10]

After a measure of introduction, a simple triplet beat sets up Tommy McLain's swamp pop rendition of "Sweet Dreams" (1966), written by country and western artist Don Gibson and recorded previously by Faron Young (1956), Gibson (1960), and Patsy Cline (1963). Embellishments include rippling scale passages from the piano, conversational fillers by guitar and saxophone, and a bell-like solo from the electric keyboard. Its two alternating sections—the A section in particular—conclude with a tag on the repeated phrase "Instead I'm having sweet dreams over you."[11] With some variations the melodic bass pattern is:

Sweet Dreams

Trumpet solos and sax fillers, complemented by the lead guitar's delicately interwoven filigree, provide the instrumentation in McLain's "Before I Grow Too Old" (1968), composed by swamp pop pioneer Bobby Charles. As in "Sweet Dreams," the bass line

Before I Grow Too Old

contains variations within each measure. A four-measure introduction leads to the repeated A section and a fadeout ends the piece. The boastful lyrics perhaps recall Charles's own aspirations prior to his rise to fame in the 1950s as a prodigious teenage songwriter and vocalist:

> I'm gonna take a trip around the world.
> Gonna kiss all the pretty girls.
> I'm gonna do everything in silver and gold.
> I've got to hurry up before I grow too old.

A swamp pop favorite, "Before I Grow Too Old" recently inspired an imaginative answer (written to the same tune) by Lafayette's twenty-something swamp guitar virtuoso Charles "C. C." Adcock. Entitled "Done Most Everything," the composition inverts the original song's lyrics to convey the world-weary laments of presumably the same Louisiana country boy after his sudden rise to rock 'n' roll stardom. Despite a fleet of Eldorados, a Hollywood estate, and the "pretty young girls back stage" (among other trappings of fame), the singer bemoans the weighty rings of silver and gold now girding his fingers and desires only to "go home . . . to Flat Town" (the small Acadiana town of Ville Platte). Playing on the original song's title, Adcock finally offers himself the cautionary words, "Lord, I've got to slow down before I grow too old."[12]

A repetitious four-measure vamp introduces Allan's "Your Picture" (1961), another Bobby Charles composition. Underlain by the piano's full triplet patterns, the saxophone furnishes a supporting continuous basic triplet rhythm of

Your Picture

Frugal harmonic changes in this one-part composition—I, V, and back to I—are relieved by breaks at the end of each eight-bar phrase. A shimmy-like sound issues from the nasal saxophone in its sixteen-bar solo. Typical of swamp pop ballads, the composition's lyrics pertain to loneliness and unrequited love:

> Your picture still stands on the table
> And forever it will be
> The only thing I ever treasure
> And love throughout eternity.[13]

With "I'm Leaving It Up to You" (1963) swamp pop team Dale and Grace offer a solid love-ballad duet—actually a cover of the 1957 Don and Dewey original—with scoops and slurs occurring in fine synchronization. As in "This Should Go On Forever," the tune is introduced by a lone augmented V chord. The bass pattern varies throughout the performance, and breaks are used between the sixth and seventh measures. Adhering to an AABA form, the guitar dominates the B section, after which vocals continue over A section harmonies. The tune concludes with a codetta on the plaintive lyrics "Or—are—we—through?"[14]

Although often overlooked by swamp pop aficionados in favor of the more distinctive ballads, swamp pop rockers are lighter in mood, livelier in spirit, and designed generally for "jitterbuggin' " (in local clubgoer parlance). Several upbeat tunes, like "Papa Thibodeaux," "Fais Do Do," "Cajun Honey," "Opelousas Sostan," "Hippy-Ti-Yo," "Cajun Man," "South to Louisiana," "The Back Door," and "Let's Do the Cajun Twist," rely on local color themes, and some even employ traditional Cajun and black Creole instrumentation alongside the standard rhythm and blues lineup. As demonstrated by the following chord progression chart, swamp pop rockers most often utilize a twelve-bar blues structure, stretched sometimes to sixteen by the repetition of a four-bar section. Swamp pop rockers are comparable to rockabilly tunes in this respect, as well as in their use of boogie woogie and walking bass lines.

Rod Bernard's "Pardon Mr. Gordon" (1958) is a rockabilly-ish novelty selection with a prolonged flatting of phrase endings. The bass carries an underlying boogie beat realized as a walking figure:

Pardon Mr. Gordon

The piano follows the chord progressions to the same rhythm. An original composition by Bernard, the song uses humor to relate the vocalist's misadventures with the ubiquitous, troublemaking Mr. Gordon.

> Well, I caught another fellow messin' with my wife.
> I said, "Look here, daddy, better run for your life."
> When he stood up he was six-foot-three,
> Weighed two hundred pounds, that was enough for me!
> I said, "Pardon, Mr. Gordon . . . keep on and I'll leave you be!"

"Pardon Mr. Gordon"											
(A Section)	I	I	I	I	IV⁷	IV⁷	I	I			
(Refrain)	IV	IV	I	I	V	IV⁷	I	I/V			
"Promised Land"	I	I	I	IV	V	V	V	I			
"Later Alligator"	I	I	I	I	IV⁷	IV⁷	I	I	V	V	I	I
"Congo Mombo"	I	I	I	I	IV	IV	I	I	V	IV	I	I
"I'm Twisted"											
(A section)	I	I	I	I	IV	IV	I	I	V	IV	I	I
Interlude	I (fourteen measures)										
(B section)	IV	IV	I	I	II⁷	II⁷	V	V			

The song's third instrumental break features an accelerated vocal clip ("Son of a gun!") reminiscent of the Chipmunks (who also scored their first hit in 1958), courtesy of inventive swamp pop producer J. D. Miller.[15]

Simpler is the harmony of Johnnie Allan's "Promised Land" (1971), with its I, IV, and V chords featuring accordion solos and guitar accompaniment. Composed and originally recorded in 1964 by Chuck Berry—who adapted the song's melody and harmonic structure from the country and western classic "Wabash Cannon Ball," popularized in 1938 by Roy Acuff—this frantic composition strongly lends itself to the swamp pop idiom, despite Berry's unsympathetic plea, "Somebody help me get outta Louisiana!" Innovative Cajun accordionist Belton Richard—backed by Allan's group, the Memories—offers a wild accordion ride reminiscent of old-time Cajun two-steps (and rearranged admirably by fellow accordionist Wayne Toups on Allan's recent rerecording of "Promised Land" for the Boogie Kings' *Swamp Boogie Blues* album [1995]).[16]

Bobby Charles's original composition "Later Alligator" (1955), recently rerecorded by Charles in zydeco-inspired form for his acclaimed *Wish You Were Here Right Now* album (1995), consists of twelve measures and exhibits a basic boogie rhythm. A notable solo by swamp pop saxophonist Harry Simoneaux relieves Charles's repetitive vocal line, the melody of which Charles borrowed from New Orleans rhythm and blues artist Guitar Slim's "Later for You Baby" (1954).

> See you later, alligator,
> After while, crocodile.
> Can't you see you're in my way now?
> Don't you know you cramp my style?[17]

Although Charles cites jazz music as a personal influence ("Jazz influenced every artist in Louisiana in one way or another. All of our music is some kind of a jazz"), he probably was unaware that the lyrical hook around which he composed this swamp pop classic originated among devotees of jazz, swing, and jive music. Early in the century *alligator* was used as slang (often disparagingly) "by black jazzmen, particularly in New Orleans, [when] referring to white jazzmen and white jazz fans, jive black people, or jitterbugs"; the slang term also meant "an assertively masculine, flashily dressed, and up-to-the-minute male," engendering *gator* and *gate,* used by black males as terms of address. Yet etymologist Stuart Berg Flexner asserts the term boasts an even more complex

Bobby Charles publicity photo, apparently taken at the Audubon Zoo, New Orleans, dated May 22, 1956. "His visit to New Orleans," reads an accompanying newspaper clipping, "is in connection with the movie, 'Rock Around the Clock,' starting Wednesday at the Orpheum." (Photo courtesy of Jeff Hannusch)

history. "Mississippi keelboatmen liked to think of themselves as tough and mean as alligators," he observes, "calling themselves *alligators* by 1808 . . . . It remained in use for any swaggering dude or sport, surfacing in New Orleans to mean a jazz musician around 1915, then a jitterbug enthusiast in the 1930s. Thus from those keelboatmen we finally got the rhyming jive farewell 'See you later, alligator' of the 1930s, which had some student use into the 1950s."[18]

A high school student himself in the mid-1950s, Charles describes the song's serendipitous origin: "We [swamp pop band Bobby Charles and the Cardinals] were walking out of a restaurant one night after a dance job and I turned round to my piano player and I told him, 'See you later, alligator!' Then they had two couples sitting in a booth in front of us, they were pretty loaded and she [a girl in the booth] said something to my ear. I was walking out and I walked back in and asked her what she had said. 'You said, "See you later, alligator," and I said, "After a while, crocodile." ' I said thank you very much, that was it. I went home and wrote it in about twenty minutes."[19]

King Karl and Guitar Gable's instrumental "Congo Mombo" (1956) possesses a quick metronomic beat of 208 quarter notes per minute, opening with a fast eighth note introduction by a conga drum (supported by other percussion) that continues under a superimposed bass figure of:

Congo Mombo

The tune's use of this "Latin" bass figure, combined with the persistent eighth note conga pattern, is characteristic of Afro-Caribbean dance pieces and also appears in the Boogie Ramblers' early recording "Such as Love" (circa 1955). The saxophone, guitar, and piano take solos—the piano most prominently, complete with glissandi (rapid slides)—and the recording ends in a fadeout like the dispersal of a rambunctious party. Despite its exotic sound, the melody of "Congo Mombo" draws heavily on that of the American folk song "Frankie and Johnny," a melody suggested by Guitar Gable when his percussionist, toying around on stage during a nightclub dance, stumbled unexpectedly on the composition's beat.[20]

Cookie and the Cupcakes' raucous "I'm Twisted" (1958) utilizes a boogie bass line with a driving emphasis on the second note of the triplet figure. Its harmonic progression is loosely improvisatory, inviting spontaneous variation. Although its rhythm, melody, and instrumentation adhere strictly to a 1950s rhythm and blues sound, the composition's bizarre, even daring lyrics seem to predict the psychedelia and Carrollian nonsense of the Beatles' "Nowhere Man" (1965) and "Being for the Benefit of Mr. Kite!" (1967):

King Karl at home, Scott, La., December 11, 1991. (Photo by the author)

I'm the barefooted boy with shoes on.
I come before you to stand behind you.
That's something I know nothing about.
Next Sunday, which is blue Monday,
There'll be a dance at the Union Hall.
For everybody who cannot attend,
The party ain't for me at all.

There's breakfast for free for nobody
And everybody will pay at the door.
There'll be plenty of seats for nobody
And everybody will sit on the floor.

Unfortunately, accounts of the authorship of "I'm Twisted" are apocryphal. No writer's credits or publishing data appear on the original 45 rpm single or subsequent reissues, nor is the song registered with either of the two leading music licensing concerns, ASCAP and BMI. During an informal interview, however, Cupcakes front man Huey "Cookie" Thierry explained that an anonymous fan handed him the lyrics during a performance, thus explaining the group's reluctance, stated Thierry, to claim the song. But during a more formal and recent interview, Thierry asserted that he actually wrote the lyrics to "I'm Twisted." Although aware of this claim to the song's authorship, Thierry's manager and longtime pianist, Ernest Jacobs, continues to regard the lyrics' origins as a mystery.[21]

This cursory appraisal of several typical swamp pop compositions shows that in general swamp pop ballads feature prominent bass lines with scale steps of 1, 3, 5, and 6 that modulate with harmonic changes. Swamp pop rockers, on the other hand, employ boogie woogie and walking bass lines. Ballads are one-part or two-part (AABA or alternating AB), each part containing eight bars, while rockers have twelve- or sixteen-bar blues structures. Naturally, tempo differs greatly between the two formats: Swamp pop ballads measure about 60 to 80 quarter-note beats to a minute; rockers, 138 to 208. Both adhere to simple harmonic structures. In fact, ballads sometimes utilize only a two-chord progression (I and V), but usually include three (I, IV, V) with occasional transitional chords (II, III, or VI). Rockers exhibit characteristic blues changes (I, IV, V). Both rely on modern instrumentation common to rhythm and blues lineups (though rockers sometimes also feature traditional instruments) and both highlight the piano's right-hand triplet chords that serve to emphasize and reinforce harmonic structures. In addition, both formats use saxophones to fill out the harmony, depend on the percussion to keep time, and contain instrumental rides (usually at least one per composition) in which the saxophone, guitar, or piano paraphrases the vocal melody in an improvisational style. Most importantly, however, both swamp pop ballads and rockers exhibit intensely emotional lyrics and vocal deliveries—a characteristic they appear to have borrowed from traditional Cajun and black Creole music.

THE BIRTH OF
SWAMP POP MUSIC

In his *Memories: A Pictorial History of South Louisiana Music,* swamp pop artist-turned-researcher Johnnie Allan compiled vital statistics of hundreds of south Louisiana performers, including swamp pop musicians. Allan's data reveal that 87 percent of swamp pop artists hail from south Louisiana and southeast Texas, regions that gave rise to the genre and have embraced it since its inception. His data also indicate that 78 percent of swamp pop artists hail from Acadiana and that of these artists 73 percent were born in a central seven-parish area consisting of Acadia, Evangeline, Iberia, Lafayette, St. Landry, St. Martin, and Vermilion parishes. It is important to note that this central region (largely composing the "Cajun Heartland" district) also produced 82 percent of traditional Cajun and black Creole musicians, of whom 42 percent were born in a northern prairie area roughly bounded by the towns of Church Point, Sunset, Opelousas, Ville Platte, Mamou, and Eunice—the same region that apparently first produced swamp pop music. Because swamp pop developed in close proximity to Cajun and black Creole sources, an adequate understanding of their influence on the genre requires at least an abbreviated survey of the region's cultural history, especially regarding its traditional music.[1]

Acadians in pre-expulsion Nova Scotia (originally the colony of Acadia, founded in 1604) possessed a musical heritage strongly rooted in medieval France. The Acadians' musical repertoire consisted of ballads and drinking songs performed a cappella at social gatherings. Dance music at first was performed orally by whistling, humming, or chanting; these tunes later were adapted for performance on instruments. After the expulsion in 1755 about 2,600 to 3,000 Acadians (roughly 15 to 25 percent of all Acadians) sailed to Louisiana over the following three decades to rebuild their pastoral refuge in the subtropics. Bringing no musical instruments on the journey, the Acadians preserved their

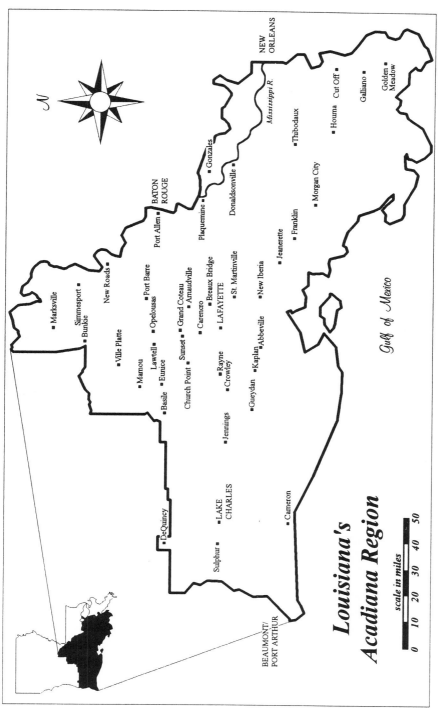

Louisiana's Acadiana Region

scale in miles

0   10   20   30   40   50

Map by Shane K. Bernard

musical tradition orally as they carved out from the wilderness two major areas of settlement: the first, established in 1765 on Bayou Teche at present-day Fausse Pointe; and the second, founded in 1765–66 along the Mississippi River between New Orleans and Baton Rouge. Contrary to popular belief, only a few Acadians settled in New Orleans, where their absorption by the city's Creole population quickly wiped out most traces of the exiles' traditional culture.[2]

Many Acadians along the Mississippi soon resettled to the northwest toward Opelousas or west toward present-day Abbeville. Moving onto the prairies, they next settled areas south of Opelousas and present-day Eunice by 1790 and the Crowley and Mermentau areas by 1803. The vastness of these semi-isolated prairies appears to have influenced the Acadians' music greatly. By the turn of the nineteenth century a few settlers had acquired fiddles, playing not only traditional tunes preserved in their collective memory but also new ones, often composed on themes of death, loneliness, and ill-fated love—effects of their brutal exile and harsh frontier experience.[3]

During the early nineteenth century Acadians began to encounter, interact with, and assimilate many ethnically diverse settlers. Despite exaggerated claims to the contrary, south Louisianians in that century did not exist in cultural isolation. An intricate system of ancient roads already linked south Louisiana to other regions and by the 1830s steamboat companies from New Orleans offered regular excursions to Opelousas and present-day St. Martinville in the heart of Cajun country. Merchant boats from the Gulf of Mexico often visited settlers along the larger bayous, providing them with consumer goods and news. Around 1880 the Southern Pacific Railroad cut across south Louisiana, connecting towns like Morgan City, New Iberia, Lafayette, Crowley, and Lake Charles to cities like Houston, New Orleans, and beyond. Naturally, these various approaches to the region encouraged the arrival of outsiders during the nineteenth century.[4]

The Acadians easily assimilated other settlers—French, Spanish, Germans, Anglo-Americans—contributing to their evolution into a distinctly new ethnic group called *Cajuns*. (A few wealthy Acadians, however, were assimilated into upper-class French Creole society and later into upper-class Anglo-American society, and thus played no part in Cajun music's development.) Importantly, Creoles of African descent also settled in south Louisiana during the late eighteenth and early nineteenth centuries, as planters bought thousands of Afro-Caribbean slaves from New Orleans. (Nonslaves of African descent, the *gens de couleur libre* or free persons of color, also settled in south Louisiana at this time.) Black

Creoles soon comprised a relatively large percentage of the population, exerting a major influence on the Cajuns' developing music. Cajuns borrowed the black Creoles' syncopated, percussive, and improvisational styles, and in turn the black Creoles borrowed the Cajuns' basic musical tradition, including their instruments. Together they adopted the diatonic accordion from German Jewish merchants (who imported the instrument from overseas). Cajuns incorporated western French folk songs and new compositions from French Creoles, and from Anglo-Americans they borrowed a variety of popular tunes, which the Cajuns performed in their own manner, often with new Cajun French lyrics.[5]

Shortly after Cajun and black Creole settlers reached the Texas border around 1890, their music entered a period of great fertility. This fertility is traceable to several factors. Toward the end of the nineteenth century Cajuns embraced the black Creole tradition of combining music, song, and dance into a single performance. They interweaved older songs and instrumentals, creating new songs with instrumental solos. Then around the turn of the century German Jewish retailers in Acadiana began to import affordable high-quality accordions, which led to that instrument's sudden rise in popularity among local musical groups. The accordion had arrived in Louisiana shortly after its 1828 invention in Vienna; early models, however, were awkward and flimsy compared to late-nineteenth- and early-twentieth-century models, which were loud, durable, and relatively easy to play. The popularity of the accordion led to a simplification of melodies to accommodate the (single row) diatonic accordion's limited tonal range. By the 1920s Cajuns had adopted the rural blues sound already popular among black Creoles, and in 1928 phonograph companies began to record and market Cajun and black Creole music in an effort to sell more players, which in effect preserved the period's repertoire for later musicians. These early recordings, observes Ancelet, received the tacit approval of listeners and thus became the standard versions of many traditional Cajun and black Creole songs, in turn discouraging the previously common use of lyrical and melodic improvisation. Standard versions of classics like "Allons à Lafayette," "Hip et Taïaut" and "Jolie blonde" originated in this period of early commercial recordings. ("Allons à Lafayette" and "Hip et Taïaut" were recorded by Joseph Falcon in 1928 and 1934 respectively as "Lafayette [Allons à Lafayette]" and "Ils la volet mon trancas"; "Jolie blonde" was recorded by Amédé Breaux in 1928 as "Ma blonde est partie.")[6]

During the 1920s and '30s, however, south Louisiana's Cajuns and black Creoles underwent a period of rapid Americanization. In short, the discovery of oil attracted workers from other states, especially Texas and Oklahoma, who migrated to south Louisiana on new highways built by flamboyant Louisiana politician Huey Long. Anglo-American workers brought with them a love for country and western music, and non-Creole African-American workers, a love for urban blues, all nurtured by radio programs broadcast into the region from cities like Nashville and New Orleans. In addition, the oil industry lured many Cajuns and black Creoles to southeast Texas, where they worked in the oilfields and refineries of the Beaumont–Port Arthur area.[7]

Responding to the influence of non-Creole African-American music, black Creole accordionists adopted a "blusier" sound. Cajun musicians, on the other hand, emulated Anglo-American string bands, advancing the role of the guitar and reinstating the fiddle as their lead instrument—at the expense of the accordion, which they banished. Cajuns also added the steel guitar, upright bass, drums and, on occasion, even banjos and mandolins. Rural electrification enabled string bands to use amplifiers on stage, encouraging them to perform and compose more delicate tunes, which now could pierce the din of crowded dance halls. At this time Cajun string bands integrated many country and western tunes into their repertoires, often transposing original lyrics into French or simply writing new French lyrics to the original melodies.[8]

By the late 1940s the accordion again dominated Cajun music, resurrected by the popularity of accordionist Iry LeJeune and by World War II (and, a few years later, Korean War) veterans seeking comfort in "old-time" music. The fiddle and guitar receded to lesser roles, but Cajun groups retained the steel guitar, upright bass, and drums, all introduced during the string-band era. Ironically, the accordion's return coincided with the advent of an increasingly popular national genre: rhythm and blues. Cajun musicians like Lawrence Walker, Bill Matte, Cleveland Crochet, and Belton Richard drew heavily on rhythm and blues elements, no doubt inspired in part by black Creole accordionist Clifton Chenier, whose style exemplifies the blend of traditional black Creole music, blues, and rhythm and blues called *zydeco.*[9]

Reaching their teens in the early to mid-1950s, young Cajuns and black Creoles noticed the rhythm and blues movement and observed a shift in the listening habits of south Louisiana teens, including themselves. Although they initially puzzled future southeast Texas swamp popper Gene Terry—he still was performing Cajun and country and western music at the time—the exotic sounds and personalities of rhythm and blues soon mesmerized him. "I said 'Whoever would make a song like "Tutti Frutti"?' . . . But I'd find myself getting back from school and turning on the Big Bopper [celebrated disc jockey and recording artist J. P. Richardson, of Beaumont's KTRM radio]. . . . [I thought] 'Well, you know, that's kind of good music there. I like the stuff.' I just crossed over. . . . That's when I started gettin' to moving, man! I wanted to be like them guys."[10]

Johnnie Allan still was performing Cajun music when he first noticed rhythm and blues in south Louisiana; in fact, he was playing steel guitar with famed accordionist Lawrence Walker and the Wandering Aces. Allan's reaction to the rhythm and blues sound parallels the response of many early swamp pop artists. "Landry's Palladium in Lafayette would bring in guys like Earl King and Gatemouth Brown," he recounts. "I went there one night and both of them were on the bill and I was so impressed. It was so packed in there you could hardly move—I could see the trend was moving away from Cajun music to that type of music. And our crowds when we played were getting smaller and smaller with the Cajun music, while the crowds at the clubs with the rock 'n' roll bill were getting bigger and bigger." Allan's departure from Cajun music required a break with Walker, a break hastened by the Wandering Aces' desire to follow Allan. "So that's what happens when you put an old horse out to grass," lamented Walker on learning that his traditional Cajun group had rechristened itself the Rhythm Rockers, soon to be the Krazy Kats—a group Allan modeled after Gene Terry's group, the Down Beats. (Allan notes, however, that the Krazy Kats' name only coincidentally resembles the Down Beats' original name, the Kool Kats.)[11]

Although the accordion (particularly the double-row, triple-row, and piano-key accordions favored by black Creole accordionists) could accommodate the rhythm and blues sound, teenage Cajuns and black Creoles took up the piano, sax, electric guitar, and modern percussion trap sets, instruments they associated closely with the alluring music from seemingly distant places like Memphis and especially New Orleans. The transformation of Allan's group typifies the changes experienced by some emerging swamp pop artists: Allan gave up steel guitar to sing and play rhythm guitar; rhythm guitarist Al Foreman changed to electric lead; fiddler U. J. Meaux switched to upright piano; and while Bhuel Hoffpauir remained on drums, the group hired Ashton Langlinais to play sax. After a few additional changes in personnel (such as switching Hoffpauir to bass, putting Austin Broussard on drums, and replacing Langlinais with saxophonist Leroy Castille), the group at last was properly outfitted to play the music later dubbed *swamp pop*. Experimenting with the rhythms, melodies, vocal arrangements, and instrumentation of the new rhythm and blues sound, the Krazy Kats unwittingly blended these elements with more familiar influences to create a fusion of rhythm and blues, country and western, and Cajun and black Creole music. Lacking a better term, the young swamp poppers called it *south Louisiana music,* a genre now known as *swamp pop.*[12]

Surprisingly, some musicians and music writers suggest that swamp pop borrowed *only* its strong emotional tone from Cajun and black Creole music, insisting that the limited range of the (single row) diatonic accordion bridled that instrument's influence on the developing genre. Music writer Larry Benicewicz seems to embrace this view, a view first articulated by swamp pop saxophonist Harry Simoneaux. Ironically, Simoneaux has referred to Cajun accordionist Belton Richard as "a real swamp popper" and, as mentioned above, coined the "half Domino, half fais do-do" definition of swamp pop. He also explains, "If there had been no French Cajun bands, there would definitely be no swamp pop."[13]

The view downplaying the accordion's influence on swamp pop begs reconsideration not only because it overlooks the popularity of the more versatile multi-row diatonic and piano-key accordions favored by black Creole artists, but because it ignores the music of Cajun musicians like Belton Richard and Blackie Forestier, who have successfully captured the swamp pop ballad's triplet rhythmic sound on the accordion. Richard, for instance, has recorded Cajun accordion versions of swamp pop songs like T. K. Hulin's "I'm Not a Fool Anymore" (1972), Warren Storm's "Lord I Need Somebody Bad Tonight" (1974), and Cookie and the Cupcakes' "Mathilda" (as "J'ai pleurer pour toi" [1972]), as well as Joe Hudson's swampy "Baby Give Me a Chance" (under the title "Give Me Another Chance" [1972]). In addition, Richard's renowned "Un autre soir d'ennui" (1970) is a Cajun French version of Jimmy Clanton's swamp pop hit "Another Sleepless Night." And Blackie Forestier's "What's Her Name" (1973) is actually an adaptation of Clarence Garlow's swamp pop composition "Please Accept My Love," first popularized in 1958 by Goldband rhythm and blues artist Jimmy Wilson; swamp poppers Elton Anderson and Johnnie Allan have covered the recording, however, and Rod Bernard cites it as an archetypal swamp pop ballad. (The Cajun group Joe Bonsall and the Orange Playboys also have covered Johnnie Allan's "Your Picture.")[14]

So accordions can accommodate the swamp pop sound—and swamp pop in turn can draw on accordion music. For example, the Cajun accordion propels Johnnie Allan's swamp pop rendition of "Promised Land" and Charles Mann's cover of the Dire Straits hit "Walk of Life"; it also appears prominently in C. C. Adcock's version of Gene Terry's minor swamp pop classic "Cindy Lou." Both the Cajun accordion and fiddle support Darby Douget's vocals on his swamp pop ballad "Mathilda Finally Came Back Home," a sequel to the Cupcakes' swamp pop anthem. In general, however, the accordion appears in relatively few swamp pop recordings (and those in which it does appear consist almost exclusively of later swamp pop recordings, symbolizing the Cajun revival spirit)—but their influence on the genre need not be explicit: noted music writer Kurt Loder thus describes swamp pop as "black rhythm and blues rendered with dense textures of accordion-based Cajun country music (but—the genius part—*without the accordions*)" (emphasis added).[15]

Those who minimize Cajun and black Creole music's influence on swamp pop also ignore a more important fact, namely, that swamp pop draws not as heavily on Cajun and black Creole accordion music as on Cajun string band music. Allan's biographical data reveal that the median year of birth for swamp poppers is 1939, which falls squarely in the string band era (circa 1935–50). Most swamp pop artists were born to parents who courted during the height of the string band era, and who after marriage probably continued to appreciate, purchase, and perhaps even perform Cajun string band music, a sound future swamp pop artists naturally absorbed growing up in their parents' homes. (Unlike children today, who regularly listen to youth-oriented sources like music television, children in the 1940s had little choice but to listen to their parents' favorite music.) In fact, a handful of future swamp pop artists performed in Cajun string bands during the late 1940s and early to mid-'50s—among them Rod Bernard, Warren Storm, and Joe Barry—and those who performed with accordion groups almost exclusively wielded instruments brought to Cajun music during the string band era.[16]

Indeed, Cajun and black Creole music and culture exerted a profound and personal influence on budding swamp pop artists. For instance, Huey "Cookie" Thierry, front man of the swamp pop group Cookie and the Cupcakes, learned the black Creole dialect from his parents and grew up listening to traditional black Creole music, which he sang informally as a child around the Thierry household. "My father played the accordion and the violin, and my mother played guitar. They used to play together, Creole dances." He adds matter-of-factly, "I am Creole, that is my nationality. I am Creole—Spanish and Indian, French, and some white, 'cause I got it all mixed up in my family." Another former Cupcakes front man, Little Alfred, also possesses a strong black Creole background. "I have the heritage," he acknowledges, "but can't speak it [the di-alect] well" (though his mother, he says, "can rattle it off"). A black Creole from Opelousas, swamp popper Lil' Bob claims several musical relatives, including zydeco pioneer Clifton Chenier, a close cousin. And swamp pop pioneers King Karl and Guitar Gable speak English as well as the black Creole dialect, and in their youth were exposed to traditional black Creole music.[17]

King Karl, for instance, was born Bernard Jolivette in Grand Coteau (located between Lafayette and Opelousas) and cites an uncle, black Creole musician John Abbs, as an early influence. "I guess that's where I took it from 'cause he played anything he picked up," observes Karl. "He didn't take it [music] in high school or nothing, 'cause he didn't go to school. He just picked it [up] on his own, but he played any instrument he picked up." Abbs, however, preferred the piano and—above all—the accordion. Yet he played not zydeco, explains Karl, but a more traditional forerunner of the genre. "It was more like French style and waltzes. It wasn't a zydeco type way back then . . . . This was around Opelousas and Lawtell, Bellevue." Despite his exposure to traditional black Creole music, as a teenager Karl preferred the new rhythm and blues sound to his uncle's accordion music. Even after learning to play the sax and guitar, however, he still joined up for a period with obscure black Creole accordionist Howard Broussard, thus advancing his knowledge of traditional music.[18]

Karl's partner, Guitar Gable, was born Gabriel Perrodin in Bellevue (named for the Prairie Bellevue, near Opelousas). Gable recalls that his father possessed a reputation locally as a formidable black Creole musician. "He played accordion and harmonica," Gable states, echoing King Karl when he explains that the elder Perrodin performed a more traditional precursor to zydeco. "French music, the French accordion music . . . . They didn't call it zydeco, they called it French music." Accompanied by a *frottoir* player, Gable's father appeared around Bellevue at house dances sponsored by other black Creoles. Gable, however, and his brother John, a long-time member of Lil' Bob and the Lollipops, fancied the electric guitar of big-city rhythm and blues over the seemingly rustic and outmoded accordion. "Zydeco wasn't out in those days when we were playing," he explains, "and French songs just wasn't catching on." (Gable points out, however, that another Perrodin brother, Oliver, played not only guitar, but also fiddle.)[19]

South Louisiana's ethnic culture also affected Cajun swamp poppers, who absorbed the strains of the accordion and fiddle as children and perhaps even utilized these instruments before embracing rhythm and blues. Bobby Charles,

Guitar Gable and His Swing Masters, poster photo, Lafayette, La., September 16, 1954. Left to right: Joseph Zeno, Albert Davis, Guitar Gable, and Freddie Lebien. (Photo courtesy of Gabriel Perrodin)

for instance, grew up in the heart of Acadiana and despite his limited knowledge of the Cajun French dialect listened as a child to Cajun music on the radio. Rod Bernard never learned the Cajun French dialect. Like Charles, however, he admired Cajun music and often experienced live performances at his grand-father's dance hall, the Courtableau Inn in Port Barre (right on the banks of Bayou Courtableau), where he listened to artists like Aldus Roger, Papa Cairo, and Jimmy C. Newman, as well as zydeco pioneer Clifton Chenier. "We used to go over there and I'd just hang on the bandstand and watch the musicians the whole time," he remembers. A few years later Bernard and his brother, clad in homemade cowboy costumes, appeared with the Blue Room Gang, an Opelousas Cajun/country ensemble that appeared regularly on local KSLO radio. Similarly, Gene Terry spoke no Cajun French, but often listened to his father and grandfather perform Cajun music, and as a child he attended Cajun house and barn dances with his uncle, R. C. DeRouen, a Cajun musician. "My uncle took me to a house dance—I didn't know what that was—one time and it pretty impressed me. My uncle at the time played guitar and sang. But that's how my dad started—barn dances, house dances." Terry eventually joined his uncle on stage at Cajun dance halls like the Clover Club in Lacassine, where they performed with Cajun artists like Jimmy C. Newman.[20]

Warren Storm, however, spoke only Cajun French until his third year of school and recalls teachers scolding him for speaking the dialect. (His parents knew only a few words of English.) Storm learned the drums and guitar from his father, a Cajun string band musician, and as a teenager he performed Cajun/country music with Larry Brasso and the Rhythmaires. Swamp popper Joe Barry also grew up in a musical household. In addition to piloting boats, trapping muskrat and hunting alligator and wildfowl, Barry's father possessed a strong interest in music (he played the Jew's harp and harmonica), an interest shared by many of Barry's relatives, including his cousin, famed Cajun string artist Vin Bruce. Barry craved live Cajun music as a child and often witnessed live performances in the dance halls of rural Lafourche and Terrebonne parishes. "When I was old enough—well, I was . . . nine years old . . . I had to go with my sister to make sure she was all right. I couldn't give a damn what she was doing. I wanted to hear the band. . . . And so I'd stick myself in front of the bandstand. I don't know what she did all night—I could care less. What I wanted was to watch the band." During the late 1940s Barry often sat in with Cajun string musicians like cousin Bruce and Blackie Dartez.[21]

Swamp pop ambassador Johnnie Allan spoke only Cajun French as a child and grew up in a family immersed in traditional Cajun music. "Whenever they'd come visiting," Allan recalls of his musical relatives, "they'd bring the guitar and the fiddle and they'd sit outside on the steps or the porch and play music. . . . All of them sang and played instruments. And, of course, my grandfather played music. He played with his brother . . . [celebrated Cajun accordionist] Joe Falcon. He played fiddle with Uncle Joe. A lot of people don't know this, my grandfather played a hell of a better accordion than Uncle Joe did, a lot better. And my mother played guitar with Uncle Joe, as did my aunt, her sister, Marie Falcon. She later recorded. She played Cajun music and recorded Cajun songs." Well versed on rhythm guitar, steel guitar, and drums, Allan as a teenager joined Cajun accordionist Walter Mouton and the Scott Playboys before teaming up with accordionist Lawrence Walker.[22]

These few examples reveal that as a rule the traditional culture and music of south Louisiana exercised a powerful sway on future Cajun and black Creole swamp pop artists. No matter how greatly they might diverge from their

Johnnie Allan (left) and Walter Mouton during the early days of the Cajun group the Scott Playboys, Girard Park, Lafayette, La., June 1, 1952. (Photo courtesy of the Johnnie Allan Collection)

traditional roots, swamp poppers retained the cultural baggage of the collective Cajun and black Creole experience. Inevitably, this baggage manifests itself repeatedly in the musical genre they created. The manifestation is sometimes obscure, sometimes quite obvious.

Although the precise time and place of swamp pop's birth no doubt will remain a mystery (as it seems unlikely the genre experienced a sudden, well-defined birth), evidence suggests an early 1950s origin around Lake Charles in western Acadiana or on the Cajun and Creole prairies of northern Acadiana, consisting of parts of Acadia, St. Landry, and Evangeline parishes. Allan's biographical data show that only 15 percent of swamp pop musicians hail from the northern prairies, compared to 35 percent of Cajun and black Creole musicians. These statistics may not properly convey swamp pop's debt to the northern prairie region, which, according to historian Carl Brasseaux, occupies a cultural crossroads where heavy interaction (musical and otherwise) occurred between Cajuns and black Creoles.[23]

An important clue concerning swamp pop's origin on the northern prairie issues unexpectedly from New Orleans rhythm and blues musician Earl King, whose "Those Lonely Lonely Nights" (1955) is often cited as a proto–swamp pop song and is even viewed by some as the first swamp pop recording. (King, however, generally is regarded by swamp pop artists and enthusiasts as a New Orleans rhythm and blues musician. Although Frankie Ford of "Sea Cruise" fame has associated strongly with swamp pop artists since the genre's heydey, King nevertheless represents perhaps the only notable New Orleans figure who attempted a crossover to swamp pop—a significant feat for King given the ascendancy of his hometown sound during the 1950s.) In fact, King states that his inspiration for "Those Lonely Lonely Nights" came from central Acadiana's northern prairie: "I was beginning to formulate a different style [after early 1954] . . . . I had been around Eunice and Opelousas and I began to get a feel for that ballad sound that those people liked to hear. If you listen closely to 'Lonely Lonely Nights,' you can hear that turn around right after the break. I wanted that to be my trademark and put it on all my records. I wanted people to associate that with me." Possibly predating the earliest true swamp pop recordings, King's composition and recollection of its origin serve to narrow the time of swamp pop's birth to 1954 or '55 at latest.[24]

King also suggests as the genre's birthplace the northern prairie region around Eunice and Opelousas: Again, the musical importance of this small, largely rural area springs from its locale and indigenous culture, which pro-moted ethnic interaction among musicians and in turn created more music and musicians than any other section of Acadiana. By the mid-1950s the demand among young Cajuns and black Creoles for innovative music attracted popular mainstream rhythm and blues artists—especially those associated with New Orleans—to the northern prairie region's myriad of live-music nightclubs. Many of these clubs stood along Highway 190, the main thoroughfare connecting western and central Acadiana to southeast Louisiana and the metropolis of New Orleans. Already steeped in ethnic musical traditions, the northern prairie region served as the point of entry for New Orleans rhythm and blues in the heartland of Cajun and rural black Creole Louisiana. That it did so may have contributed to the birth of swamp pop on the northern prairie: the introduc-tion of rhythm and blues in the early 1950s could have acted as a catalyst for the creation of swamp pop.

(Incidentally, famed recordman Johnny Vincent, owner of the New Orleans rhythm and blues–heavy Ace label, utilized Opelousas and Eunice as "breaking points" for new rhythm and blues recordings. In fact, Vincent claims the region heard new rhythm and blues recordings even before New Orleans itself: "Places like Eunice and Opelousas could bleed a record into New Orleans and force the New Orleans stations to play it," he recalls. "New Orleans, in turn, was a big national breaking point." South Louisiana deejay Buddy King similarly notes "We had every major record company in the country calling. I mean, we were like on the 'A' list. We got records as soon as, if not sooner, than New York or Los Angeles. . . . The compliment is to the people of South Louisiana . . . for being very knowledgeable about music and having a big influence on music, because they're the ones who said 'Okay, I like this.' ")[25]

Newly found evidence, however, suggests an even earlier birth than 1954 and one perhaps less confined to a specific south Louisiana locale: Lake Charles producer Eddie Shuler has discovered contracts showing that he signed the swamp pop group the Boogie Ramblers—later known as Cookie and the Cupcakes—in July 1952. He released their first, albeit obscure, single "Cindy Lou"/"Such as Love" around 1954 or '55 (probably '55) and although "Such as Love" strikes the ear as a bizarre Afro-Caribbean ballad, the rolling rhythm and blues melody of "Cindy Lou" exudes the telltale swampy feel. So while pioneer black Creole swamp poppers like Guitar Gable, brother Landry Perrodin, and Lil' Bob appeared in the northern prairie region during the early 1950s, other black Creole swamp poppers—namely, the highly influential Ramblers—were active at the same time around Lake Charles, about seventy miles to the southwest.[26]

Whether the swamp pop sound first appeared around Lake Charles or Opelousas and Eunice (or both simultaneously), its earliest development still appears to owe much to the northern prairie region's black Creole nightclubs. These almost forgotten clubs include the Gym-side Inn in Lawtell and Bradford's White Eagle in Opelousas; three early black Creole clubs, Slim's Y Ki Ki in Opelousas, Richard's in Lawtell, and Paul's Playhouse in Sunset, survive to the present as popular zydeco nightspots. (Significantly, when music writer Larry Benicewicz asked Guitar Gable if it might have been his early group, the Swing Masters, that Earl King observed near Opelousas and Eunice around 1954, Gable replied "I met him way back then and he heard me play. That's all I can say." In fact, Gable now recalls meeting King at Bradford's White Eagle, where he approached the New Orleans artist about performing with the Swing Masters at a future date.) Allan's biographical data support a black Creole origin for swamp pop: While the median year of birth for Cajun swamp poppers is 1940, the median year for black Creole swamp poppers is 1936. Black Creole

Swamp pop deejay/promoter Buddy King, then (Lake Charles, La., circa 1963) and now (Lafayette, La., 1992). Although the earlier photo appears to be a radio publicity shot—and although King was a deejay at KLOU radio in Lake Charles at the time—it actually was taken to model clothing for a local men's store. (Earlier photo courtesy of Buddy King; photo insert by the author)

swamp poppers thus matured earlier than their Cajun counterparts, a roughly four-year gap broadened by the tendency of black Creole swamp poppers to perform in nightclubs at younger ages than Cajun swamp poppers.[27]

Although today few south Louisiana and southeast Texas nightclubs sponsor live swamp pop music, the swamp pop club scene thrived in the late 1950s and early '60s. Most of these nightclubs, however, were Cajun swamp pop clubs in which both Cajun and black Creole swamp pop groups appeared. Lafayette, for instance, boasted Landry's Palladium, the Roof Garden, Whit's Lounge, and the Bayou Club; Lake Charles the Bamboo Club and the Golden Rocket; Ville Platte the Evangeline Club, the Jungle Lounge and the Rendezvous; Lawtell the Step Inn Club and the Green Lantern; and Opelousas Raphael's Inn, the Moonlight Inn, and the Southern Club. Many were rough-and-tumble joints, where some male clubgoers from rival towns or rural districts often gathered for the sole purpose of fighting. One of the toughest spots, recalls swamp popper Roy Perkins, was the Teche Club in New Iberia. "A fightin' club," he says. "We were scared to go there. A mean place." Perkins's bandleader, Phillip Comeaux, agrees: "This old guy, Rubic Blanchard, he was a tough guy, man, and he owned that club . . . . His place was a pretty nice place, nice looking. It was a nice place, but it got kinda rough at times. And boy, when you had a fight there, I mean, this was a war, it was a big to-do. . . . And he'd tell us when a fight broke out, he'd say 'Pick out a fast number and don't stop till I tell ya.' And, man! we'd be playing for 45 minutes!" Musicians tried to avoid conflict during brawls by keeping to the bandstand. Sometimes, however, they were singled out as targets of violence. Little Alfred recalls: "I ran into a thing in Basile. I can't think of the name of the club. We had a saxophone player, called him Fat Daddy—his name was Lee Bernard—and Lee would sing a lot of Fats Domino songs . . . and so this guy came up to the stage and asked him to do 'Blueberry Hill.' Now it was one of those nights Fat Daddy was drunk or whatever and he said, 'I'll get it for you.' But he didn't do it. The guy came back, the guy came back about three times and the last time he came up he said 'Look, I said I want to hear "Blueberry Hill." ' And he said, 'I'll get it for you.' He [the clubgoer] said, 'No you're not' and he hit him. And that night the club owner got on the stage with a shotgun."[28]

A few swamp pop clubs rarely saw violence, however; many, in fact, operated as respectable "dinner clubs." The most popular of these was the Southern Club of Opelousas, which, although not as obscure as the black Creole clubs where swamp pop first may have appeared, perhaps is most responsible for nurturing the genre after its inception. During the 1950s and '60s dozens of notable swamp pop artists appeared on the Southern Club's stage (or stages, as for a period it boasted two bandstands featuring alternating groups). Those performing at the club during its heyday include Warren Storm, Skip Stewart, Rod Bernard, Lil' Bob, Clint West, G. G. Shinn, Bert Miller, Johnnie Allan, T. K. Hulin, and Tommy McLain, all of whom laud club owner Lionel "Chick" Vidrine's efforts to promote and preserve swamp pop music. In fact, when Vidrine's home burned in 1991 these middle-aged artists returned to the Southern Club and on one hot August afternoon raised about twenty thousand dollars for the club owner. The event elicited praise for Vidrine and the Southern Club in the local *Daily World* newspaper. One clubgoer wrote: "Recently I read an article in the *Daily World*—about Mr. Chick Vidrine—owner of the Southern Club. The part about couples meeting there and later venture into marriage [*sic*]— sent me strolling down memory lane. For you see I met my husband of thirty-one years . . . while patronizing that famous night-spot. Yes indeed Mr. Vidrine, you and your magical Southern Club—made it possible for my spouse and I to meet, fall in love, marry and live happily ever after." Of course, the intentions of some clubgoers were not always so innocent. As one observer of St. Landry Parish notes, "In addition to locals looking for fun, soldiers and airmen from Ft. Polk in Leesville and England Air Force Base in Alexandria would come to town to hear the likes of Warren Storm and Rod Bernard play at the Southern Club. Afterwards, they might indulge themselves at one of the parish's numerous whorehouses."[29]

A popular hangout for a generation of St. Landry Parish residents, the Southern Club was built in 1949 by Vidrine's uncle, Claude Morein, who intended to operate it as a restaurant and casino, complete with bingo games, slot machines, and dice tables. Following a statewide crackdown on illegal gambling the nightclub passed though a second relative to Vidrine. He reopened the club on January 1, 1956, drawing crowds with the offer of live entertainment. Vidrine brought to Opelousas such notable artists as Smiley Lewis, Dee Clark, Fats Domino, Esquerita, Chuck Berry, Lloyd Price, the Clovers, Jimmy Reed, and even Loretta Lynn (with her sister Crystal Gayle, as yet unknown). Local swamp pop bands, however, dominated the Southern Club's stage, and a roster of Saturday night house bands includes Elton Anderson and the Sid Lawrence Band (1956–57); Lil' Bob and the Lollipops (1957/58–63); and the Shondells (1963–69/70). Friday nights featured a variety of swamp pop artists, including Rod Bernard and the Twisters; Bobby Page and the Riff Raffs; Guitar Gable

The Southern Club, 3150 West Landry Street (Highway 190), Opelousas, La., November 27, 1991. (Photo by the author)

and the Musical Kings featuring King Karl; and the Boogie Kings. (Although the Boogie Kings now perform "blue-eyed soul" music, they began in the mid-1950s as a swamp pop group; in fact, the ensemble pays homage to its swamp pop roots on its 1993 CD *Louisiana Country Soul,* featuring the track "I Love That Swamp Pop Music," and on its 1995 CD *Swamp Boogie Blues,* a collection of swamp pop cover tunes with cameo vocals by the original artists.) After a thirteen-year break from promoting swamp pop (during which he experimented with heavy metal, zydeco and Cajun music), Vidrine again brought swamp pop to the Southern Club when Johnnie Allan and the Memories took over as house band from 1982 to '83. The Shondells also held several reunions at the nightspot during the 1980s and early '90s. After Vidrine's death in January 1994 the club continued to operate for several months under his wife's direction as a tavern and hangout for local *bourré* players. (*Bourré* is a popular south Louisiana card game resembling bridge.) Today the timeworn club sits abandoned along Highway 190 awaiting a prospective buyer.[30]

Swamp pop quickly spread from nightspots like the Southern Club to primitive Louisiana recording studios, and although a few swamp poppers conducted

Elton Anderson (left) and Lake Charles recordman Eddie Shuler glancing over the swamp
popper's unsigned Capitol label contract on the front steps of the Goldband studio, 313
Church Street, Lake Charles, La., circa 1960. (Photo courtesy of the Johnnie Allan Collection)

early sessions in New Orleans (usually at Cosimo Matassa's famed studio),
most utilized local south Louisiana and southeast Texas studios. The earliest of
these studios were operated by Eddie Shuler of Lake Charles and J. D. Miller
of Crowley. (Miller is usually cited as the earlier of the two, but documents
recently unearthed by Shuler reveal that he was pressing 78 rpm records on
the Goldband label as early as March 1945, a year before Miller issued his first
recordings on his own 78 rpm label, Fais Do Do.) Shuler yielded swamp pop
hits not only for Goldband, but also for George Khoury's Lake Charles–based
Lyric and Khoury labels. He produced such well-known swamp pop recordings
as Gene Terry's "Cindy Lou," Guitar Jr.'s "Family Rules," and Phil Phillips's "Sea
of Love." Similarly, Miller directed swamp pop sessions for labels like Dago
Redlich's Viking label of Crowley, Lee Lavergne's Lanor label of Church Point,
and Floyd Soileau's Jin label of Ville Platte, as well as for his own labels, including
Zynn, Rocko (originally Rocket), and Showtime. He also licensed swamp pop
songs to Ernie Young's Nashville-based Excello and Nasco labels, which issued

numerous Miller-produced swamp blues recordings during the late 1950s and early '60s. Miller oversaw the recording of such swamp pop classics as Rod Bernard's "This Should Go On Forever," Warren Storm's "Prisoner's Song," and King Karl and Guitar Gable's "Irene," "Life Problem," and "Congo Mombo."[31]

Subsequent swamp pop producers emulated the recording styles pioneered by Eddie Shuler and J. D. Miller. Characterized by simple, even sparse production techniques, deep, murky layers of instrumentation, and—particularly in Miller's instance—a fair amount of natural reverb, these styles were influenced in part by their experiences recording and even performing traditional Cajun music. For instance, Shuler, although a non-Cajun Texan by birth, played rhythm guitar in the early 1940s with the famed Cajun string band the Hackberry Ramblers, and in the early 1950s produced the recordings of legendary Cajun accordionist Iry Lejeune. Similarly, in the late 1930s non-Cajun Miller appeared as rhythm guitarist with several Cajun groups, including Joseph Falcon and his Silver Bell Band, the Four Aces, the Rice City Ramblers, and the Daylight Creepers, and in the mid-1940s recorded groups like the Cajun string band Happy Fats, Doc Guidry and the Boys. (Incidentally, Miller, who died in March 1996, married a daughter of Cajun accordionist Lee Sonnier.) Skilled at producing and performing the region's traditional ethnic music, Shuler and Miller extracted the feeling of Cajun and black Creole music from young swamp pop artists, and in doing so contributed to swamp pop's development. Other local producers also benefited from frequent exposure to Cajun music. A Cajun accordionist's son, producer Huey ("the Crazy Cajun") Meaux performed Cajun music in his youth and even sang on recordings by the Cajun group the Rambling Aces. And although not a musician, premier swamp pop producer Floyd Soileau became involved in the music industry partly because of his childhood desire to perform Cajun music. (Soileau issues from a long line of Cajun fiddlers: His brother, father, grandfather, and great-grandfather all mastered the instrument.)[32]

By 1958 Soileau was recording Cajun and swamp pop music, and soon other producers—including Carol Rachou (of the La Louisianne and Tamm labels), Bill Hall (Hall, Hallway), Stan Lewis (Jewel, Paula, Ronn), Roland "Rocky" Robin (N-Joy), Jake Graffagnino (Carl), Myra Smith (Ram), Lee Lavergne (Lanor), George Khoury (Lyric, Khoury), S. J. "Sam Montel" Montalbano (Montel, Michelle) and Huey Meaux (Princess, Pic 1, Crazy Cajun, Teardrop)—also busily were recording swamp pop music. (In 1963 a Lafayette newspaper claimed, perhaps a bit extravagantly, "There are over 100 local labels.") These producers relied in turn on deejays like south Louisiana's Buddy King, J. P. "The

A Mike Leadbitter photo of producer Floyd Soileau spinning a 45 single at Flat Town Music Co., Ville Platte, La., circa 1967. (Photo courtesy of John Broven/Ace [UK] Records)

Big Bopper" Richardson of Beaumont, and Ken "Jack the Cat" Elliott of New Orleans to promote swamp pop over the airwaves. These artistic, technical, and promotional forces united to convert swamp pop from a rough-hewn, fledgling genre performed by Cajun and black Creole teenagers in rural and small-town nightclubs into a commercially viable sound sought after by fans around the world. Swamp pop always maintained its rough edge, however, a quality that Johnnie Allan attributes to Cajun music's influence on the genre—and attributable equally to the impact of black Creole music.[33]

Swamp poppers with few exceptions are ethnic Cajuns or black Creoles. According to Allan's biographical data, about two-thirds of white swamp pop artists possess surnames generally regarded as Cajun, while nearly three-fourths of black swamp pop artists possess surnames of black Creole origin. Obscuring this fact, however, is the widespread adoption of Anglo-American stage names by swamp pop artists. Charles Mann's actual name, for instance, is Charles Domingue; Bobby Page's, Elwood Dugas; Joe Barry's, Joe Barrios; and Little Alfred's, Alfred Babino (a black Creole version of the Cajun surname *Babineaux*). Examples exist even among southeast Texas swamp poppers: Gene Terry's actual name is Terry Gene DeRouen; Johnny Preston's, Johnny Preston Courville; and Jivin' Gene, Gene Bourgeois. Stage names also are used by musicians who today remain only on the fringes of swamp pop, such as Bobby Charles, born Robert Charles Guidry; John Fred, born John Fred Gourrier; and Beaumont's Barbara Lynn, born Barbara Lynn Ozen. (The latter surname is a variation of *Ozenne/Auzenne,* a common black Creole name in Acadiana; not surprisingly, Lynn's parents hail from the Carencro area, in the heart of south Louisiana's Cajun and black Creole country). These performers traded ethnic surnames for Anglo-American stage names not because they despised their heritage (as some maintain), but because they wished to appeal to audiences beyond south Louisiana, where the correct pronunciation of names like Guillot, Thibodeaux, and Ardoin continues to elude many enthusiasts of south Louisiana music. Some swamp poppers, however—most notably Jimmy Clanton, Dale Houston, Tommy McLain, Jimmy Donley, and Freddy Fender—were neither Cajuns nor black Creoles. These performers became swamp pop artists, however, through their immersion in Cajun and black Creole culture and their eager adoption of the swamp pop sound.[34]

Although based during his heyday just beyond Cajun Louisiana in Baton Rouge, Jimmy Clanton hailed originally from Golden Meadow in eastern Acadiana, only a few miles from Cajun swamp popper Joe Barry's hometown of Cut Off. On the eve of stardom Clanton benefited from a close friendship with future swamp pop recordman S. J. Montalbano, who not only managed the teen idol but informally assisted in producing and promoting early Clanton recordings like the swamp pop ballads "Another Sleepless Night" and "Just a Dream" (a million-selling composition inspired by King Karl and Guitar Gable's earlier swamp pop classic "Irene"). Dale Houston of the swamp pop duo Dale and Grace also hailed from Baton Rouge, where he moved from Mississippi in his early teens. Once established in Louisiana, Houston developed an appetite for swamp pop, which led him eventually to team up with Cajun swamp popper Grace Broussard of nearby Ascension Parish. As with Clanton, Montalbano managed and produced Dale and Grace, who recorded their number one national hit "I'm Leaving It Up to You" at Carol Rachou's La Louisianne Studio in Lafayette (a favorite of several swamp poppers during the 1960s, including King Karl, Rod Bernard, Warren Storm, Skip Stewart, and Lil' Bob). And as a youngster in central Louisiana, Tommy McLain listened to Cajun and black Creole artists like Happy Fats and Clifton Chenier, and later performed in south Louisiana alongside Cajun swamp popper Clint West as a member of Red Smiley's Vel-Tones. By the mid-1960s McLain had become irreversibly associated with swamp pop music—especially its archetypal gut-wrenching, end-of-the-

Some Notable Swamp Pop Artists (Stage and Actual Names)*

Stage Name(s)	Actual Name	Stage Name(s)	Actual Name
Johnnie Allan	John Allen Guillot	Lil' Bob	Camille Bob
Rockin' Dave Allen	Dave Stich	Little Alfred	Alfred Babino
Elton Anderson	(same)	Frankie Lowery	(same)
Bobby B.	Bobby Bourque	Barbara Lynn	Barbara Lynn Ozen
Joe Barry	Joseph Barrios	Mason McClain	Mason McClain Berryhill
Rod Bernard	(same)	Tommy McLain	(same)
Phil Bo	Phil Boudreaux	Charles Mann	Charles Domingue
Van Broussard	(same)	Pete Marlo	Pete Bergeron
Joe Carl	Nolan Duplantis	Lee Martin	Leroy Martin
Lee Castle	Leroy Castille	Ronnie Melancon	(same)
Bobby Charles	Robert Charles Guidry	Bert Miller	Elbert Miller
Doug Charles	Doug Ardoin	Bobby Page	Elwood Dugas
Ike Clanton	(same)	Roy Perkins	Ernie Suarez
Jimmy Clanton	(same)	Phil Phillips	Phillip Batiste
Cookie (of Cookie and the Cupcakes)	Huey Thierry	Johnny Preston	Johnny Preston Courville
Kenny Cornett	(same)	Van Preston	Preston Vanicor
Dale (of Dale and Grace)	Dale Houston	Prince Charles	Charles Fontenot
Huey Darby	(same)	Jay Randall	Jay Noel
Jimmy Donley	(same)	Don Rich	Don Richard
Shelton Dunaway	(same)	Red Smiley	Bob Shurley
Elton (of Elton and the Eltradors)	Elton Hargrave	Rocky Robin	Roland Robin
Freddy Fender	Baldemar Huerta	Buck Rogers	Lawrence Rodriguez
Kenny Fife	(same)	Bobby Scott	Floyd Begnaud
John Fred	John Fred Gourrier	G. G. Shinn	George Shinn
Guitar Gable	Gabriel Perrodin	Johnny Spain	Johnny Morvant
Kane Glaze	(same)	Jerry Starr	Jerome Verrette
Grace (of Dale and Grace)	Grace Broussard	Skip Stewart, Skip Morris	Maurice Guillory
Guitar Jr., Lonnie Brooks	Lee Baker	Sticks Herman	Herman Guidry
Hot Rod Reynaud	Sidney Reynaud	Warren Storm	Warren Schexnider
T. K. Hulin	Alton James Hulin	Gary T.	Gary Thibodeaux
Rufus Jagneaux	Benny Graeff	Travis T.	Travis Thibodeaux
Jivin' Gene	Gene Bourgeois	Willie Tee	Wilven Trahan
King Karl	Bernard Jolivette	Gene Terry	Terry Gene DeRouen
Gene King	Gene Rodrigue	Kenny Tibbs	Kenny Thibodeaux
		Lionel Torrence	Lionel Prevost
		Glenn Wells	Glenn Stilwell
		Clint West	Clinton Guillory

*For additional listings of swamp pop artists with vital statistics, consult n. 1 to chapter 3 and see Allan, *Memories*, 160–61, 202, 207, 232.

John Fred (left) and Jimmy Clanton on tour, summer 1959, Houston, Tex. (Photo courtesy of the Johnnie Allan Collection)

world ballads—cutting records under the guidance of swamp pop producers Soileau and Meaux. Classics he contributed to the basic swamp pop repertoire include "Sweet Dreams," "Before I Grow Too Old" and "Try to Find Another Man" (a duet with West).[35]

Similarly, Jimmy Donley teamed up early in his musical career with Meaux and a variety of swamp pop backing artists. Although many of his recording sessions occurred in New Orleans, Donley was supported by the Vikings, a seasoned swamp pop group led by artist/producer Lee Martin. (The Vikings previously backed swamp popper Joe Barry in the rural nightclubs of southeast Acadiana.) By the time Donley committed suicide in 1963 he had composed numerous classics of the genre, including "Please Mr. Sandman," "I'm to Blame," "Think It Over" and "Born to Be a Loser." As Johnnie Allan and Bernice Larson Webb comment in *Born to Be a Loser: The Jimmy Donley Story*, "While he entertained mainly on the Mississippi Gulf Coast in small lounges from the mid-1940s until

Grace Broussard (left) and Dale Houston, known as Dale and Grace, Catholic Youth Organization Center dance, Baton Rouge, La., 1963. (Photo courtesy of the Johnnie Allan Collection)

his death in 1963, his name became as synonymous with the indigenous swamp-pop music of south Louisiana as those of million-record sellers Joe Barry, Rod Bernard, Dale and Grace, Jimmy Clanton and Tommy McLain, to name a few."[36]

In the 1970s swamp popper Freddy Fender—born Baldemar Huerta in San Benito, Texas, near the U.S.-Mexican border—also came under Meaux's management and, as Broven points out in *South to Louisiana,* "although Fender was a Chicano . . . much of his formative career was spent in South Louisiana; spiritually, Fender's music was from the Louisiana swamp." Although he performed Tex-Mex country rock during the late 1950s, Fender recorded two early ballads swampy enough to captivate south Louisiana teens: "Holy One" and an early version of "Wasted Days and Wasted Nights." ("Holy One," in fact, is covered by Joe Carl and the Dukes of Rhythm on their circa June 1960 live recording at the College Inn in Thibodaux—the only known recording of a swamp pop nightclub act dating from the genre's golden age.) During the late 1960s Fender teamed up with Joe Barry and went on in the mid-'70s to record such enduring swamp pop classics as "Before the Next Teardrop Falls" and "Wasted Days and Wasted Nights" (the latter covered by Johnnie Allan in alternating English and Cajun French lyrics). Fender even paid homage to his swamp pop roots on his ABC label *Swamp Gold* album, on which he covered Jivin' Gene's "Breaking Up Is Hard to Do," T. K. Hulin's "Graduation Night," Jerry Raines's "Our Teenage Love" and Jimmy Donley's "Please Mr. Sandman." Fender also covered swamp pop hits like Barbara Lynn's "You'll Lose A Good Thing," Buck Rogers's "Crazy Baby," and Cookie and the Cupcakes' "Mathilda," as well as Rod Bernard's "Go On Go On." (The latter cover remains unreleased.) In addition, the swamp pop sound appears in the music of Fender's later group, the Texas Tornadoes.[37]

Swamp pop grew out of intense, sustained interaction between Cajuns and black Creoles, which, while essential for the genre's growth, occurred in the midst of racially tense conditions. Reports about the unusually harmonious relationship of Cajuns and black Creoles—especially when compared to race relations elsewhere in the South—often are exaggerated. Broven, for instance, states, "The musical integration implicit in swamp pop was facilitated by a racial climate that was more relaxed in south Louisiana than in much of the South, although the Cajuns, being white, were obliged to observe certain social ethics and traditions governing their southern neighbors." In *The People Called Cajuns*, however, historian James H. Dormon notes that evidence suggests a history of extremely poor relations among Cajuns and black Creoles. Racial differences did not prevent interaction between these groups, he observes, but Cajuns and black Creoles maintained distinct, well-defined boundaries. Summing up his findings, Dormon claims, "Despite a longstanding tradition to the effect that French Louisiana was markedly more benign in its racial attitudes and relations than other Deep South regions, there is overwhelming evidence that the French-speaking white population in general and the Cajuns in particular were as actively Negrophobic as any other post-Reconstruction white South Louisianians." And he adds, "if the Cajun people held blacks in relatively low esteem, as appears to have been the case, the blacks from all indications often harbored equally unflattering views of the Cajuns."[38]

Unlike the remainder of their societies, however, Cajun and black Creole musicians appear to have enjoyed especially amicable relationships. Cajun audiences, however, presented serious problems for black Creole musicians long before swamp pop's advent. The tragic death of legendary black Creole accordionist Amédé Ardoin provides the most poignant example. Ardoin crossed racial barriers by recording with Cajun fiddler Dennis McGee, but stepped too far when at a dance around 1941 he wiped away his sweat with a handkerchief offered by a Cajun female. Suffering a terrible beating after the dance, he eventually died from his wounds, emotional and physical. (Reports about Ardoin's death vary among sources; this account, however, draws on the most accepted versions.)[39]

South Louisiana's racial climate had not improved by the 1950s. In fact, the threat of widespread desegregation may have aggravated tensions between Cajuns and black Creoles during the mid-to-late '50s. Perhaps as a result, black Creoles playing in Cajun swamp pop clubs experienced racism on almost a nightly basis. "A lot of times we had to exit through the back door," says black Creole swamp popper Guitar Gable. "You couldn't go out the front." Gable recalls that many club owners refused to permit black Creole artists to leave the bandstand; some, however, allowed them to approach the bar or use restrooms—but only with police escorts. "You had to have a' escort generally," states Gable. "When we played in Catahoula, the police had to escort us to the bathroom and back. . . . If you had to go to the bar, they would watch over you and everything." Similarly, Gable's partner, black Creole swamp popper King Karl, recounts "[There was] one club we wouldn't go to the bar and this was in Mamou. Mamou was pretty strict about that, so we didn't bother with them, but all the other places we'd go [let us go to the bar]."[40]

Yet such prohibitions were not unique to Mamou or Catahoula. "I would say when I first started out that we ran into some trouble," recalls black Creole swamp popper Little Alfred. "Number one, we couldn't get off the stage and walk around the club. . . . We couldn't go to the bar. Oh, no. No. Couldn't go to the bar. . . . We couldn't even go out and use the restroom." Police officers often guarded black Creole musicians before and after performances, when some clubgoers targeted them for abuse. "They had to be there when you're in and out of the club," recalls Gable. "It was *terrible stuff,* but in them days they just was crazy people, you know. . . . But the policeman would be right there with you all the time, when you was loading up and unloading. . . . In those days *it just seemed so bad for the race,* you know. We just couldn't understand *why it's so bad.*" As club owner Chick Vidrine explains, the presence of black Creoles in his club concerned him less than their reception by Cajun clubgoers. "Not that it made me that much difference, but it's the crowd," says Vidrine. "That's who I was afraid I'd get some problems with." Some club owners thus restricted black Creole swamp poppers to the bandstand, usually serving them drinks onstage and perhaps allowing a small retinue of black Creole listeners to hang out backstage.[41]

"Dark days," sighs black Creole swamp popper Lil' Bob, reluctant to discuss the racism he encountered during the genre's golden age. "It didn't matter to us. All we'd do is go out there and work and get out of there." King Karl echoes Bob's stoic sentiment: "The thing it was, to know your limitations and stay there," he says. "That's all there was to it. . . . It didn't bother us. You see, we knew it, we accepted to play, so that was it. We did what was accepted to do, what we accepted to do, and leave. That's it."[42]

Despite threats of violence against those who crossed accepted racial barriers, black Creole vocalist Huey "Cookie" Thierry (front man of Cookie and the Cupcakes) entangled his group and himself in racial trouble during the 1950s and early '60s by dallying with adoring Cajun females. According to Alfred, Gable, and Vidrine, Cookie never approached these forbidden admirers; rather, they approached him—some to provoke Cajun males, claims Alfred, others to express genuine affection. Club owner Vidrine recalls: "In Lawtell they'd got the rope to hang him and everything over there one night. . . . He was messing around with a white gal. Really wasn't his fault though, 'cause those damn gals would go up and throw that shit at 'em—and they're human beings! The state police took him and brought him down the road somewheres." A former Cupcakes member, Little Alfred confirms Vidrine's account, suggesting that the incident occurred at the Step Inn Club in Lawtell. "[Cookie] also had a lot of problems in Mermentau," says Alfred, "because I remember at the River Club in Mermentau it came to the point where the band could play but he couldn't." Adds Guitar Gable, "I don't know if they tried to hung him, but I know he had to run away from Hick's Wagon Wheel a couple of times, leave all the instruments on the bandstand." In a 1986 interview with the English music magazine *Now Dig This* Johnnie Allan sums up Cookie's racial problems: "Cookie kinda messed himself up in South Louisiana because at that time he was quite popular with women and he had an affair with a white woman and the news spread around and they blackballed him from St. Landry Parish. The Sheriff told him, 'I don't wanna see you in my parish anymore. I don't want you playing in nightclubs anymore.' . . . In other words you can play in the white nightclub but don't mess with the white women. So it got to a point where Cookie just went overboard with that and finally

Rare photo of Cupcakes front
man Huey "Cookie" Thierry
at the Second Annual Eunice
Teenage Jamboree, National
Guard Armory, Eunice, La.,
December 23, 1958. (Photo
courtesy of Pete Bergeron/the
Johnnie Allan Collection)

none of the clubs would want to hire him anymore so he just left the state of
Louisiana."[43]

Although reluctant to discuss particulars (and denying he left south Louisiana
because of racial troubles), Cookie confirms the rumors about his interracial
affairs during the 1950s and early '60s, as does longtime Cupcakes pianist Ernest
Jacobs, Cookie's current manager. In fact, Cookie's exploits hurt the group's
local popularity, claims Jacobs, and led to threats of racial violence and even to
violence itself: "Threats? Not only threats! You had fights and everything," he
recalls. "Like right here in Lake Charles they turned our station wagon over . . .
our station wagon with a trailer." Jacobs verifies Allan's claim that the Cupcakes
encountered serious racial trouble in St. Landry Parish. "They blocked the road
in Eunice," he says, "[because] they didn't want us going to Lawtell . . . . It got
so bad that when we'd get ready to go into St. Landry Parish we had to have
a state deputy to meet us in Basile to go all the way with us into Lawtell and

Opelousas. And then he would drive us back." Jacobs maintains, however, that the outcry over Cookie's interracial affairs eventually subsided, and that the Cupcakes continued to perform in south Louisiana to ever increasing crowds until Cookie left for California in 1965.[44]

Similarly, Lil' Bob recalls a serious racial incident involving a member of his own band, the Lollipops. Says Bob: "Right here in '57 a guy by the name of Gabriel King, he was my lead tenor man in the band. . . . He kissed a white woman in the back of the Rendezvous Club [in Ville Platte] and they gave him one year [in jail]. Well, the woman loved him, he loved her, none of them was married and he kissed her and somebody spotted it and went to court. And we went to court, man, the courthouse was on fire. There was six black people in there—me, his daddy, his mother, his lawyer and him and [local R&B artist] Good Rockin' Bob. Man, they was hollering *'Hang him! Hang him! Hang him! Hang him!'* And he was sitting there just as cool—and they gave him a year, just for kissing." King Karl and Guitar Gable confirm Bob's account, stating they visited the saxophonist in jail. Although Karl claims that Gabriel King was framed by local authorities under a trumped-up charge of "white slavery" (enforced prostitution), no evidence exists to support this assertion. Nevertheless, Ville Platte newspaper reports and Evangeline Parish court records confirm most of Bob's, Karl's, and Gable's accounts. Police did arrest twenty-two-year-old Gabriel King for kissing a white female behind a local nightclub, but not only was she white, she also was a minor of sixteen. Without regard to the issue of race, the court accused King of the misdemeanor crime of "Indecent Behavior with a Juvenile by kissing and caressing . . . with the intention of arousing or gratifying the sexual desires of the said juvenile and/or himself." Still, it was race that converted King's violation into a small-town scandal. The saxophonist clearly understood the situation's volatility prior to his exposure and arrest, and he touches on the period's underlying tensions in a love letter to his Cajun admirer. "What a fool I was to think you could love me," he lamented. "After all, I know the condition. You hate me just as the others do. . . . I didn't think you was like the rest of the people."[45]

Pleading not guilty at his January 1957 arraignment, King stood trial in March at the Evangeline Parish courthouse. An hour beforehand over a hundred spectators had arrived, and by the time Judge J. Cleveland Frugé called the court to order all seats were occupied and the aisles and hallways were packed with onlookers. Stirred by the scene, a reporter for Ville Platte's *Weekly Gazette* waxed Shakespearian, declaring, "Friday morning the harsh sword of court procedure ripped open the belly of the drama, laying bare the dark and quivering flesh whose ancient and primitive yearnings do on occasion make poor, miserable sinners of us all." Yet some observers must have found the trial anticlimactic: The charges required no jury, little could be heard of the goings-on around the stand, and King declined to testify in his own defense. The minor took the stand, however, and according to the *Gazette* stated: "She first saw King when he played with the Good Rockin' Bob dance band in Mamou two years ago. She was never alone with him, she said, until last August. On that occasion, which was at a Ville Platte night club, she said King signalled her to meet him outside. She was alone with him about 20 minutes, she told the judge, and this time was spent behind the club. King, she declared, kissed her twice during this interval while holding her around the waist." Backing up Lil' Bob's account, the *Gazette* goes on to report: "She also testified she had been in love with King, but would not admit they planned or discussed eventual marriage."[46]

Although no one witnessed the events that transpired behind the Rendezvous that night in 1956, the prosecution managed to produce incriminating evidence: the saxophonist's love letter. Court records show that the minor's father, a local farmer, reported the tryst to police, apparently turning over as evidence the confiscated letter and a snapshot of King wielding his saxophone on stage. Just as Bob, Karl, and Gable claim, Judge Frugé—while waiving a five hundred dollar fine to assist King in paying his attorney's fees—sentenced the saxophonist to a one-year jail sentence. (King died in 1988.)[47]

As historian Dormon points out, racism also existed among black Creoles. "When I first started out," says Lil' Bob, "if a black person was caught in a [Cajun] place like the Rendezvous in Ville Platte—oh, they'd hang him! [And] vice versa—[if] a white person was caught . . . in a black place, they might not would hang him, but they'd cut him." In fact, Cajun swamp poppers performed for black Creole audiences only at civic dances, when separate shows were staged for the different races. For instance, regarding a circa 1960 swamp pop benefit in Lafayette featuring Johnnie Allan, T. K. Hulin, Rod Bernard, Bobby Charles, Skip Stewart, King Karl, Warren Storm, and others, a local newspaper notes that "May 26 is scheduled for the Negro youth of the area, and May 27 will be for white teenagers."[48]

Most Cajun and black Creole swamp pop musicians, however, tried to disavow racism and often worked together to make swamp pop music. For instance, Cajun swamp popper Rod Bernard often collaborated with King Karl and Guitar Gable. In fact, Karl's compositions greatly influenced Bernard, who

Lil' Bob and the Lollipops, apparently on the set of KLFY's live "Saturday Hop" dance program, Lafayette, La., 1964. Front row, left to right: Joseph Richard, John Clinton Perrodin, and Lil' Bob. Back row: "Blind" John Hart, Zellus Preston, John Bell, and Gabriel King. (Photo courtesy of the Johnnie Allan Collection)

found national success with "This Should Go On Forever" and followed it immediately, albeit less successfully, with "My Life Is a Mystery," another Karl composition. (After Bernard's recording of "This Should Go On Forever" hit the national charts, Excello quickly issued Karl's own version—actually a demo, says Karl—but it never received much airplay or attention.) Illustrating the long tradition of interaction among Cajun and black Creole musicians, Karl and Bernard even collaborated as songwriters, composing "(I Have a Vow) To Have and Hold" and "Gimme Back My Cadillac." "A lot of times he would come with his guitar and we'd sit down and play guitar," recalls Karl. "I was living in Opelousas. He'd come over and sit down and play guitar . . . . Sit on the side with Gable. We'd play music. We used to fool around with writing songs." Karl claims that Bernard also helped him to write "My Life Is A Mystery," although Bernard is not cited as co-writer and does not recall contributing to the song.[49]

Unfortunately, Cajun and black Creole swamp poppers rarely performed together on the bandstand. "If you had a mixed band—man, you could wait for trouble," says Vidrine. As late as 1967 when Little Alfred joined the Boogie Kings—touring at the time as "American Soul Train" because, according to bandleader Ned Theall, *boogie* often was considered a racial slur outside Louisiana—the group expressed concern about playing in south Louisiana clubs fronted by a black Creole vocalist. (Attitudes clearly have changed, however: I recently witnessed a white female leap from the Southern Club's crowded floor to dance onstage with Lil' Bob, who was backed that day by an integrated band. This occurred without incident before hundreds of the same clubgoers who might have been revolted at the sight during the 1950s and early '60s.)[50]

Despite the taboo against Cajuns and black Creoles performing together in local nightclubs, they often collaborated in south Louisiana's small-town recording studios. Like fellow recording pioneer Cosimo Matassa of New Orleans, J. D. Miller used integrated bands in his Crowley studio; indeed, his studio band from 1958 to '62 regularly consisted of black and white musicians. (This openness foreshadowed a similar movement in Memphis studios like Stax and American during the 1960s.) For instance, Cajun swamp popper Warren Storm drummed on sessions for black artists like Slim Harpo, Lightnin' Slim, Katie Webster, Lazy Lester, and Lonesome Sundown. Some of these artists in turn backed Cajun swamp poppers like Johnnie Allan, who recalls, "I've had Lazy Lester . . . play drums [actually a cardboard box] with me, I've had Katie Webster, [she] played keyboards on sessions for me, I've had Lionel Torrence, one of the top-notch swamp pop saxophonists anywheres, [he] played with me . . . . I'm sure there were some others." In addition, six-string virtuoso Guitar Gable played on Miller-produced sessions for fellow swamp poppers Warren Storm and Bobby Charles.[51]

Although they usually could not perform together in nightclubs, Cajun swamp poppers often admired their black Creole counterparts from the dance floor, and that admiration crossed genre boundaries. Allan, for instance, notes: "I've played in clubs where the larger section of the club was for whites, but then you had a little room in the back where the blacks would play their zydeco music. . . . So when we took intermission, where did we head? Looking at [through] the cracks in the wall or at the door, listening to them." Similarly, Rod Bernard recalls: "I would go listen to black bands play in white nightclubs.

An interracial recording session for Pete Marlo at J. D. Miller's famed Crowley, La., studio, 1958. Left to right: L. J. Doucet, Earl McFarland, swamp bluesman Lazy Lester, Nelson Bergeron, and Pete Marlo. (Photo courtesy of Pete Bergeron/the Johnnie Allan Collection)

Like Guitar Gable's band was all black, Good Rockin' Bob, Lil' Bob and the Lollipops . . . . We never thought of it being a black-white thing, there was just good music that everybody enjoyed." Nevertheless Bernard admits, "Back in the fifties, the black people didn't try to come in the white clubs, I don't think they even wanted to. We never thought about that, I mean we didn't think about going into theirs."[52]

Although relations between black and white Southerners remained tense during swamp pop's heyday, Cajun and black Creole swamp pop musicians openly admired each other's artistry and overcame racism to collaborate actively offstage, particularly in south Louisiana's small-town recording studios. This process of ethnic interaction encouraged the borrowing of musical styles and permitted swamp pop to develop into a dynamic interracial musical genre. "We all played together," remarks Allan, "so we had to learn a little something from each one of them [the black Creole musicians]." Despite the segregation of south Louisiana society, young Cajun and black Creole swamp poppers, like older traditional Cajun and black Creole musicians, crossed racial barriers and in doing so benefited richly from exchanges crucial to swamp pop's development.[53]

CAJUN AND BLACK CREOLE ELEMENTS IN SWAMP POP MUSIC

Many vintage swamp pop songs reflect the influence of Cajun and black Creole culture, revealing that in general swamp pop artists viewed their heritage in positive terms—long before the explosion of interest in all things Cajun and Creole that occurred in the 1970s and '80s and persists to the present. In fact, swamp poppers embraced their traditional culture prior to the "Cajun revival" of the late 1960s, when the efforts of out-of-state folklorists and the founding of CODOFIL (Council for the Development of French in Louisiana) provided a badly needed boost to the Cajun community's faltering self-esteem. (Although triggered in part by the successful appearance of Cajun musicians at the 1964 Newport Folk Festival, the Cajun revival actually materialized around 1968, reaching an early milestone in 1974 with the occurrence of the first Tribute to Cajun Music festival in Lafayette. Organized attempts to preserve black Creole culture, however, occurred only in the late 1980s with the founding of Creole, Inc., and *Creole Culture Magazine*.) Although most swamp poppers clearly are proud of their heritage, some musical purists argue otherwise: Advocating a twisted form of cultural elitism, this small, ill-defined, but well-entrenched faction regards swamp pop artists as apostates—Cajuns and black Creoles who turned their backs on their heritage in exchange for a greater chance at national fame and commercial success—and so deny swamp pop music and artists the benefit of the preservation and promotional efforts afforded to traditional Cajun and black Creole music.[1]

Such sentiments rarely appear in print or other media, but an obvious example can be found in Les Blank and Chris Strachwitz's documentary *J'ai été au bal* and its short version *French Dance Tonight*, which cover the genre (albeit briefly) as though it were a mere aberration of traditional Cajun and black Creole music. In addition, the documentaries take a direct swipe at swamp pop music and artists when Cajun performer D. L. Menard states during a filmed interview that "there's a lot of Cajuns that was ashamed to play our music." At that moment Blank and Strachwitz choose to flash a well-known photograph of swamp popper Gene Terry posing with a tilted microphone, horn-rimmed glasses and dapper western-style stage costume—implying that all swamp poppers were ashamed of their heritage. Of course, some swamp poppers no doubt were ashamed of their heritage, just as were some Cajun musicians and some segments of the entire Cajun community, but these Cajuns hardly constituted a majority of swamp pop artists. (The films' unwarranted censure of swamp pop artists may have issued from co-producer Strachwitz, who in a 1970 article for the *American Folk Music Occasional* derides what appears to be a swamp pop group in Lafayette as "only a band trying to imitate Fats Domino.")[2]

A "non-purist" creating a personalized blend of Cajun and country and western music, D. L. Menard insists he did not target swamp pop artists during his interview with Blank and Strachwitz. Rather, Menard claims he aimed his comments solely at traditional Cajun artists who gave up the "old-time" music in disgust around 1949 or '50 for country and western music. And many of those musicians *were* ashamed of their heritage. Dormon makes this observation in *The People Called Cajuns*: "It is thus of great significance that Cajun music in the '50s also came to bear the stigma of something déclassé . . . . Some musicians refused to have their names associated with it, even on recordings." During the 1950s and early '60s, however, many swamp pop artists were recording modern versions of traditional Cajun compositions and writing new compositions about Cajun culture, this work taking place in an era described by Dormon as possibly the "nadir in the ethnohistorical experience of the Cajun people . . . when the stigma still attached to rural Cajun culture was utterly pervasive and outside observers were even predicting the demise of the subculture altogether."[3]

In the early 1960s, for instance, Cajun swamp popper Rod Bernard penned several songs about Cajuns and Cajun culture with fellow songwriter Jack Clement. According to Bernard, it was Clement who suggested they compose a series of Cajun-oriented tunes, but it was Bernard who infused the songs with genuine Cajun elements. "Jack Clement was Bill Hall's recording engineer at the time and Jack's from Memphis," recalls Bernard.

> He was the engineer at Sun studios when Johnny Cash did all his things. In fact, Jack wrote songs like "Ballad of a Teenage Queen," "Guess Things Happen That Way," things like that. And he and Elvis and Roy Orbison and Jerry Lee [Lewis], he did all those original Sun things. He was the engineer. So Bill Hall hired him and brought

him to Beaumont and they built that studio for Big Bopper [music company] in Beaumont. And Jack was really fascinated with Cajun things and he would corner me and we'd talk *a lot* about south Louisiana and about gumbo and then the fais do-do thing came up and he said, "Well, what is that?" So I explained what a fais do-do is and he was fascinated by that term, by the terminology, and he said, "We ought to write a song about that." So he asked me about Cajun people and about the mamas watching their daughters at the dances and things of that nature and I filled him in every way I could, then we sat down and we wrote "Fais Do Do."[4]

Recorded in 1962 for Bill Hall's Hall-Way label, the Bernard-Clement composition "Fais Do Do" is one of the best examples of swamp pop songs about Cajun culture. (Along with its standard Cajun French spelling, Bernard rendered the song's title phonetically on the original 45 rpm release as "Fay Doe Doe," reflecting his desire to target listeners both in south Louisiana and beyond.) This upbeat composition relies heavily on a bouncy rhythm borrowed from traditional Cajun two-steps, and its lyrics express a Cajun's concern for the deterioration of his culture.

Fais Do Do

> Got a girl in Opelousas, Louisiana,
> She's the queen of the Teche Bayou.
> Prettiest girl in South Louisiana,
> The youngest daughter of Rufus Thibodeaux.
>
> But she don't like to ride in my pirogue.
> Don't even know how to cook gumbo.
> She upsets her Cajun papa.
> When she does the Twist at the fais do-do.
>
> Elle aime pas aller dans ma pirogue.
> Connait pas comment fait des gumbos.
> Elle fais fâcher sa 'Cadien papa
> Quand elle fait la Twist à la fais do-do.
>
> She was born and raised on the bayou,
> She's a tenth-generation Thibodeaux.
> Used to do the Cajun two-step
> Till she heard "The Twist" on the radio. . . .[5]

Bernard provides an accurate depiction of Cajun culture's status around
1960, apparently with concern for historical accuracy. For instance, he describes
the song's subject as a "tenth-generation" Thibodeaux; that is, she represents
the tenth generation of Thibodeauxs residing in Louisiana. Because the name
Thibodeaux is Acadian in origin, and because twenty years roughly comprises
a generation, the subject's family must have arrived in south Louisiana around
the 1760s, when the exiled Thibodeauxs did indeed immigrate to the region.
Bernard thus adds a degree of realism to the song while making a personal
observation about the decline of his traditional culture. Through the narrator—
apparently an un-Americanized Cajun—Bernard reveals the effects of Americanization on the Thibodeaux girl, who no longer enjoys traditional Cajun activities
like riding in a *pirogue* (a narrow flat-bottomed boat) or cooking gumbo. (Interestingly, Bernard named the song's father figure in tribute to Cajun musician
Rufus Thibodeaux and originally named another Cajun-oriented song for the acclaimed fiddler, but Bernard's producer, Huey Meaux, requested that he change
the title for legal reasons to the less specific "Papa Thibodeaux.")[6]

The song's narrator observes that his girlfriend angers her father by performing the nontraditional "Twist" at the *fais do-do,* or communal dance. The
composition thus exhibits a "generation gap" theme common to youth-oriented
music and, like the narrator of the traditional Cajun song "Colinda" (who
wishes to dance "to make the old ladies mad"), the Thibodeaux girl no doubt
intends to disturb her " 'Cadien papa." Yet the song concerns not only a gen-
erational gap, but a cultural gap separating the girl from her father and from
her boyfriend. Although the listener safely can assume that the Thibodeaux
girl and narrator are roughly the same age, they no longer share the same
culture: The girl has embraced American culture as represented by Chubby
Checker's early 1960s hit song "The Twist" and the dance craze it inspired, a
fad introduced to her through radio, a powerful Americanizing force. (Checker's
"The Twist," originally recorded in 1958 by Hank Ballard and the Midnighters,
reached number one on the charts in 1960 and again in 1962, inspiring
Bernard's reference.)[7]

Like "Fais Do Do," Johnnie Allan's "Cajun Man," written by Allan and Ingrid
Guidry and released in 1965, conveys an exceptional degree of lyrical realism.
The song also documents many positive attributes ascribed to Cajuns: A close
relationship with the environment, a spiritual outlook, an intense *joie de vivre,*
and a strong work ethic. (The latter attribute, however, is a matter of contention. Some observers claim that although Cajuns are hard workers, they

nevertheless lack a middle-class work ethic; that is, they typically are nonmaterialistic and work primarily to subsist, not to acquire material goods or social prestige.)

Cajun Man

He works the land with blistered hands.
He don't know night from day.
He keeps that water in that rice.
You have no time to play.
His tired face, his sunburned hands,
Now show the stress and strain.
Lord have mercy on this man,
Send him down some rain.

. . . .

Weather is his friend and foe,
Till that rice is cut.
He knows no peace, he gets no rest,
But that's the farmer's luck.
When all his work is done at last,
The rice is in the mill,
He celebrates at festivals.
Let him have his fill.[8]

This tribute to hard-working Cajuns and in particular to Cajun farmers no doubt appealed to Allan because of his rugged childhood near Rayne, where his father, a sharecropper, raised corn, hay, cotton, and sweet potatoes. "We'd work one year to pay last year's debts," says Allan. "It was gettin' up at 4:30 in the morning. My brother and I would do the work in the barn, feed the animals, and then we'd go in the fields, if it was cotton pickin' time we'd pick cotton until about 6:30, come back to the house, get dressed and go to school . . . . My parents worked hard, both of them . . . . I saw my mama work many times in the field many times sick . . . . It was not an easy life, it was a life of a lot of hard work."[9]

Rice farmers inhabited the prairie surrounding Allan's hometown; in fact, the region's high claypan—which contributed to the development of the prairies by blocking tree growth—encouraged rice farming by permitting the required long-term flooding of fields. The town of Crowley, located only about six miles from

Rayne, promotes itself as "Rice Capital of the World" and sponsors an annual rice festival.[10]

The realism of "Cajun Man" also shows up in songs like "Crawfish Festival Time" and "Alligator Bayou," both written around 1970 by country and western star Eddy Raven, a former resident of Lafayette and an acquaintance of many swamp poppers. Suited naturally to the swamp pop idiom, T. K. Hulin recorded an upbeat swamp pop version of "Alligator Bayou" in 1976, and since then the composition has become strongly associated with Hulin's highly energetic stage performances. Like Allan's song, "Alligator Bayou" portrays Cajuns as hard-working, close to the earth, and spiritual, yet full of *joie de vivre*. The composition also mentions Cajun pastimes like playing *bourré* and depicts the blue-collar toils of the Cajun oil-field worker, constructing wooden roads for south Louisiana's oil exploration crews.

> Working on a board road through the swamp
> For a dollar and a half an hour.
> A Cajun man with a love for life
> And a whole lot of muscle power.
> I'm a good-time, hard-loving Cajun man.
> . . . .
> Saturday night you can find me downtown
> Playing *bourré* at Beno's Lounge.
> Sunday morning I go to church
> And pray the Lord don't strike me down.
> I'm a good-time, hard-loving Cajun man.[11]

Allan offers a more idealistic view of south Louisiana and Cajun culture in "South to Louisiana," recorded for the Viking label of Crowley in 1962 to the tune of Johnny Horton's "North to Alaska."

South to Louisiana

> Joe Boudreaux left Breaux Bridge
> In the spring of '44
> With Jean-Pierre, his partner,
> And his cousin Robichaux.
> They crossed the Atchafalaya
> As they paddled their pirogue
> Through the swamps and the bayous

To the town of Thibodaux.
They paddled through marshlands
And the swamps of *Louisiane*
With the handles of the handmade oars
Making blisters in their hand.
But they had to get to Thibodaux,
So they went on through the swamps
'Cause tonight they were taking their Cajun girls
To a crawfish sauce piquante.

Where the bayous are flowin',
Big crawfish keep a'growin'.
South to Louisiana,
To the town of Thibodaux.

Then Joe fell in love
With a girl they call Maureen.
She came down from Opelousas
To be crowned the crawfish queen.
They danced and sang at Abbeville,
Did the same in Jeanerette.
Got married in the springtime,
Settled down in Lafayette.
Then Joe turned to Pierre
With a crawfish in his hand.
Said "Pierre, you're a'lookin'
At a mighty hungry man.
I'll take the crawfish by the neck,
And tear his tail like this,
Then pass 'em on to little Maureen,
Let her make a crawfish bisque."[12]

Although three writers receive credit for "South to Louisiana," it actually was penned by Cajun rockabilly artist Clifford "Pee Wee" Trahan. As Broven notes in his book *South to Louisiana* (named for Allan's recording) the composition "did nothing to dispel the romantic Louisiana images of blue bayous, steamy cypress-swamps, slow-moving pirogues, and tasty sauce piquantes. Only the snapping alligators and dripping Spanish moss were missing from the popular conception of the state. Louisianians are willing to tolerate such poetic license because they know that reality, if less exotic, is just as enticing."[13]

Bernard presents a similarly idealized view of Cajun culture in songs like "Diggy Liggy Lo," credited to producer and songwriter J. D. Miller, but actually composed by the Clément Brothers—traditional Cajun musicians who recorded swamp pop at Miller's studio during the late 1950s as the Tune-Tones. New Iberia–based Randy and the Rockets' "Let's Do the Cajun Twist," released in 1962, also idealistically portrays the *joie de vivre* theme common to traditional Cajun compositions:

> Let's go to Lafayette
> And do the Cajun Twist.
> We'll twist with Jolie Blonde
> And twist all night long.
> We'll go to Grand Coteau
> And eat some good gumbo.
> Then go to 'tit Maurice
> And do the Cajun Twist.[14]

Unlike "Fais Do Do," which views the Twist as a corruptive influence on Cajun culture, this song suggests a positive, productive union of Cajun and mainstream American influences with its reference to "the Cajun Twist." (Oddly, a traditional south Louisiana group, the Cajun Trio, featuring accordionist Harrison Fontenot, recorded a composition called "The Cajun Twist" on the Swallow label in 1962, the same year "Let's Do the Cajun Twist" appeared on Swallow's sister label, Jin.) For their composition the Rockets borrowed the tune of the traditional Cajun song "Allons à Lafayette," but replaced its original Cajun French lyrics—concerning a Cajun bachelor's desire to marry a reluctant fiancée—with new English lyrics that emphasize central Acadiana's local color. The three communities mentioned in the song, for instance, are found in the "Cajun Heartland" area. In addition, the composition boasts the seemingly incongruous lyrics, "They sing about the storms / They sing about the fish." These are frequent topics of discussion, however, among the inhabitants of subtropical south Louisiana. The lyrics also refer to "jolie blonde" (literally "pretty blonde"), the name of the classic Cajun song widely regarded as the culture's unofficial anthem. Over the years, however, the phrase *Jolie Blonde* has evolved into the proper name of a cultural icon. The personification of Cajun culture, she appears in modern Cajun artwork as a blue-eyed, golden-haired Cajun maiden (not all Cajuns are dark-eyed and dark-haired) wearing delicate, old-fashioned apparel. Today her image graces posters, t-shirts, beer labels, and a variety of consumer goods bearing the stamp "A Product of Cajun Louisiana" (on which she appears playing a diatonic accordion). Randy and the Rockets' evocation of Jolie Blonde (a character first appearing in Cajun recordings as early as 1929) to personify Cajun culture reinforces the composition's local color themes and demonstrates the link between swamp pop and its folk influences. (Incidentally, Jolie Blonde also appears in the 1960 Goldband track "Slop and Stroll Jolie Blonde" by obscure swamp popper Gabe Dean—real name Gabriel D. Leneau of Marksville—who sings "Jolie Blonde is now a real gone cat / Now she's wearing bluejeans / 'Cause she is a cool queen / Of all them bayou pirogue strollin' cats.")[15]

One modern swamp pop band from south Louisiana expresses concern about its heritage by parodying popular, often derogatory misconceptions about Cajuns—much in the same manner that D. L. Menard pokes fun at Cajun stereotypes in his classic "La porte d'en arrière (The Back Door)."

Cajun Rap Song

A Cajun is a person
Who likes to have fun.
They have a accent [sic]
That's far from none.

. . . .

We spend all of our time
Down deep in the sticks,
Where the cypress trees grow
And the big fat ticks.
Yeah, we eat *choupique*
And alligator, too.
We like to party down
And so should you.

. . . .

We boil our crawfish,
Mais, in a bucket.
Then we pull off their heads
And then we suck it.

. . . .

I eat *couche-couche.*
I like that, me.
And barbecued possum
Is a delicacy.
We kill *moustiques*
And drink beer all day long.
Mais, how you think we had time
To write this Cajun rap song?
When the moon goes down
We do our dance.
We drink home brew
And go into a trance.[16]

Recorded for the Jin label in 1988 by Cypress City of Marksville, this song draws more on inner city rap music than it does swamp pop. As mentioned, however, music writer Jeff Hannusch regards "Cajun Rap Song" as swamp pop—probably because it originated in south Louisiana, concerns south Louisiana, and qualifies as *pop* music. Allowing at least temporarily for Hannusch's extremely broad definition of swamp pop, "Cajun Rap Song" captures some of south Louisiana's local color with references to *choupique* (a type of fish), *moustiques* (mosquitoes) and *couche-couche* (cornbread sopped in milk). But the song primarily derides several negative stereotypes: Cajuns as country hicks; Cajuns as uncontrollable partiers; Cajuns as drunkards; Cajuns as swamp dwellers. Compare these lyrics with Rufus Jagneaux's largely English swamp pop rendition of "The Back Door" (which captures the spirit of Menard's original):

Me and my brother went out last night.
Got real loose, almost got into a fight.
Drank so much couldn't swallow anymore.
When I came home had to use the back door.
J'ai passé dedans la porte d'en arrière [I went in through the back door].[17]

In addition to recording original swamp pop compositions about Cajun culture, swamp pop artists also expressed pride in their culture by rerecording swamp pop songs in Cajun French. In 1960, for instance, Joe Barry recorded a Cajun French version of his swamp pop classic "I'm a Fool to Care" called "Je suis bêt pour t'aimer," which he backed with another Cajun recording, "Oh Teet Fille" (unrelated, he claims, to Clifton Chenier's early zydeco recording "Ay-Tete-Fee"). And Johnnie Allan covered Freddy Fender's swamp pop hit "Before the Next Teardrop Falls" in alternating English and Cajun French verses. (Fender similarly had recorded this Charley Pride song in alternating English and Spanish.) Allan also utilizes bilingual lyrics in his swampy rendition of Merle Haggard's "Today I Started Loving You Again."[18] Swamp pop artists also incorporated traditional Cajun and black Creole instrumentation into otherwise straight swamp pop recordings: Allan's "Promised Land" and Charles Mann's "Walk of Life" both feature heavy accompaniment by Cajun accordionists.

Many traditional Cajun and black Creole songs also made their way into swamp pop repertoires, a natural result of swamp pop's descent from the ethnic cultures of south Louisiana and southeast Texas. For instance, the aforementioned "Let's Do the Cajun Twist" borrows the melody of "Allons à Lafayette," the first recorded Cajun song, which in turn derives from an older traditional tune, "Jeunes gens de la campagne." Similarly, in 1965 Warren Storm, Rod Bernard, and Skip Stewart (otherwise known as the Shondells) recorded the largely instrumental "A-2-Fay" for Carol Rachou's La Louisianne label. ("A-2-Fay" is a play on the pronunciation of *étouffée,* a popular method of preparing crawfish or shrimp in south Louisiana.) This composition, however, is actually an electrified version of "Mamou Two-Step," a traditional Cajun instrumental by accordionist Lawrence Walker. Amazingly, the Shondells' subtly duplicate the sound of "old-time" Cajun music using nontraditional instruments, adding to the ethnic character of this swamp pop remake. Short, bouncy saxophone bursts substitute for the puffing of a Cajun accordion; swirling electric guitar riffs create a reeling Cajun fiddle sound; and the sharp, repetitive striking of another electric guitar rings out like a Cajun *petit fer,* or triangle. This imitative device, however, is not unique to "A-2-Fay" or the Shondells: Other south Louisiana artists have used the harmonica to mimic the Cajun or black Creole accordion sound. Rufus Jagneaux's "Opelousas Sostan," "Port Barre," and "The Back Door," and Rockin' Sidney's "You Ain't Nothin' but Fine," are obvious examples.[19]

Swamp poppers also recorded undisguised swamp pop versions of Cajun and black Creole songs, including "Colinda," "Diggy Liggy Lo," "Jolie blonde," "Grand Mamou Blues," and "Hip et Taïaut." Of course, the electric guitars, pianos, saxophones, and strong rhythm and blues backbeat of swamp pop replaced the accordions, fiddles, and modest percussion of traditional south Louisiana music. Typically, however, swamp poppers recorded these songs with alternating Cajun French and English lyrics, preserving the strong ethnic character of the composition while striving to appeal to a wider, non-francophone audience. An examination of Bobby Page and the Riff Raffs' "Hippy-Ti-Yo" and Rod Bernard's

The Riff Raffs, somewhere on Highway 165 between Alexandria and Monroe, La., en route to a dance at Northeastern Louisiana University, 1959. Left to right: Ulysses Broussard, Jimmy Patin, Bessyl Duhon, Roy Perkins, and V. J. Boulet. (Photo courtesy of the Johnnie Allan Collection)

"Colinda," for instance, reveals the complex cultural forces that helped to create swamp pop music.

In the spring of 1958 Page and his group released "Hippy-Ti-Yo," a swamp pop version of the traditional tune "Hip et Taïaut," on Myra Smith's Ram label of Shreveport. Recorded in Cajun French and English and drawing on the rollicking, frantic rhythms of earlier traditional versions, "Hippy-Ti-Yo" is rendered by Page in a wild, carefree manner to the backing of modern electric instruments:

> *Translation:*
> v. 1. It's Hip and Taïaut, dear,
>   Who stole my sled, dear,
>   When they saw I was hot, dear,
>   They returned my sled, dear.

Hippy-Ti-Yo

MM=200

Solo
C'— est les Hip et Taï— aut, chère, qu'— a vo - lé mon traî— neau, chère.

Quand ça vu que j'é - tais chaud, chère, ça m'a rame - né mon traî— neau, chère.

C'— est les Hip et Taï- aut, Taï- aut, Taï— aut qu'a vo—lé mon— traî— neau, traî – neau, traî–

neau. Quand ça vu que j'é – tais chaud, chère, ça m'a rame- né mon traî- neau.

Duet
It was the girls from Mire_____ that stole my sled. _____

And when things got hot_____ they re - turned my sled. _____

It was the girls from Mire, from Mire, from Mire that stole my sled, my sled, my

sled and when things got hot, got hot, got hot they re - turned my sled._____

v. 3. It's the girls from Bosco, dear,
Who stole my sled, dear,
When they saw I was hot, dear,
They returned my sled, dear.
[Not shown on sheet music]

(Incidentally, Mire and Bosco are two small prairie communities in central Acadiana; and *traîneau* more precisely translates as "drag-sled," a primitive, wheelless mode of transportation formerly used even in subtropical Louisiana.)[20]

Cajun and black Creole culture deeply influenced the Riff Raffs, who grew up in the central Acadiana region. In fact, the strain of Cajun French utilized by lead singer Bobby Page is peculiar to prairie Cajuns. Like many traditional Cajun and black Creole compositions, "Hippy-Ti-Yo" possesses an extremely complex genealogy, reflected in part by the various renderings of its title: "Hippy Ty-Yo," "Hippy Ti Yo," "Hippy Tai Yo," "Hippitiyo," "Les huppés taïauts." The song also goes by the titles "Tayeaux Dog Tayeaux," "Ils ont volé mon traîneau," "Il la volés mon trancas," "T'as volé mon chapeau" and "Les filles d'Arnaudville." Black Creole versions of "Hip et Taïaut," however, bear the titles "Les haricots sont pas salés" and "Zydeco est pas salé." In addition, Cajun string band-era songs like Leo Soileau's "Hackberry Hop" and Link Davis, Sr.'s, "Come Dance with Me" borrow the melody of "Hip et Taïaut." With the exception of the latter two compositions, the remainder consist basically of variations on a stock melody and stock lyrics. The origin of these stock elements remains a mystery, but Cajun accordionist Joseph Falcon, during a 1962 interview with folklorist Lauren Post, suggests at least an early twentieth-century birth among light-skinned black Creoles, known more specifically as Creoles of color.

> *Lauren Post:* Did you know that you play three songs that are supposed to be Negro folk songs? One of them is "Hip et Taïaut."
>
> *Joseph Falcon:* That's one that I just picked up like that and played it. . . .
>
> *LP:* How much of that did you learn from someone else?
>
> *JF:* I just picked it up like that. They wasn't playing no public dances. I just heard the tune.
>
> *LP:* Was it a white person or a colored person?
>
> *JF:* Colored. It was Babineaux . . . . It was Oscar Babineaux's son, and then there was Sidney Babineaux, the accordion player—and he could play, too!
>
> *LP:* Was Oscar Babineaux light complexioned?
>
> *JF:* Yes, kinda like that.
>
> *LP:* So they were playing 'Hip et Taïaut' before you got hold of it?
>
> *JF:* Yes, that's how I heard it.
>
> *LP:* And you developed it your way?
>
> *JF:* Well, I played it a little different.[21]

Renowned folklorist Alan Lomax offers interesting speculation about "Hip et Taïaut," suggesting an earlier origin among nineteenth-century Cajun and black

Creole prairie cowboys. Lomax proposes that the popular Anglo-American cowboy yell "Hippy Ti Yo!" (and apparently its variations, such as "Whoopee Ti Yi Yo!" found in the Western classic "Git Along Little Dogies") may derive from the Cajun or black Creole phrase "Hip et Taïaut." (The two phrases are pronounced in virtually the same way.) Lomax theorizes that Texan cowboys may have picked up the expression while driving cattle across south Louisiana's prairies to stockyards in New Orleans. (Kansas City stockyards eventually replaced those in New Orleans.) South Louisiana cowboys inhabited the prairie country during that period, and many of these cowboys were black Creoles, who to the present enjoy a reputation as excellent horsemen. In fact, some modern black Creoles integrate horseback riding into their celebrations, such as their annual *Courir du Mardi Gras* (Running of the Mardi Gras) and frequent weekend "zydeco trailrides." Adding strength to Lomax's argument, the cowboy interjection "Hippy Ti Yo!" means nothing in any literal sense in English, but in Cajun French *taïaut* means "tallyho" and is a Cajun idiom for "hound dog." (The English *tallyho* apparently derives from the standard French *taïaut*, "a cry used to excite hounds in deer hunting.") Also, according to Cajun musician and preservationist Raymond E. François, the word *hip* (or *huppé*, as he spells it) means "clever." "Hip et Taïaut" thus has been translated as both "Clever Hounds" and "Hip *and* Taïaut" (the proper names of two hound dogs). If correct, Lomax places the origin of "Hip et Taïaut" long before it initially appeared on record in 1934 (as "Ils la volet mon trancas" by Joseph and Cléoma Falcon).[22]

Delving deeper into the complex cultural forces affecting south Louisiana music, Cajun music enthusiast Paul Tate suggests that the various stolen items mentioned in "Hip et Taïaut" are sexual double entendres. The verses containing these double entendres generally take the form of "It was the girls from _____ who stole my _____." Stolen items like *capot* (coat) and *gilet* (vest) bear no apparent sexual connotations, yet the piecemeal theft of the singer's garments by "the girls" in itself may be regarded as suggestive. Other items, however, like *chapeau*, present better candidates, as do *traîneau* (dragsled), *candi*, and *yo yo*. Adding weight to Tate's view, blatantly sexual Cajun songs like "Faire l'amour dans l' poulailler" ("Making Love in the Chicken Coop") and "Faire l'amour dans les rangs d' coton" ("Making Love in the Cotton Rows") contain similar double entendres. "Poulailler," for instance, contains the lines "*C'est la fille à Nonc' Edouard qu'a frotté mon 'tit frottoir*" ("It's Uncle Edouard's daughter who rubbed my little rubboard") and "*C'est la fille à Nonc' Hilaire qu'a touché ma 'tite cuillière*" ("It's Uncle Hilaire's daughter who touched my little spoon").

"Coton" contains the lines *"Ouais, les filles de Lafayette avait cassé son 'rated X'"* ("Yes, the girls from Lafayette broke his 'rated X'") and *"C'est les filles de Vatican qu'avait cassé son 'tit piquant"* ("It's the girls from Vatican who broke his little sticker"). A rather obvious double entendre also appears in the Cajun composition "La banane à Nonc' Adam" ("Uncle Adam's Banana"). In his article "Zydeco/Zarico: Beans, Blues and Beyond," folklorist Barry Jean Ancelet notes the presence of double entendres in zydeco and observes that "much of Afro-American expressive culture features double-entendre and sexual imagery"; he also suggests that the word *zydeco* (from the French *les haricots,* meaning "beans") itself bears sexual connotations. Thus, the double entendre in Cajun and black Creole music is hardly confined to one composition.[23]

Bobby Page and the Riff Raffs' seemingly innocuous swamp pop version of "Hip et Taïaut" derives from this complexity of Cajun and black Creole influences, adding to the rich ethnic character of swamp pop music. A study of "Colinda," however, offers perhaps the most thorough glimpse of the cultural forces that helped to create swamp pop music, as well as traditional Cajun and black Creole music. Also known as "Danser Colinda" or "Allons danser Colinda," the song remained largely unknown outside south Louisiana and southeast Texas before Rod Bernard released his swamp pop rendition in 1962. According to Bernard, his version—recorded at Bill Hall's Big Bopper studio in Beaumont and featuring as-yet-unknown artists Johnny and Edgar Winter on a variety of instruments—sold about eighty to one hundred thousand copies, mainly along the Gulf Coast and in Canada. It attracted enough national attention, however, to prompt an invitation from Dick Clark's "American Bandstand," which Bernard reluctantly turned down because of his recent induction into the military.[24]

Bernard's recording owes much of its popularity to bilingual lyrics, which caught the attention not only of French-speaking audiences in south Louisiana, southeast Texas, and Canada, but also of an Anglo-American audience, which found the alternating English and Cajun French lyrics too exotic to ignore. Bernard grew up at a time, however, when Cajun children were punished at school for speaking French. Although he never learned to speak the dialect, he sings in Cajun French on "Colinda" and a few other swamp pop songs. "Colinda" is an animated Cajun two-step performed on modern electric instruments. The second stanza in Bernard's version may allude to the period's prevailing anti-Cajun sentiment:

Brooding pose by the usually jovial Riff Raffs leader Bobby Page, shown here wielding Bessyl Duhon's guitar, Webster's Four Corners Bar, Cecilia, La., Circa 1960. (Photo courtesy of Elwood Dugas)

Translation:

v.1. Let's dance, Colinda,

While your mother isn't around

To make the old ladies mad.

Not everyone can dance

All the old two-step waltzes.

While your mother isn't around

Let's dance, Colinda.[25]

Like several other Cajun and black Creole songs, "Colinda" derives from Old World sources. In fact, the word *Colinda* originally identified not a girl,

Colinda

but a dance—the *Calinda,* which appeared over four centuries ago in Guinea on the Gold and Slave coasts of western Africa. When Guinea began to supply slaves to the New World in 1562, the Calinda spread throughout the West Indies and to Louisiana. An early reference to the dance in the New World dates from 1678, when the Conseil Souverain de Martinique outlawed the *Kalinda*, which it considered not only indecent, but capable of inciting slave rebellions. Martinique's colonial government reinstated the ban in 1758 and again in 1772.[26]

Several New World colonists provide eyewitness accounts of the Calinda, including Père Jean Baptiste Labat, whose 1698 description of the dance in Martinique portrays it as a social gathering suggestive of a fertility ritual. In New Orleans, however, the Calinda assumed other characteristic functions. For instance, nineteenth-century writers Charles Dudley Warner and George Washington Cable associate the dance with the practice of voodoo. After witnessing a New Orleans voodoo ritual in 1885 Warner wrote, "A colored woman at the side of the altar began a chant in a low, melodious voice. It was the weird and strange 'Danse Calinda.'" A year later Cable recorded: "In Louisiana . . . Voodoo bore as a title of greater solemnity the additional title of Maignan and . . . even in the Calinda dance . . . was sometimes heard, at the height of its frenzy, the invocation 'Aïe! Aïe! Voodoo Magnan!'" [*sic*]. (Interestingly, folklorist Harold Courlander claims the Calinda survives in modern Haiti as a dance associated not with voodooism, but with zombiism.)[27]

In 1921 folklorist Mina Monroe published a different account of the dance, which she obtained from "an old darky once an expert at the Calinda." Monroe states: "In Louisiana, the Calinda was a war-dance in which men alone took part, stripped to the waist and brandishing sticks in mock fight, while at the same time balancing upon their heads bottles filled with water." (This account corresponds to descriptions of the Calinda in Trinidad, where it survives to the present as a dance associated with stick fighting.) The Calinda thus arrived in the New World from Guinea and evolved into many related dances throughout the West Indies. It became an occult dance in New Orleans and Haiti; a warfare dance in New Orleans and Trinidad; and in many locations a social-oriented dance with overtones of a fertility ritual.[28]

Although the dance apparently still exists in the Caribbean, it disappeared in Louisiana in the mid-to-late nineteenth century. Its name persisted in black Creole songs, however, a few of which contain lyrics similar to the Cajun phrase "*Danser Colinda.*" The oldest of these songs seems to be "Lizette to quité la plaine," first published in Louisiana in 1859. Surprisingly, the song was published in Philadelphia in 1811 as "Chanson nègre" and appeared even earlier as "Chanson créole" in a circa 1740 treatise by Jean-Jacques Rousseau concerning his invention of a new system of musical notation. The first quatrain of the third stanza, rendered in the black Creole dialect, mentions the dance:

Dipi mo pêrdi Lizette,	[*Trans.*] Since I lost Lizette,
Mo pa batte Bamboula,	I don't beat the Bamboula [drum],
Bouche a moi tourné muette,	My mouth has become mute,
Mo pa dansé Calinda.	And I don't dance the Calinda.[29]

Dating from the early or mid-nineteenth century, two other black Creole songs mention the Calinda and contain a variation of the phrase "*Danser Colinda.*" These songs, entitled "Michié Préval" and "Michié Baziro," are closely related, having similar lyrics and melodies. A favorite of slaves who gathered on Sundays in Congo Square in New Orleans to dance the Calinda, "Michié Préval" satirizes the city's upper class by relating the riotous events of a slave dance sponsored by "Monsieur Préval," identified as an actual nineteenth-century New Orleans magistrate. The song also pokes fun at a certain "Monsieur Mazuro," identified as Attorney General Etienne Mazureau (1772–1849), who is likened "in his big office" to a "bullfrog in a bucket of water." The first verse, however, reads in black Creole:

Michié Préval li donnain grand bal,	[*Trans.*] Monsieur Préval gave a big dance,
Li fé nég payé pou sauté in pé.	He made the blacks pay to stomp their feet.
Dansez Calinda, boudjoum, boudjoum!	Dance the Calinda, boudjoum, boudjoum![30]

Although the melody and lyrics of the Cajun "Colinda" bear no resemblance to "Michié Préval" or "Michié Baziro" (except the phrase "*Danser Colinda*"), the Cajun song apparently derives to some extent from these sources and in fact shares a few common characteristics with them. For instance, all three songs express disregard for authority figures: "Préval" and "Baziro" satirize the upper-class citizens of New Orleans, and the narrator of "Colinda" wants to dance "to make the old ladies mad." "Préval" and "Colinda" also exhibit a "forbidden dance" theme: Préval is thrown in jail for sponsoring a slave dance "*sans permis,*" and the narrator of "Colinda" urges his partner to "dance all the old two-step waltzes . . . while your mother isn't around"—apparently because Colinda's mother (like the old ladies) considers the archaic dances indecent. Speculation is required at this point: Cajuns and rural black Creoles in the late nineteenth century either forgot or never directly experienced the Calinda dance, but heard the lyrics "*Dansez Calinda*" (the name of a dance), which they interpreted as "*Danser Colinda*" (a girl's name). They then composed a new song around this refrain or incorporated the refrain into a preexisting song.

A black Creole composition called "Anons au bal Colinda" may represent a stage in the song's evolution. Like the Cajun "Colinda," this tune interprets the word *Colinda* as a girl's name, refers to dancing, and exhibits an underlying sexual theme—remnants of the forgotten dance repeatedly banned because of its perceived sinister and lascivious nature. Captured during a 1956 field recording of obscure black Creole accordionist Godar Chalvin of Abbeville, the melody of "Anons au bal Colinda" vaguely resembles that of "Allons danser Colinda." Its lyrics, however, read:

Anons au bal, Colinda.	[*Trans.*] Let's go to the dance, Colinda.
Ti vas matin le brouillard.	You go in the morning fog.
Ta robe était déchirée.	Your dress was torn.
Pourquoi, ti me dis pas, Colinda,	Why won't you tell me, Colinda,
Où t'a été hier au soir?	Where were you last night?
Alle y va matin dans le petit jour.	She left at the break of dawn.
Sa robe était déchirée.	Her dress was torn.[31]

These lyrics closely resemble those of Cajun musician Nathan Abshire's "Pine Grove Blues," recorded for the O.T. label in 1949; in turn, Abshire's song derives from "Tite negresse," an earlier recording by fellow Cajun musician Columbus Frugé. Whether "Anons au bal Colinda" or "Tite negresse" appeared first is unknown, but the question to be asked is: Could "Anons au bal Colinda" be the melodic source for the Cajun "Colinda," or could both songs derive independently from a third, earlier song?[32]

Joseph Falcon again provides vital information during his 1962 interview, agreeing with Lauren Post that "Colinda," like "Hip et Taïaut," may issue from a black Creole source. He also helps to document the song's evolution, referring to "Colinda" as both a Cajun song and a Cajun dance (though he may imply that "Colinda" merely served well for dancing "two-step waltzes"): "That 'Colinda,' that's what the old folks call a 'two-step waltz.' I had one of my musicians say that there wasn't no such thing as that. I said, 'Hold it, brother, I'm older than you.' He said, 'There ain't no such thing as a two-step waltz. What number could it be?' I said, ' "Allons danser Colinda." That's a two-step waltz from the old times.' " The song's lyrics actually mention the "two-step waltzes" referred to by Falcon: *"C'est pas tout le monde à danser / Toutes les vieilles valses à deux temps"* ("Not everyone can dance / All the old two-step waltzes.") A few versions of "Colinda," however, omit this reference.[33]

Falcon also states " 'Allons danser Colinda'—I knew that tune since I was a little boy. I played it many times." Born in 1900, Falcon thus confirms the song's existence shortly after the turn of the century. Indeed, traditional Cajun fiddler Dennis McGee's "Madame Young donnez moi votre plus jolie blonde," recorded for the Vocalion label in 1929, borrows the tune of "Colinda." The first actual recording of the song, however, dates to 1946, when the Cajun string band Happy Fats, Doc Guidry and the Boys recorded "Colinda" in Cajun French for J. D. Miller's new 78 rpm Fais Do Do label of Crowley. Although Happy Fats claims that he and Guidry composed the song's tune and lyrics around a preexisting title, Guidry testifies they created neither, stating, "It was a mistake when they put 'Words and music by Happy and Doc.' " Nevertheless, Happy, Doc and the Boys' classic recording of "Colinda" inspired Louisiana's singing governor, Jimmie Davis, to cover the folk song in 1953 with Guidry on fiddle. Although utilizing a Cajun French chorus, Davis sang new English lyrics devised with Guidry while en route to a recording studio.[34]

Swamp popper Rod Bernard became aware of "Colinda" partly through his childhood appearances on Happy and Doc's talent program, broadcast live on KSLO radio between approximately 1948 and 1950 from the old Rose Theater in Opelousas. The regional success of the song's early recorded versions helped to convince Bernard to record his own bilingual swamp pop version, just as the enduring local popularity of "Hip et Taïaut" prompted Bobby Page and the Riff Raffs to record their bilingual swamp pop version of that folk composition. As demonstrated, both songs derive from an intricate process of ethnic interaction between Cajuns and black Creoles.[35]

Although some critics argue that swamp poppers merely "jumped on the bandwagon" after the rebirth of Cajun and black Creole culture, these artists actually blended traditional elements into their music from its inception. This process occurred naturally: after all, the traditional elements were inherent in their shared experiences as Cajuns and black Creoles. Swamp poppers would not have composed new songs about their culture or recorded new versions of traditional songs if they despised their heritage, as some maintain. Of course, a few swamp poppers did return eventually, but not exclusively, to more traditional music. Johnnie Allan, for instance, wrote several Cajun French songs for accordionist Aldus Roger, including the popular "Une autre chance," and during the 1980s Allan released two albums of Cajun French and Cajun-oriented music entitled *Johnnie Allan Sings Cajun Now* and *Cajun Country,* the latter of which features Wayne Toups on accordion. In 1989 he teamed up with fellow swamp poppers Warren Storm and Clint West to record the *Cajun Born* album, which features mostly Cajun French compositions. (Incidentally, West covered the Cajun favorite "Bayou Pon Pon" for the Jin label in the early 1970s.) In 1975— years before zydeco's surge in popularity—Rod Bernard joined zydeco pioneer Clifton Chenier to record *Boogie in Black & White,* a collection of swamp pop/zydeco recordings that pays homage to swamp pop's black Creole roots. And in 1982 Jay Randall released an album entitled *Cajun Boogie,* which featured traditional Cajun compositions. Yet swamp poppers took pride in their heritage even before all things "Cajun" (a term often used incorrectly to mean "Cajun or black Creole or both") became trendy worldwide.[36]

THE FUTURE OF SWAMP POP

Despite the passage of over four decades since its birth, swamp pop music remains a regional sound. The interaction of Cajun and black Creole swamp pop artists during the genre's formative years mirrors the society that produced the music and its performers—a society composed of two distinct yet tightly intertwined ethnic groups. Swamp pop's inception during a period of enforced racial segregation, however, parallels the origins and development of other regional genres, including New Orleans rhythm and blues and Memphis rockabilly. Like swamp pop, these genres arose from the confluence of diverse elements during racially tense periods to form new, distinct regional sounds. Many local sounds sprang up during the 1950s, as music scholar Robert Palmer notes in *A Tale of Two Cities: Memphis Rock and New Orleans Roll*: "Before the coming of radio, records, and subsequent refinements in electronic media, music in America was largely an at-home phenomenon. Regions, counties, towns, and even neighborhoods developed their own musical personalities . . . . But the coming of 'the media,' rapid as it was even in the more remote rural areas, did not immediately wipe out all traces of regionalism. In fact, as late as the 1950s, a music as commercial as rock-and-roll developed largely along regional lines."[1]

These observations apply strongly to swamp pop, which remains a regional sound because its most crucial elements—the elements without which it would not be swamp pop but merely an unimaginative clone of New Orleans rhythm and blues—derive from Cajun and rural black Creole culture and music. Readily accessible in past decades only to inhabitants of Acadiana and southeast Texas, these vital elements precluded the existence of swamp pop artists from places like, say, California or New Jersey or even New Orleans. Performers around the world have imitated the swamp pop sound, but few have managed to duplicate it to any high degree of accuracy because they lacked the direct influence of Cajun and rural black Creole music and culture.

Palmer observes that the advent of records and commercial radio initiated a complex process of homogenization that obscured regional sounds. Although swamp pop survives to the present in an unadulterated form, some swamp pop artists suffered during the early 1960s at the hands of slick Mercury label producers, who isolated artists like Rod Bernard, Jivin' Gene, and Warren Storm from their traditional roots, recording them in Nashville with smooth but over-arranged studio bands complete with violin sections and female choruses. Storm calls the Nashville sessions "mechanical" and observes, "It wasn't *swamp pop*. It was more *pop* than anything else." Fortunately, the failure spurred artists to re-turn to the studios of local south Louisiana and southeast Texas producers, who again recorded them utilizing more time-tested and successful studio arrange-ments. Thus, swamp pop artists never were fully assimilated into mainstream pop culture; they did manage, however, to make a small but measurable impact on that pop culture both prior to and even after their decline in popularity.[2]

The golden age of swamp pop stretched from 1958 to 1963, a period ended by the Beatles phenomenon, the ensuing British Invasion, and the evolution of more innocent, more naive *rock 'n' roll* music into more cosmopolitan "sex-and-drug-oriented" *rock* music. These factors account largely for swamp pop's initial decline in popularity in the mid-to-late 1960s, a condition noted by Rod Bernard in his 1966 Chuck Berry–type rocker entitled "Recorded in England": "If you want food on your table / Better stamp this on the label / Recorded in England with your electric guitar."[3]

Musical trends during the mid-1960s impacted swamp pop enormously: Most swamp pop artists refused to adapt to the new sounds, while others tried but failed in dismay. At least one group, however, made a successful transition from the south Louisiana sound to the Beatlesesque, namely, John Fred and the Playboys, who scored a worldwide success in 1968 with "Judy in Disguise (with Glasses)," a tune inspired by the Beatles' "Lucy in the Sky with Dia-monds." And although one unveiled swamp pop recording managed to climb national charts during the psychedelic era—Tommy McLain's "Sweet Dreams" (1966)—the singer found himself crooning the anachronistic '50s-style ballad in arenas with groups like Paul Revere and the Raiders, Tommy James and the Shondells, and the Yardbirds. McLain recalls: "I was on a two-week tour with them [the Yardbirds] when I met [Jimmy Page] .... He would play his guitar, he would make it get that thing a feedback going through his amp, and he would

Tommy McLain, publicity
photo for the release of
"Sweet Dreams," shot at Floyd
Soileau's recording studio,
Ville Platte, La., 1965. (Photo
courtesy of Tommy McLain)

play that thing with a violin bow. And Robert Plant was on that thing, playing harmonica and singing. And I didn't know what the hell they were doing—I was doing 'Sweet Dreams.' I was doing South Louisiana music. I was doing swamp pop music then. Nobody was familiar with what I was doing. It was all the Beatles and the Yardbirds and that stuff. And I was hanging in there doing my act."[4]

Rooted in the sounds of the 1950s and early '60s, swamp pop could not compete with the emerging rock sound and began its slow decline, losing artists one by one to more reliable full-time jobs outside the music scene: King Karl became a night watchman; Guitar Gable, a TV repairman; Warren Storm, a printer; Charles Mann, a policeman; Lil' Bob, a used-car salesman; Roy Perkins, a draftsman; Bobby Page, a plumber; Jivin' Gene, an insulator; Johnny Preston, a construction worker; Gene Terry, a chemical plant technician. Some wandered into these positions, others wisely had cultivated a second occupation in case a musical career proved unprofitable. Almost all returned to the stage at one time or another, but a handful, such as Clint West, Little Alfred, and Tommy McLain, managed to perform swamp pop full-time throughout the decades.[5]

Most swamp poppers, however, now perform only on special occasions—band reunions, fund raisers, agricultural festivals—claiming they gave up music for a variety of reasons, and not solely because of the changes popular music underwent during the mid-1960s. By that time, after all, swamp poppers no longer were carefree teenagers. Some had married and started families, which discouraged touring and late-night gigs at roadside honky-tonks. Swamp pop artists remaining in music after the mid-1960s, however, inevitably encountered widespread drug abuse and alcoholism. Swamp pop performer Skip Stewart sums up the attitude of many south Louisiana artists during this period: "I was a little bit burnt out on it [the music business] and to be perfectly frank . . . at the time drugs were just creeping into the scene around here, around this part of the country. Not so much hard drugs, but speed and marijuana and that sort of thing, and it really scared the hell out of me, because I was, I figured, too smart to get into that and I knew that as long as I was exposed to it, there was a possibility I might get mixed up in it . . . . I wanted to go home and try to lead a respectable family life."[6]

Unfortunately, some swamp poppers were not as cautious as Stewart. For instance, Joe Barry, Rod Bernard, Jimmy Donley, Tommy McLain, and Bobby Page became heavy drinkers, hard-drug users, or both. Barry's notorious use of drugs and alcohol induced him to destroy countless hotel rooms—years before rock drummer Keith Moon perfected the art. Barry excelled at ripping out phones, shooting TVs, and setting fires. "I started pretty heavy into some heavy stuff," he explains. "Got strong, real strong, shooting up and just going out of it." Long, difficult days and nights on the road and on the stage led to Bernard's chronic addiction to a variety of prescribed uppers and downers. "I got to a point where I had to take pills just to stay awake between jobs," he admits. "And as my tolerance level became heavier, I had to take more and more just to stay awake." Bobby Page struggled with a similar addiction, and Tommy McLain recalls: "I got on pills so bad nobody would fool with me . . .'66 and '67 I barely remember. 'Cause I was on a plane going somewhere every weekend of my life for a couple of years. I was everywhere. And if I wasn't on an airplane I was on a tour bus going somewhere. And I was eating speed like candy and taking sleeping pills . . . . I started going downhill faster than I went up."[7]

Other swamp poppers quit music over sour business deals, certain that crooked producers had swindled them of hard-earned rewards. Although a few swamp pop producers possess spotless reputations, others are widely regarded by artists as con men who stole songwriting credits, altered or reneged on contracts, failed to report profits, and refused to disburse royalty payments properly. Unable or unwilling to enter drawn-out legal battles, many artists discounted their losses but, refusing to risk further exploitation, dropped out of recording and the music scene altogether. Not all crooks, however, were producers: Around 1975 one dishonest studio musician took off with Rod Bernard's demo of "Sometimes I Talk in My Sleep," a song written by Eddy Raven especially for the swamp popper. Quickly rerecording the song, the crafty musician licensed his "bogus" version to ABC before Bernard's original appeared, and the pirated song soon hit the country and western Top 40. "That crushed Bernard," says producer Floyd Soileau, "and it crushed his last effort to really get up again."[8]

Swamp pop's decline thus can be traced not only to the advent of the Beatles, the ensuing British Invasion, and the evolution of rock 'n' roll into rock music, but also to the desire of swamp poppers to settle down and raise families, their frustration with the seemingly inherent dishonesty of the music industry, and the growing epidemic of drug and alcohol abuse among musicians (which ruined some and drove away others). These factors combined to curtail swamp pop's popularity, just as they similarly led to the decline of genres like jazz, rhythm and blues, and rockabilly.

Some swamp poppers, however, continued to release new recordings after the genre's golden age, finding loyal audiences throughout south Louisiana and southeast Texas, not to mention overseas. As late as July 1968, with Herb Alpert's "This Guy's in Love with You" at number two and the Rolling Stones' "Jumping Jack Flash" at number three, Rod Bernard's "Play a Song for My Baby" occupied the top spot on Lake Charles's KLOU playlist. "South Louisiana is a unique place," says Bernard. "The things that sold here a lot of times didn't sell anywhere else. . . ." Freddy Fender reached the national charts in 1975, however, with his swamp pop classics "Wasted Days and Wasted Nights" and "Before the Next Teardrop Falls," and Johnnie Allan hit in Europe on four separate occasions in the 1970s and early '80s with his phenomenal swamp pop cover of "Promised Land." Although few later swamp pop recordings fared as well as these examples, "golden oldies" compilations have appeared in abundance since the mid-1960s, beginning with the 1965 Jin release *A Rockin' Date with South Louisiana Stars*.[9]

Swamp pop music continued to impact other musical genres despite its ebbing popularity. For instance, it exerted a strong but as yet unacknowledged influence on the "Cajun rock" or "progressive Cajun" sound that first surfaced during the early 1970s. This style drew on ingredients found in swamp pop (albeit in different measure), but relied more heavily on traditional melodies and instrumentation, and blended these elements with 1960s and early '70s mainstream and folk rock sounds. The swamp pop (and proto–Cajun rock) group Rufus Jagneaux of "Opelousas Sostan" fame bridged the gap between 1950s-style rhythm and blues–based swamp pop and more contemporary Cajun rock. Like other swamp pop groups, Rufus combined rhythm and blues, country and western, and Cajun and black Creole elements, but it also drew on mainstream rock and folk rock music, sounds that appeared too late to influence other swamp poppers. In Jagneaux's wake followed other, more progressive bands like Coteau, Cajun Brew, Filé, Atchafalaya, Red Beans and Rice Revue, and the Bluerunners, all of which no doubt benefited from examples set by pioneering swamp pop groups. Although their styles differed from swamp pop, these younger artists followed a trend first established almost two decades earlier by swamp pop artists, who also blended mainstream and local traditional elements (albeit less consciously) to create exciting new south Louisiana sounds.[10]

Music writer Larry Benicewicz suggests that swamp pop even may have inspired popular, innovative Cajun artists like Wayne Toups and Zachary Richard, citing Rod Bernard and Clifton Chenier's 1976 *Boogie in Black & White* album as a possible source for Toups's combination of Cajun and zydeco elements, as well as for Richard's own distinctive sound. "Such a masterpiece," observes Benicewicz, "no doubt . . . spawned other 'experiments' like Wayne Toups' 'ZydeCajun' style or, perhaps, a Zachary Richard 'Zack Attack,' a similar fusion of Cajun, zydeco and R&B." (Broven calls Richard's style "a hybrid, rock-influenced form of Cajun music," and folklorist Ancelet describes it as "innovative rock and country arrangements of Cajun dance tunes.") Former Coteau and Cajun Brew member Michael Doucet (better known as fiddler/leader of the Cajun group Beausoleil) has mixed rock and rhythm and blues elements into his groups' Cajun-oriented recordings. This mixing appears most prominently in Cajun Brew's blend of Cajun French lyrics and 1960s rock standards, including its locally popular rendition of the Kingsmen's "fratbrat" anthem "Louie Louie." Doucet's earlier band, Coteau, also combined musical elements in the manner of swamp pop groups and, as Ancelet observes, "attracted a substantial young audience with its exciting fusion of traditional Cajun music and southern rock and roll."[11]

In addition, swamp pop appears to have influenced young Cajun artists like Bruce Daigrepont and the band Mamou. The latter group may have pursued the swamp pop ideal to the extreme, mixing traditional Cajun elements with the brash hard-rock sounds of Jimi Hendrix and Eric Clapton. (Incidentally, Rufus Jagneaux founder Benny Graeff notes that several Rufus members later performed with Cajun rock or progressive Cajun groups: Bruce McDonald joined Coteau; Gare Hernandez joined Beausoleil; and brothers Victor and Ronnie Palmer formed Red Beans and Rice Revue. Victor even joined up eventually with Zachary Richard's band.)[12]

Drawing heavily on New Orleans rhythm and blues, swamp pop reciprocated by contributing minor stylistic traits to its metropolitan cousin. These details appear in recordings by artists like Fats Domino, Earl King, Lloyd Price, Frankie Ford, and Dr. John, who occasionally recorded songs that blurred distinctions between the genres. Domino, for instance, recorded swamp pop–ish songs like "Walking to New Orleans" (1960), "Before I Grow Too Old" (1960), "It Keeps Rainin'" (1961), and "Those Eyes" (1962), all composed by swamp popper Bobby Charles and all but the latter *Billboard Hot 100* hits. (Charles actually wrote only the melody to "It Keeps Rainin'": Originally named "Little Rascals," Domino received the demo tape minus Charles's intended vocal track; admiring the melody, however, the pianist supplied new lyrics and a new title and promptly recorded the composition, much to Charles's surprise.) Domino also recorded no less than seven tunes composed by swamp popper Jimmy Donley, including "What a Price" (1961), "Rockin' Bicycle" (1961), and "Nothing New (Same Old Thing)" (1962), all three of which broke into the *Hot 100*.[13]

Other New Orleans rhythm and blues classics bearing the swamp pop imprint include Lloyd Price's "Just Because" (1957), Little Richard's "Can't Believe You Wanna Leave" (1957) and "Send Me Some Lovin'" (1957), Clarence "Frogman" Henry's "I Don't Know Why but I Do" (1961) and "On Bended Knee" (1961)—both compositions by Bobby Charles—and, of course, Earl King's "Those Lonely Lonely Nights" (1955). More recently, New Orleans bluesman Ford "Snooks" Eaglin covered King Karl and Guitar Gable's swamp pop classic "Irene" for the Black Top label's *Blues-A-Rama—Live at Tipitina's* album. Swamp pop also influenced other Louisiana artists, including swamp bluesmen like Slim Harpo, Lazy Lester, and Silas Hogan, and rockabilly performers like Rocket Morgan and Al Ferrier, all of whom recorded with J. D. Miller's swampy session band, featuring Warren Storm on percussion. (Swamp pop's influence is particularly evident on notable swamp blues recordings like

Joe Hudson and His Rockin' Dukes' "Baby Give Me a Chance" [1957], Hogan's "Everybody Needs Somebody" [1964], and Harpo's quintessential swamp blues composition "Rainin' in My Heart" [1961].) Famed rockabilly artist Jerry Lee Lewis of Ferriday, Louisiana, covered three swamp pop ballads: Cookie and the Cupcakes' "Mathilda" and "Got You on My Mind" and Jimmy Donley's "Born to Be a Loser." (Lewis's cousin, country and western artist Mickey Gilley, recorded another Donley swamp pop classic, "Think It Over," also covered by Tommy McLain in 1966.)[14]

Swamp pop's influence, however, stretched far beyond south Louisiana, southeast Texas, and neighboring regions. In 1955, for instance, Bill Haley and the Comets issued their influential cover of Bobby Charles's swamp pop classic "Later Alligator," thus more firmly establishing in popular culture the catch phrase "See you later, alligator!" and its inevitable dovetail reply "After a while crocodile!" (Etymologist Eric Partridge notes the composition's significance in his *Dictionary of Slang and Unconventional English* when he observes: "Reinforced by use as the chorus of a very popular 'rock' rhythm song, [the catchphrase] swept the English-speaking world.") The swamp pop sound exudes from Elvis's 1977 version of the Johnny Ace song "Pledging My Love," covered two years earlier by Rod Bernard and (rightfully or not) often associated by south Louisiana audiences with swamp pop music. (Although Elvis's version of "Pledging My Love" bears no resemblance to Bernard's, Johnnie Allan claims Presley covered "Promised Land" in 1975 solely in response to the belated success of Allan's 1971 swamp pop version.) And bluesman Anson Funderburgh has recorded King Karl's swamp pop compositions "This Should Go On Forever" and "Life Problem"—the latter track featuring fellow blues artist Sam Myers. The swamp pop sound also shows up in recent country and western hits like T. Graham Brown's "I Tell It Like It Used to Be," Mark Collie's "Shame Shame Shame Shame," and Billy Joe Royal's "Burned Like a Rocket." (Royal encountered the genre in the late 1960s while performing with Tommy McLain in clubs around Monroe.) In southern Texas along the Mexican border swamp pop influenced the ballad-heavy Tex-Mex sound, and Hispanic swamp popper Freddy Fender has recorded swamp pop-styled music with Doug Sahm (formerly of the Sir Douglas Quintet) and his Texas Tornadoes. (I recently witnessed an accordion-based Tex-Mex band break into Fender's "Wasted Days and Wasted Nights" to the extreme pleasure of a previously indifferent San Antonio audience.) And perhaps it most bespeaks swamp pop's impact on American pop culture that at the height of their fame Donny and Marie Osmond—those wholesome icons of mid-1970s American pop culture—had a transatlantic hit with their cover of Dale and Grace's swamp pop classic "I'm Leaving It Up to You," which the Osmond siblings also used as the title of their album.[15]

(Some observers have attempted to link Creedence Clearwater Revival's peculiar sound to the influence of swamp pop. Charlie Gillett vaguely expresses this sentiment in his *Sound of the City*, writing that "[CCR's] style merged a Memphis country rock instrumental sound with a lead singer who tried to sound as if he came from somewhere like Baton Rouge or Lake Charles." Baton Rouge area swamp bluesmen probably did influence CCR front man John Fogerty, and north Louisiana artists like Dale Hawkins and Tony Joe White clearly impacted the California-based group, which attempted to associate itself with Louisiana by coining song titles like "Born on the Bayou" and album titles like *Mardi Gras* and *Bayou Country*. But no strong evidence exists, even among the group's recordings, to suggest an actual link between CCR's style and the swamp pop sound.)[16]

In England, where swamp pop has retained a small but faithful audience almost since its inception, the swamp pop sound echoes in the music of performers like Chas & Dave, who reached the English Top Ten in 1982 with "Ain't No Pleasing You," a song later covered by Johnnie Allan. In fact, the sound appeared in English recordings as early as 1965, when the Rolling Stones covered Barbara Lynn's "Oh Baby (We Got a Good Thing Goin')." Perhaps the most intriguing example of swamp pop's impact overseas, however, is "Oh! Darling," a Lennon-McCartney song from the Beatles' 1969 *Abbey Road* album. Actually a McCartney composition, "Oh! Darling" sounds like a genuine 1950s swamp pop ballad recorded in a primitive south Louisiana studio like Eddie Shuler's or J. D. Miller's. Swamp pop producer Floyd Soileau states: "What we're calling South Louisiana music [i.e., swamp pop] has been around for some time—and it's obvious that other artists have been picking up on it. The Beatles' 'Oh! Darling' is a good example. When that song came out, people around here swore that someone from South Louisiana did it. It was so typical of the sound, the rhythm patterns, the arrangements that you find in a lot of this area's music."[16]

The inspiration of "Oh! Darling" remains a mystery, but George Harrison—who played synthesizer and lead guitar on the track—describes the composition as "a typical 1950s-'60s-period song because of its chord structure." None of the Beatles, however, is known to have mentioned a south Louisiana source. But according to John Fred, who met Lennon, McCartney, and Harrison in London in June 1968, the Beatles expressed a strong interest in Louisiana music, declaring an infatuation with Baton Rouge bluesman Slim Harpo, who recorded songs like "Raining in My Heart" at Miller's studio with swamp pop accompaniment. Regarding the Beatles' knowledge of swamp pop, however, Fred relates: "They were very familiar with a lot of records, like 'Irene' by Guitar Gable . . . . That freaked me out—I didn't think that song ever left Mamou. I knew what it was because we used to play 'Irene' all the time . . . . They were very familiar with South Louisiana music."[17]

Following the Beatles' release of "Oh! Darling," numerous swamp pop fans called south Louisiana radio stations to request the song and contacted record shops to inquire about its availability as a single. Observing this regional demand, Church Point producer Lee Lavergne called in Opelousas swamp popper Jay Randall, who covered "Oh! Darling" for Lavergne's small Lanor label. The single was issued in January 1970. Thus, a strange musical process may have come full circle: a swamp popper copying the Beatles copying swamp poppers. (The theory is not farfetched: Accordionist Aldus Roger recorded a Cajun French version of Hank Williams's country and western hit "Jambalaya," which Williams in turn had based on the traditional Cajun song "Grand Texas," also known as "L'Anse Couche-Couche.") Of course, McCartney merely may have wished to capture the sound of a typical 1950s slow ballad, and perhaps by adding to the melody a slight New Orleans inflection by chance produced a sound similar to swamp pop. But "Oh! Darling" sounds incredibly like swamp pop and not quite like New Orleans rhythm and blues. The simpler and more probable explanation is that McCartney drew on swamp pop music as the source for "Oh! Darling." (Incidentally, Warren Storm heard from a now-forgotten source that Ringo Starr once noted his admiration for Storm's drumming. Although Storm provides percussion on many classic recordings—including Harpo's "Raining in My Heart"—this account may stem from the source's confusion over the name of Starr's early group, *Rory Storm and the Hurricanes,* which closely resembles *Warren Storm and Bad Weather,* one of numerous bands the swamp popper has fronted over the decades.)[19]

"Oh! Darling," however, exerted no measurable effect on popular music except as part of a larger opus, the Beatles' highly successful and influential *Abbey Road* album. But in 1984 former Led Zeppelin front man Robert Plant provided a more concrete example of swamp pop's impact on popular music when his Honeydrippers successfully covered Phil Phillips's swamp pop classic "Sea of Love." Similarly, a 1981 cover of the same composition by early rock 'n' roller Del Shannon (of "Runaway" fame) reached number thirty-three on national charts. Rocker Tom Petty produced Shannon's version, which featured backing by Petty's group, the Heartbreakers. Phillips's original recording appears prominently in the 1989 Al Pacino film of the same title, and an anonymous cover sets the mood for a Chanel No. 5 perfume commercial that aired on major American TV networks. In addition, Lil' Bob's "I Got Loaded"—as covered by Los Lobos on their acclaimed *How Will the Wolf Survive?* album—shows up in the 1988 Kevin Costner film *Bull Durham.* And Johnny Preston's "Running Bear" sets the theme for a ritzy strip-tease act in the risqué 1989 film *Scandal* and appears in several other motion pictures. Swamp pop also has made its way into popular fiction: "I ordered a chicken-fried steak and a cup of coffee and listened to Jimmy Clanton's recording of 'Just a Dream' that came from the jukebox next door," writes detective fiction author James Lee Burke in *Black Cherry Blues,* one of his Dave Robicheaux mystery novels.[20]

These examples no doubt fall short of conveying the full extent of swamp pop's impact on pop culture and music. Despite its far-reaching if only minor influence, however, the genre remains a regional phenomenon. To experience live swamp pop music usually requires a visit to its natural habitat: the smoky nightclubs of south Louisiana and southeast Texas, where now middle-aged swamp poppers still perform old favorites for die-hard devotees. Some swamp pop artists even have ventured overseas to perform at international folk and blues festivals. Johnnie Allan, Warren Storm, Tommy McLain, Lil' Bob, and Charles Mann, for instance, have traveled to Europe. Between them, they have performed for receptive crowds in England, Scotland, Wales, Ireland, Finland, Sweden, the Netherlands, Austria, and Germany. In recent years numerous overseas record companies have secured distribution rights for swamp pop recordings. These labels include Ace/Kent, Flyright, Zane, Deep Elem, Gumbo/Cooking Vinyl, Krazy Kat, Stiff, Oval, and OvalStiff (all of the UK), as well as Polydor and Trikont (both of Germany), Sunjay and Rock & Country (Sweden), VIP and Disky (Holland), Fortune (Switzerland), and Blues Interactions (Japan).[21]

While promoting Cajun and zydeco, however, American compact disc labels like Rhino, Arhoolie, and Rounder for the most part have ignored swamp pop. For instance, Rhino chose only two tracks—Allan's "Promised Land" and "It's Christmas Time"—to represent swamp pop on its eighty-nine-track south Louisiana–oriented *Alligator Stomp* collection. Three swamp pop tracks, however, appear on Rhino's *Sound of the Swamp* release, namely, King Karl and Guitar Gable's "Congo Mombo" and "This Should Go On Forever," and Warren Storm's "Prisoner's Song." In addition, Lil' Bob and the Lollipops' "I Got Loaded" appears on Rhino's *New Orleans Party Classics,* but for unknown reasons, as the

Lollipops hail from Opelousas and recorded the track in Lafayette. Similarly, Rod Bernard's "This Should Go On Forever" and "Pardon Mr. Gordon" appear on MCA's recent *Chess New Orleans* collection, despite the fact that Bernard hails from Opelousas and Lafayette and never recorded within a hundred miles of New Orleans. Arhoolie's *J'ai été au bal* soundtrack also contains one swamp pop song and one swamp pop–influenced Cajun track: Allan's "Do You Love Me So" and Belton Richard's "Un autre soir d'ennui." These few examples seem to comprise the entire stock of swamp pop tracks available at present on major American compact disc labels, excluding the occasional appearance of swamp pop tunes on various 1950s and '60s "golden oldies" compilations. Fortunately, small south Louisiana labels like Jin and Goldband finally are issuing swamp pop on compact disc. At present, however, limited financing and distribution preclude the release of more obscure vintage tracks, and packages often lack the detailed liner notes appreciated by serious music enthusiasts. Imports usually provide such bonuses, ironically luring many swamp pop fans to European labels for this distinctly American sound.[22]

Sadly, the American folk and music festival scene, even in south Louisiana, similarly has neglected swamp pop, featuring it only sporadically or excluding it completely from its venues while regularly promoting Cajun and zydeco music. Often the genre simply is overlooked in favor of its seemingly more exotic sister genres; some circles of music enthusiasts, however, clearly have singled out swamp pop for exclusion. Swamp popper Benny Graeff, front man of Rufus Jagneaux, claims his group was ostracized in the early 1970s after the success of its sing-along favorite "Opelousas Sostan." Performed to the easy rhythm and melody of an old-time Cajun waltz, the song (written by Victor Palmer and Graeff during a Lafayette rehearsal break, not, as rumored, in a Tennessee hippie commune) features a harmonica mimicking the diatonic accordion sound and boasts the seemingly innocuous lyrics:

> Opelousas Sostan
> Used to come this way,
> On his way
> To sing his song,
> "I can hear the jukebox play."
>
> "*Mais*, I can hear the jukebox play.
> *Allons 'vec moi* [Go with me].
> *Bon temps rouler*" [(Let the) good times roll].

"Cajun hippie" swamp pop group Rufus Jagneaux, probably at a Monroe, La., festival, circa 1972. Left to right: Victor Palmer, Steve Salter, Benny Graeff, and Bruce McDonald. Drummers Gary Graeff and Ken Blevins are visible behind Benny Graeff and McDonald. (Photo courtesy of the Johnnie Allan Collection)

The popularity of "Sostan" with the south Louisiana public infuriated some cultural activists and musical purists, who regarded the song as an offensive parody of Cajun music and culture. (The popularity of Rockin' Sidney's Grammy-award-winning "My Toot Toot" sparked similar protests in 1985; still, the general public purchased thousands of copies of it, spawning covers by the likes of John Fogerty and Fats Domino.) A Cajun through his mother's Toups family and a close cousin of performer Wayne Toups, Graeff was stunned by the vicious-ness of unexpected attacks from fellow local musicians and music enthusiasts, recalling:

> Some of the more-Cajun-than-thou people thought we were ridiculing Cajuns and that we were prostituting it [Cajun culture] and all this stuff. And that couldn't be further from the truth. The songs that my grandmother taught me, one of them was [sings] "Oh, Madame Sosthène—" And I'm a kid . . . . There were certain memories that I had about Louisiana from the pictures and the sounds and stuff that I retained

in my head. And that was one of the things. And when I'd think of grandma . . . that little song, I could see her sing it and the little tunes—she taught me "Colinda." I had an aunt that played "Colinda" on harmonica all the time. These things stuck with me. And "Jolie blonde." . . . [But] there was a lot of negative backwash to us that was really kind of unjust. Some of it was probably jealousy. Some of it was they just didn't understand what was fixing to happen. We played all over and people were booking us for the uniqueness of being from Louisiana. There's people out there now making big bucks 'cause they're from Louisiana. Well, we went out there and got our faces dirty. We basically went down and kicked down doors in universities and places. And they were booking us as being "From Louisiana!" We were bringing them the best representation of our culture. We didn't ridicule Louisiana music. We didn't put on overalls and go "*Mais*, dis and dat, *cher!*" . . . We played original music and people started seeing that there's something really good from Louisiana. We played as much Cajun-oriented [music]—we took a bunch of 'em and did 'em instrumental, we converted some of 'em to English so that we could really sing 'em instead of being up there faking that we could speak French . . . . And there were a lot of the holier-than-thou people that were killing us.[23]

Similarly, Johnnie Allan has encountered strong opposition to his promotional and preservation efforts, particularly from cultural activists in swamp pop's own south Louisiana homeland. "We've been trying for years [to receive recognition]," he complains, "but they've [festival organizers] totally ignored us . . . . But swamp pop music is just as indigenous to South Louisiana as . . . Cajun or zydeco, and swamp pop has more big selling records . . . than Cajun or zydeco put together!" Yet swamp pop's past commercial success actually may work against its inclusion at folk and music festivals: the view persists that swamp pop artists renounced their heritage in exchange for monetary gain and greater chances at national fame. Swamp pop also lacks the "folk" appeal of Cajun and zydeco because its artists perform infrequently in French and rarely utilize the fiddle, accordion, and *frottoir*. This opinion is not shared by European listeners, however, who tend to find swamp pop just as exotic as its sister genres.[24]

Despite unfavorable biases, swamp pop preservationists have achieved moderate success in recent years thanks in part to the popularity of John Broven's *South to Louisiana,* Johnnie Allan's activism, and the support of several pro–swamp pop south Louisiana deejays. For instance, Allan organized the first swamp pop festival—the First South Louisiana Music All-Star Show—in Thibodaux in 1981, and in 1994 the festival was revived by the Acadian Village in

Lafayette. Swamp poppers also have made appearances (albeit sporadic) at the New Orleans Jazz and Heritage Festival, the Louisiana Folklife Festival, *Festival International de Louisiane,* and *Festivals Acadiens.*[25]

In addition, the annual Louisiana Hall of Fame (located at Acadian Village), the South Louisiana Music Association (based in Brittany in Ascension Parish), and the biennial *Times of Acadiana* music awards (of Lafayette) regularly honor swamp pop artists for their contributions to south Louisiana's musical tradition. And although overlooked by the Cajun French Music Association, a new, similar organization—the Acadian Music Heritage Association, based in Church Point—was formed in 1995 with the goal of equally promoting and preserving Cajun, zydeco, and swamp pop music. In fact, the Louisiana state legislature proclaimed the organization's planned museum "the official home of Cajun, zydeco, and swamp pop," prompting a Baton Rouge senator to quip to reporters that he previously thought swamp pop was "Coca-cola and whiskey mixed together and bottled in Lafayette." (This jest provoked a harsh response from Johnnie Allan in the letters section of Lafayette's *Daily Advertiser.*) Similarly, in 1995 the legislature—urged chiefly by KVPI swamp pop disc jockey Mark Layne—proclaimed Ville Platte the "Swamp Pop Capital of the World." Layne's activism is mirrored in other contemporary pro–swamp pop deejays like Louis Coco (KLIL, Moreauville), Danny White (KREH, Oakdale), Paul Marx (KJEF, Jennings), Roland Doucet (WKJN, Baton Rouge), Keith Manuel (KKAY, Donaldsonville), Rick Russeau (KKAY), Camay Doucet (KROF, Abbeville), Todd Mouton (KRVS, Lafayette) and Herman Fuselier (KRVS). A few swamp poppers also host (or in recent years have hosted) swamp pop radio programs, including Johnnie Allan (KRVS), Tommy McLain (KREH), Huey Darby (KROF), and Mason McClain (WKJN).[26]

Nevertheless, many enthusiasts striving to preserve Cajun and zydeco music may be condemning a third major indigenous south Louisiana genre to extinction. Cajun music has its Roddie Romeros and Kristi Guillorys and zydeco its Geno Delafoses, but swamp pop—still rarely featured outside south Louisiana and southeast Texas nightclubs—has in recent years attracted only a handful of younger swamp pop artists: Kane Glaze and Coozan, Gary T. and Deuce of Hearts, Mason McClain and Makin' Memories, Kenny Cornett and Killin' Time, Kenny Fife and Bac Trac, Ronnie Melancon and Nite Moves, and Don Rich, almost all in their thirties (though Gary T.'s act includes his fifteen-year-old son, swamp pop drummer/vocalist Travis T.) and almost all hailing from Ascension Parish, the last stronghold of swamp pop music. These artists combine

Tommy McLain (left) and Rod Bernard at a political fund raising rally with a swamp pop theme, Eunice, La., May 1992. (Photo by the author)

"oldies" swamp pop material with more recent, sometimes original swamp pop compositions, and often hawk their recordings from the bandstand on cassette and compact disc. And although not a swamp popper, C. C. Adcock draws heavily on the swamp pop sound, which he highlights on his recent Island label debut album featuring guest vocalist Tommy McLain and percussionists Clarence "Jockey" Etienne (longtime drummer for King Karl and Guitar Gable) and Warren Storm.

These few examples represent practically all swamp pop artists roughly under the age of fifty-five performing the genre regularly and contributing new songs to the basic swamp pop repertoire. Otherwise, the older, original swamp pop artists mainly churn out faithful renditions of local favorites in south Louisiana and southeast Texas nightclubs; the effect is more nostalgic than innovative. "I'm just a little afraid," confides Rod Bernard, "that these beautiful songs might all die with us." Bernard's fear is not unfounded: Swamp poppers are appearing in public on increasingly fewer occasions while folk and music festival organizers (who could provide comfortable venues for these now middle-aged performers, and in doing so reintroduce swamp pop to music enthusiasts) continue to overlook their musical contributions. Authors, filmmakers, and photographers also ignore the genre, typically examining Cajun and zydeco music without reference to swamp pop. Their reasoning may be that Cajun and zydeco music are traditional genres, while swamp pop is not—but how true is this assessment?[27]

Cajun music continues to evolve, and, as Ancelet notes, "Purists who would resist new instrumentation, styles and compositions neglect to consider that change and innovation have always been an integral part of Cajun music." As for zydeco, it appeared only when pioneers of the genre like Clifton Chenier and Boozoo Chavis mixed traditional black Creole music with rhythm and blues elements. Clearly then, zydeco's appearance could not have preceded the birth of rhythm and blues around 1945–50, only a few years prior to swamp pop's own advent in the early 1950s. (Although Clarence Garlow recorded the zydeco-ish "Bon Ton Roula" in 1949, Chenier and Chavis first recorded in 1954, *only one year* before the Boogie Ramblers, Roy Perkins, and Bobby Charles yielded the first swamp pop recordings.) Today zydeco is performed increasingly in English, not the black Creole dialect, and often sounds much like mainstream soul or rhythm and blues despite the presence of an accordion and *frottoir*.[28]

At best it can be argued that Cajun and zydeco are merely *more* traditional than swamp pop music, yet that impression does not merit swamp pop's dismissal as a musical form unworthy of equal footing with its antecedents. Once it is regarded as a major indigenous genre of south Louisiana music descending in part from traditional Cajun and black Creole music—and once it is recognized as a positive expression of the entire Cajun and black Creole experience, rather than an aberration from traditional sources—swamp pop at last may receive the recognition it deserves and perhaps even benefit from preservation efforts similar to those that rescued Cajun and black Creole music from extinction.

CASE STUDIES

Huey "Cookie" Thierry

Without doubt one of the most popular swamp pop artists, Huey "Cookie" Thierry, front man of pioneer swamp pop group Cookie and the Cupcakes, remained until recently perhaps the genre's most mysterious performer. After he disappeared from the south Louisiana music scene in the mid-1960s, neither his former bandmembers nor his own family knew his exact whereabouts or fate. Rumors held that shortly after swamp pop's decline, Cookie—besieged by racial difficulties—drifted to California and settled somewhere in Los Angeles, where (depending on the rumor) a tragic automobile accident left him confined to a wheelchair or, worse yet, he died years ago in total obscurity. As it turns out, however, the rumors were only in part accurate: Cookie indeed had settled in Los Angeles in the mid-1960s and did suffer from a series of debilitating accidents (which had occurred both prior to and during his West Coast sojourn), but he had not perished on skid row. In fact, after an almost thirty-year hiatus Cookie—renowned vocalist on swamp pop classics like "Mathilda," "Belinda," "I'm Twisted," "Got You on My Mind," and "Betty and Dupree"—returned from obscurity to perform again as lead vocalist of the reorganized Cookie and the Cupcakes, an event that transpired quietly as the author completed his initial field research for this study.[1]

Although he remained in self-imposed exile in California for many years, Huey Peter Thierry was born on August 16, 1936, on the south Louisiana prairie between Jennings and Welsh, near the little-known community of Roanoke. A black Creole of mixed-race ancestry, Cookie grew up, like many future swamp poppers, in a working-class household imbued with the sounds of traditional music.

Shane Bernard: Could you tell me a little about your family musical history? Did your parents perform music?

Huey "Cookie" Thierry: Yes, my father played the accordion and the violin, and my mother played guitar. They used to play together, Creole dances.

SB: What was your father's regular occupation?

HCT: He was a construction worker.

SB: Your parents spoke French?

HCT: Oui, very much.

SB: And it was the Creole French?

HCT: Creole French.

SB: Do you think of yourself as a Creole? Is that how you refer to yourself, like I say I'm a Cajun?

HCT: Well, I am Creole, that is my nationality. I am Creole—Spanish and Indian, French, and some white, 'cause I got it all mixed up in my family.[2]

Cookie sang black Creole music around the Thierry household and listened to it on phonograph recordings (probably those of accordionist Amédé Ardoin), but he never performed black Creole music publicly and downplays the genre's influence on his musical career. He regarded the old-time black Creole music as acceptable, but not until Cookie heard Fats Domino's 1949 recording "The Fat Man" did he experience a musical awakening. "Mother and Father had old [French] records," he recalls, "them old phonographs, they would play that kind of stuff. When the first time I heard Fats Domino, I told Mama, 'Get one of that guy there's records.' Man, I can imitate Fats Domino better than he can do his own self!" Still, black Creole and rhythm and blues music were not the only sounds absorbed by Cookie during his childhood in rural south Louisiana.

SB: So did you listen [a lot] to . . . Amédé Ardoin or was it white [Cajun] guys?

HCT: No, most of the songs that came out back then was Hank Williams and, you know, all hillbilly—. I started to become the first [black] hillbilly singer, but I said that wasn't my—

SB: So you liked country and western?

HCT: Yeah, country and western. Yeah . . . I'm just a plain old country boy . . . I'm just a plain old—I'm a Louisiana boy. Went to school in Jennings, went to school in Roanoke in a little church house and went to the seventh grade and quit. I say, I told my daddy, "I'm going to sing for a living." He said, "Boy, you going to starve." I say, "Watch me." And I haven't starved yet . . . . 'Cause, see, I was going to be a country and western singer, 'cause all I listened [to] was Gene Autry and

Roy Rogers and all them, Eddy Arnold. And I would listen to all them. And so when they bought that Fats Domino I changed my whole style and Fats Domino just stuck in my blood. And rock 'n' roll got into me, man.

SB: You think any of that country stuck with you, though? The country feel?

HCT: Oh, yeah! It's a lot of songs that I do now I put country in it . . . . Most every song that I sing it's got a little, you can notice it in the way I sing it, it's a little bit of country and western, and the rock 'n' roll and blues and just, hey, just *soul,* man. 'Cause I sing from here [the heart]. If I can't feel it, I can't sing it.

When questioned about his personal musical heroes, Thierry cites only two dissimilar artists: Fats Domino and Hank Williams, Sr.[3]

Despite Cookie's declaration to his father, he only casually cultivated his interest in music over the next several years; but sensing a gift for singing, he felt self-assured in his calling. "*I knew I could sing.* 'Cause I'd sing to myself, going bring my daddy his lunch out in the country, and sing on the open field and you'd hear it echo and it would come back to you. I knew I could sing then. So from then on it just stuck in my mind to become a singer." Yet it was not until around 1952 that Cookie became a professional vocalist. Escorting his two sisters to a dance at a now-demolished black nightspot in Lake Charles called the Horseshoe Club, Cookie winced at the discordant vocals provided by that night's entertainment, a small, recently formed local band called the Boogie Ramblers. The group featured Ernest Jacobs on trumpet and piano, Shelton Dunaway (a talented singer in his own right) on saxophone, and Marshall LeDee on electric guitar, as well as the elderly Simon "Kedee" Lubin on drums. The selection performed by the group was none other than Domino's "The Fat Man."

SB: How and when did you join the Cupcakes, and were they even the Cupcakes at the time?

HCT: No, they were called the Boogie [Ramblers], they were—let me see, I went to a dance. Ernest Jacobs was playing the trumpet. He had a guy there we'd call Kedee, he was the drummer, and they had a guy was up there singing and I say—I knew this song by Fats Domino, "They Call Me the Fat Man"—so I told the guy, I say, "Hey, man, I can sing that better than him." I say, "He's not singing it right." I didn't know he wasn't singing in the right key, 'cause I didn't know nothing about no key. I said, "I can sing that, but I can make it sound better than that." So the drummer told me, "Old po' boy, come up here." So I went up there, he says, "Sing the song." He say, "What key?" I say, "I don't know." I say, "Right where you were playing that [previous song], play that." I didn't know about no keys. I said "Play it there." And so they kicked the thing off and did it and then I took off [*sings*] *"They call, they call me the Fat Man/'Cause I weigh two hundred pounds/All the girls they love me/Cause I know, I know my way around!"* And man, the house came down when I did that. They said, "Do another!" I didn't know no other songs, that's the only song I knew! So I made up a song, right there . . . . [I said,] "Just play something fast." Kedee got off swingin' blues, I just put up a song with that, and that's it. And that started my musical career.[4]

Despite Cookie's immediate success with clubgoers, bandleader Jacobs—who still serves as the Cupcakes' pianist and manager—was reluctant to place his new discovery in the group's forefront. In fact, after that night he cautiously elected to appoint Cookie the group's stagehand. Jacobs recalls, "His job was to set the instruments up. That was his job. I'd give him a dollar, a dollar and a half a night. [Then] he learned two or three other numbers, you know. As a matter of fact, he wasn't even on payroll."[5]

The Boogie Ramblers signed with Eddie Shuler's Goldband label of Lake Charles in July 1952, apparently a short time before Cookie joined the group, as all the early members except Cookie signed the document. But the band did not record until around 1954–55 (probably '55), when Shuler released its debut single "Cindy Lou"/"Such as Love." An original composition by the Cupcakes, "Cindy Lou" would become a minor swamp pop classic as covered rockabilly-ish style by southeast Texas swamp pop group Gene Terry and the Down Beats. The flip side, however, "Such as Love," another original composition, comes across as an Afro-Caribbean ballad, complete with characteristic bongo-type percussion and affected Calypso-style vocals. Oddly, Shelton Dunaway provides lead vocals on these early Boogie Rambler sides, while Cookie, still unestablished as the group's indispensable voice, appears only as saxophonist (and also as a backing vocalist on "Cindy Lou"). Noteworthy as one of the earliest swamp pop recordings—it may even be *the* earliest—"Cindy Lou" failed to impact national or local charts, and for years Shuler issued no additional Boogie Ramblers recordings from this period.[6]

By around 1956 Cookie had worked his way up to fronting the group, which, at the suggestion of Cajun/country artist Jimmy C. Newman, altered its name to "Cookie and the Boogie Ramblers" to reflect this arrangement. (Jacobs, however, doubts the veracity of Cookie's claim about Newman—although he does recall performing in the same clubs with Newman.) A short time later, however, the group adopted its present name after hearing it shouted in jest on the street. "How we got Cookie and the Cupcakes," explains Cookie, "[this] guy's standing on the corner signifying 'Cookie and the Breadcrumbs! Cookie and the Pies!' Some guy says, 'Cookie and the Cupcakes!' I say, 'Hey, man, that'll go good. Let's go with Cookie and the Cupcakes.'" Around this period the group also stumbled on the composition that would become their first national hit (number forty-seven in *Billboard* in January 1959) and the undisputed anthem of swamp pop music: the quintessential swamp pop ballad "Mathilda."

HCT: You know what the name of "Mathilda" is? "But Still I Cried and Cried for You."

SB: That's the original title?

HCT: That's the name of the song. I was singing, "But still I cried and cried for you!" So Shelton, he told me, "You know what you sound like you're saying? It's like you're saying 'Mathilda.' And I say, the only woman I knew named Mathilda was Miss Mathilda Gray, and civil rights hadn't passed and I wasn't about to sing about that white woman! He said, "You're not singing about her. Just call the song 'Mathilda.'" I disagreed with him and disagreed with him. He said, "Go ahead and say it." I said "Alright, I'll say 'Mathilda.'" And I changed it to "Mathilda," and that's where it took off. The name of it was "But Still I Cried and Cried for You." . . . [Jacobs] was messin' on the piano one night, 'cause he always, when he gets through with a song he goes to banging on the piano. So he hit me, and I was hurt by a broad, and so I started, "But still I cried and cried for you." And so, hey, Marshall filled in with the guitar, and the bass fell in, and the drum fell in, and, hey, we had a song. We did, what, a year or two before we cut it, just doing it in the clubs.

Ernest Jacobs: Maybe two years.

HCT: Yeah, just doing it in the clubs.

EJ: Didn't even have it on tape or nothing.

HCT: That's right. And we got so popular, here's a song they would ask for *every night we'd get up.* "Play that song you played the other night!" . . .

SB: So you probably wrote it around '56.

HCT: Yeah, we almost went through a studio and cut it.

SB: What studio?

HCT: I think he tried at Eddie Shuler. Eddie Shuler here. They said, "Cookie, we can't make a record outta that."[7]

The Cupcakes presented their new song to several other producers, including Duke/Peacock label owner Don Robey of Houston, all of whom turned down proposals to record the group. Finding a supporter, however, in Lake Charles recordman George Khoury, owner of the Lyric and Khoury labels, the Cupcakes finally yielded an acceptable version of "Mathilda" at KAOK radio in Lake Charles (they had recorded the song for Khoury in other studios without success), and it is this version, according to Thierry and Jacobs, that now is regarded as the archetypal swamp pop recording. ("Mathilda" first appeared on Lyric before Khoury licensed the track to Jud Phillips's new Judd label of Memphis, which shortly went bankrupt on the deal, much to the Cupcakes' dismay.) Despite claims to the contrary, however, earlier swamp pop recordings—particularly King Karl and Guitar Gable's "Irene," issued on Excello in 1956—also possess the same telltale piano triplets, undulating bass lines, and bellowing saxophones that appear in "Mathilda." Yet it was "Mathilda" that became the standard for all subsequent swamp pop ballads, inspiring numerous south Louisiana and southeast Texas teenage musicians to compose strikingly similar plaintive ballads.[8]

Quizzed about the origin of the swamp pop ballad sound associated so strongly with "Mathilda," Cookie defers to the opinion of pianist Jacobs, whom he credits more than any other musician with popularizing the style.

> *SB* [*to Jacobs*]: Where did what's called the swamp pop ballad sound, the "Mathilda" sound, where did that come from? That piano sound and the saxes—especially the piano triplets and the bass line.
>
> *EJ:* I think it accidentally happened. I'm going to explain to you what I mean by that. When we recorded "Mathilda," we didn't have all these different soundtracks.
>
> *HCT:* Oh, no!
>
> *EJ:* Alright? We had one big microphone that looked about [like] a small basketball. All the sound came through that one microphone. That's why it was all in the little cubicle, so to speak, in a radio station. KAOK radio station. It wasn't in no studio . . . . What it was, the cone, you can pick the sound up all the whole way around. Today it's just, you know, right out front. But the microphones during that time, anywhere you stand it'll pick up . . . . They're directional mikes today. If you not right in front of that microphone, it's not going to sound—
>
> *SB:* So it was an accident?
>
> *EJ:* I think it was purely an accident because like the piano for instance, you're playing on an upright piano and the microphone is way over there. What make it sound deep was, you so far away from the microphone. And you gotta play *real hard,* okay, but it still picking the sound up. The guitar, he's way back, you know,

the only ones that was a little bit closer was the horns, okay? And I think that's what created that, like playing inside of a *drum,* so to speak. *Like a muffled sound.* That's what they mean by that *swamp* sound.

SB: What about the particular bass lines that you picked out? It's sort of like [imitates the bass line of "Mathilda"] and the piano would follow that, too. Where did you get that from?

HCT: The piano was *leading* it.

EJ: The piano led . . . . When I'd take a break I still wanted to play on the piano and I just started playing something.

SB: "Irene" by Karl and Gable has a similar sound . . . . Were you all getting that from the same source, do you think they got that from you, or did you all get it from someone else? Was it the Fats Domino sound or was it different from Fats Domino?

HCT: He [Jacobs] plays in Fats Domino style.

EJ: I think it's different from Fats Domino. They were a little bit better equipped. You know, they might had maybe *two tracks,* okay, for Fats Domino, maybe one for just him and the other track is for the instruments and stuff like that, alright? And I think that created a little bit different *sound* . . . . Back during that time they just didn't have the microphones, they didn't know nothing about putting padding on the wall and stuff like that and make a soundproof room. They didn't know anything about that, see. But later on, like when we did "Got You on My Mind," they had everybody in a separate room *with earphones on! We thought that was the funniest thing in the world! Hell, I can't hear that drummer!* You know? "Yes, you will, you gonna hear him right here, through the headphones." That was strange to us![9]

The Cupcakes went on to record several more swamp pop classics, including "Belinda," "Betty and Dupree," and "Got You on My Mind," the latter of which, leased to Chess records near the close of swamp pop's golden age, barely broke into the *Billboard Hot 100* in May 1963 to reach number ninety-four. (Cookie duets with Shelton Dunaway on both "Betty and Dupree" and "Got You on My Mind.") During this period local black Creole swamp popper Little Alfred—cousin of Simon Lubin, the group's early drummer—left a Cupcakes-inspired but otherwise unrelated group called the Berry Cups to join the band as saxophonist and vocalist. Alfred, in fact, recorded a half-dozen singles for the Lyric and Khoury labels with backing by the Cupcakes, but his most popular recording remains the Berry Cups' swamp pop ballad "Walking Down the Aisle."[10]

In the mid-1960s swamp pop began its slow decline and in August 1965 Cookie moved to Los Angeles, leaving the Cupcakes to continue without him until their dispersal around 1972–73, says Jacobs, who himself left the group in 1970. Cookie confirms the truth of rumors regarding his affairs with female Cajun admirers during the 1950s and early '60s, and also confirms that these romances led to serious racial trouble for himself and the group; but he denies leaving the state because of racial tensions. "I'm a Leo, I just want to roam," he matter-of-factly explains. "I'm the lion. I gotta go and see what's out there. And my whole thing was just to see the other part of the world." Severing most contacts with his south Louisiana homeland, Cookie vanished from the swamp pop music scene until his unexpected 1992 comeback. During the twenty-seven-year interim, however, swamp pop enthusiasts elevated Cookie to legendary status and entertained rumors to explain his mysterious disappearance. One had it that a tragic automobile accident left Cookie confined to a wheelchair. Actually, Cookie's left leg was broken when an automobile struck him and four other members of the Cupcakes' entourage outside the Raven Club in Lake Charles; and years later he broke his right leg when he tripped over a heavy oak coffee table in his Los Angeles home. Although not confined to a wheelchair, Cookie today finds walking a difficult task, and often supports himself with a sturdy cane. As for the rumors of his demise, Cookie jokes:

HCT [*to Jacobs*]: I've been dead for how many years?

EJ: Quite a few.

HCT: Ten or fifteen years, I was dead. So I came down here when my baby brother got killed, they said, "Cookie, Cookie, they told us you was dead!" And I said, "Man, c'mon!" I said, "You can't kill the devil! [*laughs*] He's going to be around all the time!" I went back to California—I stayed here, what, about six months, I went back to California, then my brother put out that I had got killed in a car wreck. I called his house one day and I said, his wife's name was Laura, I said, "Let me speak to Laura." [He says] "Who's this?" I said, "This is Cookie." "*Man, I thought you were dead!*" "Yeah, I'm calling you from the graveyard!" . . .

SB: But people were still thinking that you were dead up until you came back [recently].

HCT: 'Til I came back, yeah.

EJ: Up until three years ago they still thought he was dead.[11]

Even Jacobs was uncertain of Cookie's fate, and a Los Angeles vacation presented the now-middle-aged former Cupcakes pianist with an opportunity to locate his missing friend. Acting on vague rumors heard for years around Lake Charles, he searched the notorious south central region of Los Angeles for three days before stopping by chance at the very car wash where Cookie worked as a washer. Unfortunately, Cookie was absent that day, but tips gleaned from other car washers and a gas station attendant led Jacobs to Cookie's home on a side street so obscure that Jacobs's up-to-date Los Angeles city map omitted it.

> *EJ:* I knocked on the garage door. I say, "Cookie!" He says, "Yeah!" I said, "This is Ernest! Turn around!" He say, "Yeah, I know, yeah, Ernest, yeah, uh-huh, okay, yeah, tell me anything!" I said, "Cookie! Turn around, man!" I said, "This is Ernest!" *He still wouldn't turn around.* So I said [*sings*], "Luv honka mon, tee na nee na nay!"
>
> *HCT:* Yeah, I knew it was him, 'cause that's a little song we made up called "Luv Honka Mon."
>
> *EJ:* And look here! He turned around—that turned him around—and the little old song, it was just *nothing!*
>
> *HCT:* It's nothing. It's just something we just made up.
>
> *EJ:* We used to make that up when we be going fishing . . . . But that's the only thing made him turn around. And when he turned around, the tears rolled. And when I saw his tears roll, my tears rolled. I said, "C'mon on out here, man!"[12]

Cookie and his former pianist renewed their friendship over the remaining days of Jacobs's vacation, during which Cookie expressed an interest in returning to Louisiana to resume his position as lead vocalist of the revived Cupcakes. (Several ex-members of the group recently had reunited under Jacobs's direction for a fund raiser.) Jacobs offered to finance Cookie's move and the band's reorganization—but only if Cookie could prove beyond a doubt that he still possessed his vocal prowess. Jacobs recalls: "He said, 'I got the voice.' I say, 'Mm-hmm.' I say, 'But you going to have to prove it to me.' So I took him to the park, I say, 'Sing! Sing loud! Scream!' We went to the beach, remember the beach? I said, 'Sing to them seagulls!' I said, 'I want to hear you *scream!*' And he would just open up . . . . I was waiting for it to crack. If it'd 'a cracked, he'd 'a still been in California. 'Cause I wasn't going to bring him here if he's no good to nobody, over here . . . . *And his voice never did crack!* I stayed with him another two days, singing every day."[13]

Jacobs promptly flew his vocalist back to Lake Charles and reorganized the Cupcakes, which, while augmented by a few newcomers, features two original members in addition to Thierry and Jacobs: saxophonist and singer Shelton Dunaway and guitarist Marshall LeDee. Although these veteran Cupcakes are in their late fifties and early sixties, they currently perform throughout south Louisiana, southeast Texas, and beyond on a hectic, demanding schedule. "That's what bothers me as a promoter and a manager," confides Jacobs, who also works for a Lake Charles plastics manufacturer, "'cause I don't know if we'll be able to handle it. It's gonna call for dedication, it's gonna call for a lot of traveling, and we're not a hundred percent ready for it." Despite these concerns, the group intends to record a new album in the near future and recently appeared overseas at the Utrecht *Blues Estafette*. Its four original members recently made cameo appearances on the Boogie Kings' swamp pop tribute album *Swamp Boogie Blues,* for which Cookie and the group covered "Mathilda."[14]

King Karl and Guitar Gable

King Karl and Guitar Gable are two of the earliest and most important swamp pop performers. Black Creoles from south Louisiana's northern prairie region, they worked as a musical team to help formulate the blend of rhythm and blues and traditional Cajun and black Creole music that in part characterizes swamp pop. Both musicians fit patterns common to many swamp poppers: They grew up in an area of intense cross-cultural mixing, speak English as well as French, and as youngsters were exposed frequently to traditional Cajun and black Creole music.[1]

King Karl, for instance, was born Bernard Jolivette in Grand Coteau—located between Lafayette and Opelousas—on December 22, 1931. According to Karl, only one relative, an uncle named John Abbs, performed music. Abbs had a definite impact, however, on the future swamp popper.

> *King Karl:* I guess that's where I took it from 'cause he played anything he picked up. He didn't take it [music] in high school or nothing 'cause he didn't go to school. He just picked it on his own [*sic*], but he played any instrument he picked up. . . .
>
> *Shane Bernard:* What kind of music did he play?
>
> *KK:* He used to play like country and blues.
>
> *SB:* Was there any one instrument that he played above all the rest?
>
> *KK:* I'd say he was about as good on each. But he played more accordion and piano.
>
> *SB:* Did he play with anyone notable back then, like Clifton Chenier or anybody like that?

KK: No, it was more like French style and waltzes. It wasn't a zydeco type way back then.

SB: Where was all this—this was around Grand Coteau?

KK: This was around Opelousas and Lawtell, Bellevue.

SB: Where was he from?

KK: He was from Opelousas. But I think he was born around Elton.

(The "French" music to which he refers is no doubt a precursor of zydeco such as that recorded by legendary black Creole accordionist Amédé Ardoin; in addition, all the locations Karl names—Opelousas, Grand Coteau, Lawtell, Bellevue, Elton—fall within or border the northern prairie region.)[2]

After his birth Karl's family left Grand Coteau to settle in nearby Sunset. In school he bolstered his talent for singing with alto saxophone lessons and around age thirteen formed an unnamed band with Peter Guilbeau and John and Charlie Bob (relatives of swamp popper Camille Bob, better known as Lil' Bob). The group soon disbanded, however, and Karl gave up his saxophone to play guitar with black Creole accordionist Howard Broussard.[3]

Like his uncle, Karl played many instruments—saxophone, guitar, even piano and harmonica.

SB: How did you learn to play all that?

KK: Just pick 'em up and play 'em. The first one, my mother used to play harmonica, so when she got two, her brother had given her one, so she gave me one. I was about eight years old. So I started playing harmonica. And then like I say when I was thirteen and we had started that little band, everybody had a sax, so I took my sax and I trade it to Prof Erny [of Prof Erny's music store in Lafayette] for a guitar, the type that had them pickups on it.

SB: What kind of guitar was it—I mean, what brand?

KK: It just was a gui-tar. [Laughs.] They had them pickups they'd put on 'em. You could put it on and take it off. And a little bitty amplifier. . . .

SB: It was an acoustic?

KK: It was a box type. That's the guitar I started playing with Howard Broussard.[4]

At about age eighteen Karl, like numerous Cajuns and black Creoles, moved to southeast Texas in search of work, which he found at a veterinary hospital and at a railway company. In his spare time, however, Karl composed songs (mainly ballads) and performed in local black nightclubs like the Raven. In 1950 he joined Lloyd Price's band, working as Price's relief singer around Beaumont and occasionally in New Orleans. Karl regards Price as a major influence on his vocal style and also cites B. B. King, Ben E. King, and Otis Redding as inspirations.[5]

When his father died in the early 1950s Karl gave up music and settled for a short time in Opelousas, where his family had moved from Sunset. He soon departed for Lake Charles to work in construction, but received his draft notice in 1953. Karl served at Fort Hood, Texas, and in Korea until he was discharged on May 14, 1955. Returning to south Louisiana, he found work at a Sunset sweet potato kiln. (Sunset and nearby Opelousas both have called themselves the sweet potato or "yam" capital of the world.) He also began to sing in local nightclubs, and around this time he met Guitar Gable, his future musical partner.

> *KK:* Guitar Gable had been playing little jobs with some little guy out of Lafayette. Anyhow, there was this priest, Father Millet, and he came one day [to the kiln] and he said, "I was told you was fixing to be in a band." So I said, "Yes." He said, "I got a good boy. I would like for you to go play with him." He said, "I would like for you to get together, 'cause I don't like the company he's with." I said, "Okay" . . . So we went to Gable and it happened that Gable would be playing that night. So I went cleaned up. I went on the job with Gable and I sung. This was in Rayne at a place called Joe's Place.
>
> *SB:* About what year was this?
>
> *KK:* This was '55, when I came back. So the place went crazy. So this night Gable didn't waste no time, he told the boys he was quitting, he was forming his own band. And he [the band leader] says, "No, you going with him [Karl]!" And Gable says, "No, if it's anything, he's gonna come with me—I'm building my own band."[6]

Six years Karl's junior, Guitar Gable was born Gabriel Perrodin on August 17, 1937, in Bellevue (named for the Prairie Bellevue), a few miles south of Opelousas. Although he recalls no musically inclined grandparents, Gable notes that his father, a Creole of mixed black, white, and native American heritage, possessed a reputation around Bellevue as a formidable musician.

> *SB:* In your family, does anyone else play music?
>
> *Guitar Gable:* My father played accordion . . . . He played accordion and harmonica. . . .
>
> *SB:* Was he playing what's now called zydeco?
>
> *GG:* French music, the French accordion music, then. They didn't call it zydeco, they called it French music.[7]

The elder Perrodin performed with a *frottoir* player at house dances sponsored by other black Creoles around Bellevue. Unlike his father, however, Gable
never picked up the accordion or harmonica, preferring the guitar, which he
taught himself to play around age twelve on a cheap Gene Autry–style model.
A brother, John Clinton "Fats" (or "Yank") Perrodin—longtime bass player for
Lil' Bob and the Lollipops—shared Gable's preference for rhythm and blues
over their father's accordion music. "Zydeco wasn't out in those days when we
were playing," he explains, "and French songs just wasn't catching on." Gable
points out, however, that another brother, Oliver, played fiddle as well as guitar.
Gable supplies a lengthy list when asked which performers he favored: B. B.
King, Guitar Slim, Earl King, Fats Domino, Little Richard, Sonny Boy Williamson,
Jimmy Reed, Little Walter, John Lee Hooker, Bo Diddley, and even Elvis Presley.[8]

By 1953, at age sixteen, Gable had mastered the guitar and—wielding a box-
type model with a self-installed pickup—was appearing in nightclubs with yet
another brother, guitarist Landry Perrodin. Gable recalls that his first public
performance took place in Abbeville at the Gypsy T Room (probably named
for the Gypsy Tea Room, a popular rhythm and blues club in New Orleans).
By 1954 Gable had adopted his stage name, fronting a four-piece band called
Guitar Gable and His Swing Masters—the group disbanded by Gable after he
met King Karl.[9]

All but the Swing Masters' deposed bandleader/lead vocalist followed Karl
and Gable, who assembled a few additional musicians and billed themselves as
"Guitar Gable and the Musical Kings featuring King Karl." Gable now wielded
a sleek, white Fender brand Telecaster (though he later switched briefly to a
Gretsch model). Surprisingly, the group lacked a designated pianist, although
Karl occasionally played piano on the bandstand and the group utilized the
instrument during recording sessions. Playing mainly white nightclubs throughout south Louisiana and southeast Texas, the Musical Kings accrued a sizable
repertoire of original songs, as well as a local following. Many of their fans
were young Cajuns who soon would form bands of their own modeled on the
Musical Kings and Cookie and the Cupcakes (formerly the Boogie Ramblers).

> **GG:** At that time Cookie and the Cupcakes and my group was recording and we
> were pretty much the hottest little thing going in the little area, at that time. We
> was recording and it was quite new. And then Jimmy Clanton came in and he
> started doing it and Bobby Charles. They were after us, as far as I remember.
> And they did good, too.

SB: Now you're talking about back when you were sixteen, seventeen?

GG: [Yes.]

SB: That's the period you're talking about—and then they came in?

GG: Yeah.

SB: You were still pretty young then when Bobby Charles came in?

GG: Yeah. Oh, yeah, I was playing out there. I was doing some recording then when Bobby was recording for somebody else. Rod [Bernard] did his tunes after, too, I believe.[10]

Karl composed most of the Musical Kings' songs, which consisted mainly of the slow mournful ballads most easily identifiable as swamp pop. Wishing to record for Eddie Shuler's Goldband label of Lake Charles, the Musical Kings prepared two sides in 1956 for a prospective 45 rpm single: "Life Problem" and "Congo Mombo." A classic swamp pop ballad later covered by swamp popper Elton Anderson, "Life Problem" was written by Karl during a night school class. "We wasn't busy in school. We wasn't doing nothing, so I was writing," he recalls. "So the teacher come to me, she say 'You wasting my time?' I said 'No, I ain't wasting your time.' I said 'You going to hear this on record.' 'No, boy. Throw that piece of paper somewhere!' " Karl retained the lyrics, however, and the band soon included "Life Problem" in its growing repertoire.[11]

Although he states in John Broven's *South to Louisiana* that TV depictions of African musical performances inspired their popular instrumental "Congo Mombo," Gable now supports Karl's recollection that the tune originated by accident.

KK: The way we done that, one night we were in New Iberia—I'll never forget—and Jockey was just doing that with the drums by hisself.

SB: What's his last name?

KK: Jockey? That's Clarence Etienne. He was just making the same beat he be doing [on the recording]. He was by hisself, though. So I looked at Gable and I say, "Gable, play something like 'Frankie and Johnny' behind that." So Gable started playing that and they did it again and everybody started dancing behind it.

SB: You're right. It does sound like "Frankie and Johnny." I never thought of that.

KK: Yeah. So the next day I told Gable, man, we going to cut that. So they rehearsed it over and over, added a little bit here and there, and we recorded it.[12]

When the Musical Kings drove to Lake Charles to audition for a Goldband session, they learned of Shuler's absence and disappointedly turned back

King Karl, rejected poster
photo, Crowley, La., late 1955.
(Photo courtesy of Bernard
Jolivette)

towards Opelousas. Driving down Highway 90, they happened to stop in
Crowley, where they learned about J. D. Miller's local studio and approached
him about recording "Congo Mombo" and "Life Problem." Miller auditioned
the group and agreed to record them, leasing the sides to Ernie Young's Excello label of Nashville. The record became a hit nationally and the Musical
Kings followed it with other Miller-produced vocal/instrumental pairings. Sides
like "Guitar Rhumbo" only mimicked the more successful "Congo Mombo,"
prompting Miller to drop the instrumentals—which had highlighted Gable's
six-string prowess—in favor of ballads showcasing Karl's strong vocals and
impassioned lyrics.

> **SB:** How many songs did you do [as composer] . . . compared to Bernard Jolivette
> [King Karl]?
>
> **GG:** Well, what we were doing at the time was trying to do an instrumental on one
> side and a vocal on the other side. But that got caught up in the middle of us
> having a good instrumental. So what Miller did, he just went ahead and did the
> songs, let King Karl write some songs, he did a slow and a fast, started doing

that. If he'd have run across a pretty good instrumental down the line that he thought would have did something for us, he would have put it on . . . . I couldn't sing that good so we just let it stay like that.

SB: What do you think the reason was for that—do you think you were maybe intimidated by the fact that it was going down on tape?

GG: I don't know what happened. Miller didn't like the style I sang in, so—

SB: But you were better live?

GG: Yeah, on the bandstand I'd help Karl sing. I'd do a few numbers. I'd do Chuck Berry, I'd do Fats Domino. I'd sound pretty good on the bandstand, but come to the recording on tape I didn't come out too good. Miller didn't want to use that.

SB: You don't know why you sounded different on tape?

GG: I don't know. I sounded different on the tape. I mean, it surprised me because on the bandstand I sounded pretty good.

Despite his problem with studio vocals, Gable often worked as a studio musician for Miller, backing artists like Bobby Charles, Warren Storm, Lazy Lester, Slim Harpo, Classie Ballou, Tabby Thomas, Chuck Martin, and Joe Hudson. Gable's intricate solos inspired many emulators and helped to create the "swamp sound" so closely associated with Miller's productions.[13]

After their initial release on Excello, Karl, Gable and the Musical Kings went on to record several notable songs in the swamp pop idiom, the most notable of which were "Irene" and "This Should Go On Forever," both penned by Karl. According to Karl, "Irene" became their biggest seller, and Gable insists that Jimmy Clanton borrowed its melody for his million-selling swamp pop recording "Just a Dream." Karl's compositions also greatly influenced swamp popper Rod Bernard, who found success with "This Should Go On Forever" and followed it immediately (albeit less successfully) with "My Life Is a Mystery," another song written by Karl. (After Bernard's recording of "This Should Go On Forever" hit the national charts, Excello quickly issued Karl's own version—actually a demo, says Karl—but at the time it never received much airplay or attention.)[14]

Illustrating the long tradition of interaction among black Creole and Cajun musicians, Karl and Bernard collaborated as songwriters, composing the tunes "(I Have a Vow) To Have and Hold" and "Gimme Back My Cadillac." (Karl even claims that Bernard helped him to write "My Life Is a Mystery," but Bernard is not cited as co-writer and does not recall contributing to the song.)

SB: Do you remember . . . [Rod Bernard] going over to your house and learning how to play the—

KK: Oh, he used to come home all the time.

SB: Tell me about that.

KK: A lot of times he would come with his guitar and we'd sit down and play guitar.

SB: Where were you living at the time?

KK: I was living in Opelousas. He'd come over and sit down and play guitar . . . . I was living in a little old sharpshooter house.

SB: Like a shotgun house?

KK: Yeah . . . . [Rod] used to come home all the time. Sit on the side with Gable. We'd play music. We used to fool around with writing songs.[15]

The Musical Kings broke up in 1960 when Gable received his draft notice. By that time Miller had fallen out with Excello's Ernie Young, who decided to promote and record King Karl under the pseudonym "Chuck" Brown. Despite an extensive tour, Young released only two Brown singles, "Lead Me to Lover's Land"/"Hard Times at My Door" and "The Moon without You"/"Oh! No Love," around 1962 on Excello. Karl believes other "Brown" recordings remain unreleased in the Excello vaults.[16]

Gable returned from the military around the time Karl soloed on Excello, and the Musical Kings soon reunited to back Karl (now billed as King *Carl*) on several 45 rpm singles released on Carol Rachou's La Louisianne and Tamm labels of Lafayette. Around 1968 the group disbanded again—this time for good, recalls Karl, because Gable and he found too few reliable musicians to induct as Musical Kings. After the breakup, Karl found work painting vehicles for a Lafayette business, but continued to perform at night with Good Rockin' Bob, Roscoe Chenier, and C. D. and the Bluerunners (not to be confused with the present-day Bluerunners of Lafayette). In recent years he worked as a night watchman for St. Landry Security of Opelousas and often could be found patrolling the sidewalks outside the Evangeline Maid Bakery near downtown Lafayette. Karl recently moved to Arizona, however, for reasons of health. Gable, on the other hand, appeared in the early 1970s with the Outcasts (a local rhythm and blues group popular among Lafayette's college crowd) and Lynn August before joining Lil' Bob and the Lollipops for seven years. He also found day work as a Montgomery Ward TV repairman in Lafayette. Gable retired from music and repair work in 1980 after suffering a back injury in an auto accident.[17]

Although Karl and Gable no longer appear in south Louisiana clubs, Karl's son Larry has played bass with Cowboy Stew Blues Revue, featuring Lil' Buck Senegal (former guitarist with Clifton Chenier) and guitarist Sherman Robertson;

and Gable's son, Guitar Gable, Jr., also known as "Pandy," has performed with several zydeco musicians, including Rockin' Dopsie, Roy Carrier, and Beau Jocque, and now appears both with Zydeco Force and Warren Ceasar. Joined by Pandy, however, Gable teamed up with Karl at the ninth annual *Festival International de Louisiane*, held in Lafayette in April 1995, for their first performance in over a quarter-century.[18]

Bobby Charles

As a recording artist and particularly as a songwriter, Bobby Charles exerted a profound influence on swamp pop, especially during its formative years. Although best known for penning such memorable tunes as "Later Alligator," "I Don't Know Why but I Do" and "Walking to New Orleans," other, more locally popular songs like "On Bended Knee," "Why Did You Leave," "Why Can't You," and "Before I Grow Too Old" inspired numerous south Louisiana imitators, who in turn expanded the swamp pop repertoire and impacted regional and national charts. Although Charles refuses to confine himself solely to writing swamp pop–styled music—and although he is skeptical about his role in swamp pop's development—he nonetheless deserves credit for his contributions to the fledgling genre.[1]

Born Robert Charles Guidry on February 21, 1938, in Abbeville, he was reared by nonmusical parents in the heart of the Acadiana region. According to Charles, as a child he enjoyed listening to Cajun music on the radio, despite his limited knowledge of the Cajun French dialect.

> **Shane Bernard:** You speak French?
>
> **Bobby Charles:** *Ouais, 'tit peu* . . . a little bit. . . .
>
> **SB:** [Rod Bernard] told me how . . . [children were punished for] speaking it on the playground.
>
> **BC:** That's right, that's right. At school we were taught not to speak French. . . .
>
> **SB:** What type of music did you listen to when you were growing up, teenage years and before that even?
>
> **BC:** When I was a kid I used to listen to French music and country music—and one day I turned the radio dial and found this rhythm and blues music station . . . . Changed my life, like that.

Surprisingly, however, in addition to Fats Domino and Hank Williams, Sr., Charles names such artists as Nat King Cole and Louis Armstrong as influences.

"Jazz influenced every artist in Louisiana in one way or another," he says. "All of our music is some kind of a jazz."[2]

During his early teens Charles began to pen numerous rhythm and blues–influenced tunes, developing a songwriting process that would remain largely unchanged over the years: He composed quickly, in a matter of minutes, relying on handwritten lyrics and a memorized tune until he preserved the completed song on tape. Oddly, Charles never learned to read music or play an instrument. In fact, he insists that a basic understanding of music has always eluded him. "But I can tell when somebody's playing a wrong note," he says, "or a wrong chord or something, like when we go in the studio. It's really funny, I have to tell Willie Nelson and Neil Young, somebody, they're playing the wrong chord. They ask me, 'What's the chord?' and I say, 'Well, I don't know, man. You hit me all the chords you know and I'll tell you which one it is when you hit it!' "[3]

Early in his career Charles occasionally sought the assistance of other, more technically adept south Louisiana performers. For instance, fellow swamp pop performer and songwriter Roy Perkins recalls an as yet unknown Bobby Charles asking for impromptu piano lessons between Perkins's sets at the Airport Club in Abbeville. (Ironically, Perkins at the time played with the Cardinals—later known as the Clippers—who eventually backed Charles on stage and in the studio.) And hometown swamp popper Warren Storm often assisted while Charles composed. "I had a tape recorder and he didn't have one," says Storm. "We'd go to his house and he'd hum the melody and I'd strum the chords." Storm remembers assisting Charles on "Walking to New Orleans," "Before I Grow Too Old," "I Don't Know Why but I Do," and several other compositions.[4]

Charles compensated for his technical handicaps with sheer songwriting talent, and although aware of his genius, he declines to assume credit for his abilities. "It's like a gift, it's a God-given gift," he explains, "because I can't read or write a note of music, I can't play a musical instrument. It's strictly a gift. I get an inspiration for a song, it's like it's been living in me all my life and it comes out. It's not like it's a song to me, it's more like a spirit or something almost. But when I get the inspiration for it, it's always been like that, I can write a song in fifteen minutes, or twenty minutes, it doesn't take me long at all and I don't change hardly any words. It's just a gift, it just comes out." Stressing the importance of genuine emotion and spontaneity in songwriting, Charles notes that he often goes for months without penning a lyric. Even when inspired, however, he usually finds the process exhausting. "I don't try to write a song," he points out. "I have to really be inspired. I mean it drains me. It moves me. It has to move me real, real deep, or it doesn't come out."[5]

Charles's first notable success as a songwriter and performer came in 1955 with "Later Alligator," an upbeat composition containing the heavy piano triplets found in later swamp pop ballads, but in this instance rendered at an extremely rapid tempo. When a Crowley record shop owner, Charles "Dago" Redlich, heard Charles perform the song on stage, he recommended "Alligator" and the young artist to Chicago recordman Leonard Chess—of rhythm and blues–heavy Chess, Checker, and Argo labels—who listened over a telephone to the fifteen-year-old sing the composition. Thinking he had discovered an up-and-coming black artist, Chess later was shocked when, during a promotional tour, a white teenager stepped off an airliner to greet him in Chicago; in fact, his response marked the first occasion Charles heard a certain expletive beginning with the word *mother.*[6]

Undaunted, Chess booked Cosimo Matassa's New Orleans studio and re-cruited Fats Domino's band for the session. Although this lineup later appeared on his other Chess sides (including "Laura Lee," "Take It Easy Greasy" and "One Eyed Jack"), Charles refused to record without the Cardinals, who had accom-panied him to New Orleans. Today he suggests a smoother sound might have been obtained with Domino's group, but the Cardinals exhibited an unaffected simplicity and rawness captured on later vintage recordings by other swamp pop groups like the Twisters, the Riff Raffs, and the Down Beats. (Other successful Bobby Charles tracks from this period include "Why Did You Leave"/"Don't You Know I Love You," "Take It Easy Greasy," "No Use Knockin'," "Why Can't You," "You Can Suit Yourself," and "One-Eyed Jack.")[7]

"Later Alligator" fared well on local charts, but achieved its greatest success when covered by Bill Haley and the Comets. This hardly disturbed Charles, who flourished on songwriting royalties. In fact, Charles subsists today mainly on royalties collected from other performers who have recorded his songs, including Joe Cocker, Muddy Waters, Delbert McClinton, Bo Diddley, David Allan Coe, Tom Jones, Kris Kristofferson, Rita Coolidge, Etta James, Clarence "Frogman" Henry, and Ray Charles. At one time Colonel Tom Parker and even Elvis Presley himself courted Charles as a prospective songwriter.

> *BC:* The flip side [of "One Eyed Jack"], I had "Yea Yea Baby." I had written that . . .
> for Elvis, because Elvis had asked me to write a couple of songs for this one al-
> bum he was doing. And when I wrote the songs, I sent them to [Leonard] Chess

in Chicago and he said, "No, the hell with Elvis!" He didn't want to send them to Elvis. I said, "Why, are you crazy?" But he never would send them to him.

SB: I never read about that before. You met Elvis somewhere?

BC: In Memphis.

SB: At Graceland?

BC: No, I met him at this theater. He used to have this theater that would show some movies after hours, after midnight. He would have some movies flown in from Hollywood and him and some of his friends would go over and watch them and I got invited to one of those and I met him. I met him a couple of times. Colonel Parker sent me a telegram one morning, my mother woke me up, asking me for some songs for Elvis. But for some reason Chess just would never send them the songs.[8]

One famed performer who did record several of Charles's songs is Fats Domino. Their relationship began in the early 1960s, shortly after Charles signed with Lew Chudd's Imperial label, the same label that promoted Domino. "That was a real rush for me," says Charles, "to write a song for somebody that was an inspiration to me, like Fats Domino." Charles penned several compositions for Domino between 1960 and '62, including "Before I Grow Too Old," "Walking to New Orleans," and "Those Eyes." He also wrote "Little Rascals" for Domino, who inexplicably received the demo tape without Charles's accompanying vocal track. Domino liked the melody, however, wrote new lyrics, and released the tune as "It Keeps Rainin'," much to Charles's surprise. Yet composing for Domino came belatedly for Charles, who remembers trying unsuccessfully to peddle the unrecorded "Later Alligator" to the famed pianist.

Charles "C. C." Adcock: How did you just start writing all those great songs for him [Fats Domino]?

BC: I don't know. I went to see Fats when he was playing in Abbeville, when I had first wrote "See You Later Alligator." He was playing at this black club called Robinson's Recreation Center. And I was the only white kid in there. But, man, I liked him. I was getting in there one way or the other. I met him, I was about fourteen years old . . . and I told him about this song I had written, "See You Later Alligator," and he laughed. He said he didn't know about doing anything about alligators. And I said, well, I said I was going to try to put down the song so that he could hear it with some music so that he could tell what it was, because you can't tell if a song's good just by saying what it is. So, anyway, he blew it off. But the next time he saw me, [*laughs*] he remembered me![9]

Charles often visited black clubs around south Louisiana and occasionally ran into trouble at white clubs while traveling with black musicians like Chuck Berry, Frankie Lymon, and Ray Charles. "I've been called a lot of things," says Charles. "I've been thrown out of several places because of some of my black friends. I mean, I was just brought up with them, like in my music career. I was the only white guy on the bus. I was the only one there—and I enjoyed it. I learned a lot. I learned things you can't learn in school." Charles also grew up with and played on stage with numerous local swamp pop artists, many of whom later would cover his compositions. For instance, Rod Bernard recorded Charles's "On Bended Knee," Johnnie Allan, his "Your Picture," Tommy McLain, "Before I Grow Too Old," and John Fred, the upbeat "Good Lovin'." Although from 1955 to the mid-'60s he drew frequently on the swamp pop sound—and to a lesser extent continues to draw on it today—most Bobby Charles fans, and many swamp pop enthusiasts, regard Charles as too diverse an artist to classify solely as a swamp popper. As former Cardinals saxophonist Harry Simoneaux notes, "Bobby is such an incredible talent—that's why it's hard to categorize him." Charles himself dismisses the swamp pop classification. "I never know what kind of song I'm going to write," he states. Yet he also admits his uncertainty about the meaning of *swamp pop*.

> **SB:** Even though you say you write different kinds of music, most of your better known songs have that south Louisiana sound . . . . Would you consider yourself a swamp pop musician, and even if you don't, how would you define that swamp pop sound?
>
> **BC:** I don't know, I really don't know [what it is]. I guess it's just a Louisiana sound from this particular area . . . . I had never heard that [term] before, I didn't know what it was. Somebody told me I was a swamp pop musician, I said "Oh, *really?*" I mean, I didn't know what the hell they were talking about . . . I just thought it was people who lived in the swamp who had a pop record, I don't know! They just label it like rhythm and blues, or whatever—rock 'n' roll, swamp pop, zydeco . . . . If you got to name your children, I guess you have to give it [swamp pop] a name, too![10]

Although the late 1950s and early '60s remain his most productive period, Charles continued to release new material over the subsequent decades. In the early 1970s, for instance, an extended sojourn in Woodstock, New York, resulted in friendships with rhythm and blues performer Paul Butterfield and members of The Band, who—along with musicians like David Sanborn and

Dr. John—appeared on his ensuing 1972 *Bobby Charles* album, reissued on CD in 1995. Music critics praised the release (recorded in Bearsville, New York, for Albert Grossman's new Bearsville label) but sales were disappointing. The track "Small Town Talk," however, became one of Charles's most well-known compositions. In 1976 Charles performed at The Band's farewell concert; he appears on their *Last Waltz* album, which captures the concert, and in the accompanying documentary.[11]

Despite success as a songwriter of international repute ("The Japanese know more about me than I do," he quips, referring to his many Asian enthusiasts), Charles eventually retired to the countryside near his hometown of Abbeville. Although seldom heard from during the late 1970s, he founded the Rice & Gravy label in the 1980s to promote locally produced south Louisiana music. "Louisiana was a major spoke in the wheel of the music industry, the music world," he says. "Louisiana was the heart and soul of it all almost. We just lost the business [side] of music." Indeed, his earlier label, Hub City—founded in the mid-to-late 1960s with the help of Carol Rachou's La Louisianne records of Lafayette—was short-lived, and Charles cites the unwillingness of south Louisiana radio stations to promote "local records" as the primary cause of its demise. The same problem also plagued Rice & Gravy. "I told them [south Louisiana radio stations] they were wrong," he complains. "It's not a local record, it's a *local* radio station that we're standing in, [but] this is an *international* record." A planned Rice & Gravy album, *Lil' Cajun,* recorded in 1984 with cameos by Willie Nelson and Neil Young, remains unreleased, although Charles issued the title track in 1986 as a Rice & Gravy single. In the early 1990s he planned to release several recordings from these sessions on a Rice & Gravy album entitled *I Wanna Be the One,* and while the album never materialized, a number of the recordings finally appeared in 1995 on his well-received Rice & Gravy/Stoney Plain album *Wish You Were Here Right Now.* In 1994 his composition "I Don't Know Why but I Do," as rendered by Clarence "Frogman" Henry, appeared on the popular *Forrest Gump* motion picture soundtrack.[12]

Residing for years on Bayou Vermilion—which snakes its murky way through central Acadiana—Charles grew increasingly concerned about the environment and recorded three environmental songs, "Clean Water," "The Solution to Pollution," and "Environmental Harmony," the first of which appears on his *Clean Water* album (issued at present only in Japan). Charles has developed around these songs a global education program aimed at instilling environmental awareness in children. According to him, the United Nations recently embraced the program, entitled *Solution to Pollution: The Children's Environmental Program.* Charles now resides at Holly Beach, located in Cameron Parish on the Gulf of Mexico, living off royalties and awaiting a burst of inspiration that will yield another south Louisiana classic.[13]

Warren Storm

Most swamp poppers are praised solely as vocalists, but Warren Storm is renowned for both his vocals and drumming, recording several swamp pop classics (he remains producer J. D. Miller's top-selling swamp popper) and backing other musicians in the studio and on the bandstand. Artists he has supported over the decades include fellow swamp poppers Johnnie Allan and Rod Bernard, as well as legendary swamp blues artists like Katie Webster, Silas Hogan, Slim Harpo, Lonesome Sundown, Lightnin' Slim and Lazy Lester. Failing to reappear on national charts after his early success with "Prisoner's Song," Storm nevertheless remains a vital swamp pop artist in south Louisiana and southeast Texas, where dedicated fans continue to purchase his releases on local independent labels. Indeed, most admirers know Storm for his many regional hits rather than for his isolated national hit.[1]

Storm was born February 18, 1937, in the small Cajun town of Abbeville as Warren Schexnider, a common Cajun surname of German Creole origin. He spoke only French until his third year of school and recalls impatient teachers scolding him for speaking the Cajun dialect. (His parents never learned to speak more than a few words of English.) Storm's father, Simon Schexnider, played drums throughout south Louisiana in Cajun and country and western string bands.

> *Shane Bernard:* What about Cajun music? Your dad played drums for the Rayne-Bo Ramblers, right?
>
> *Warren Storm:* Yeah, he played for the Rayne-Bo Ramblers and Happy Fats and Al Terry and Doc [Guidry]. It was a string band. It was country, then he played Cajun after that.
>
> *SB:* So it wasn't like there was an accordion in the group?
>
> *WS:* Right. They had two guitars, a fiddle, drums. They had . . . an upright bass then. Most of the stuff wasn't electrified. They just had one little amplifier when they started. . . .
>
> *SB:* Did you come from a musical family? Were there other people in your family who played . . . ?

WS: No. My daddy played music all his life. He played the guitar, the fiddle, the harmonica, the accordion and the drums.

SB: What about grandparents?

WS: No.

SB: So as far as you know, your father was the first one [in your family] to play music?

WS: Right.[2]

Simon Schexnider taught his son to play the drums and guitar, and in 1948 Storm began sitting in with small country and western groups around Abbeville, singing tunes by artists like Faron Young, Lefty Frizzell, and Hank Williams, Sr. (That same year Storm briefly met Williams at a show promoting Hadacol health tonic.) In 1952, at age fifteen, however, Storm became interested in playing music professionally after he sat in for his father at a dance. Continuing to perform Cajun and country and western music throughout high school, he joined Larry Brasso and the Rhythmaires from about 1951 to '53. He then moved on to saxophonist Herb Landry's band, the Serenaders, around 1953 to '56, when he played rhythm and blues for the first time, both with the Serenaders and occasionally with Bobby Charles and the Cardinals. Roughly the same age, Charles and Storm often traveled together to New Orleans, where they encountered many notable rhythm and blues performers.

SB: You had mentioned that you and Bobby Charles, you'd go to New Orleans to listen [to rhythm and blues musicians]. . . .

WS: That's right. We'd go down there and we saw Fats Domino recording at Cosimo's studio. Then after the session we'd go at the Brass Rail—that was after-hours. And some of Fats's band [performed there]. Paul Gayten played piano. Lee Allen on the saxophone. And Charlie ["Hungry"] Williams—that's where I learned a lot of my drumming techniques from. Charlie Williams, that old blues drummer from New Orleans. He worked with Fats Domino and a bunch of artists.

SB: I was going to ask you—where'd you learn your drumming . . . ?

WS: Well, I learned it from my daddy, the beginning of it. But as I'd go to New Orleans, I'd pick their style up, which is a very good style. It's like a shuffle beat with a heavy foot and a lot of cymbals.[3]

In 1956 Storm founded his first group, a swamp pop band called the Wee-Wows. (*Wee-Wow*, explains Storm, was the cry of clubgoers when he soloed

Warren Storm with the Cajun/country string group Larry Brasso and the Rhythmaires, 1952. Left to right: Larry Brasso, Warren Storm, Nelson Lange, and Dalton Delcambre. (Photo courtesy of the Johnnie Allan Collection)

on the drums.) At this time he exchanged the drawn-out *Schexnider* for *Storm,* a name he took from pop singer Gale Storm. The Wee-Wows soon became the Jive Masters, playing throughout the Acadiana region of south Louisiana. "We played everything from Cajun, country, Fats Domino rhythm and blues to Elvis Presley music," says Storm, "and were booked at all the nightclubs around Lafayette, Crowley, Kaplan, and Ville Platte."[4]

Around the spring of 1958 a Kaplan recording artist and clubowner introduced Storm to Crowley producer J. D. Miller, who invited the twenty-one-year-old to audition at his studio. Storm obliged, strumming a guitar as he sang tunes by Hank Williams, Fats Domino, and Elvis Presley. Pleased with Storm's voice, Miller picked out a song for him to record: the old country and western standard "Prisoner's Song." A traditional Cajun group from Storm's hometown, the Alley Boys, had recorded a Cajun French version of the song for the Vocalion label in 1939 called "Tu ma quité seul," yet Storm recalls learning his version from a circa 1920s English recording (probably the 1924 hit rendition by early "hillbilly" artist Vernon Dalhart).[5]

Requiring a flip side, Miller wrote "Mama Mama Mama (Look What Your Little Boy's Done)." Storm recorded the two songs at Miller's studio in May 1958 with swamp poppers Guitar Gable and pianist Roy Perkins on the session with the Jive Masters' lead guitarist, Al Foreman, and bass player, Bobby McBride. (Foreman and McBride, along with Storm, would comprise the core of Miller's regular studio band in the late 1950s and early '60s.) Miller leased the tracks to Nashville recordman Ernie Young, who issued them on Nasco, sister label of his famous Excello blues label. Touring the country to promote the record, Storm appeared on several TV dance programs, including a Memphis program hosted by future game show emcee Wink Martindale. After the program Martindale presented Storm with a handwritten pass to Graceland, the estate of one of Storm's musical heroes.

> **WS:** And he [Elvis] was there [at the mansion] and they had a little party going on and he was sitting at a piano. And when the chauffeur brought us in, he [Elvis] told me to come sit by the piano while he was playing. And he had seen our show that afternoon. It was a Saturday. . . . And they had about ten or fifteen people around him.
>
> **SB:** Do you remember anything that he sang?
>
> **WS:** He took off on "The Prisoner's Song." He sang a little bit of "The Prisoner's Song."[6]

By August 1958 "Prisoner's Song"/"Mama Mama Mama" had broken into the Billboard Hot 100; one of the earliest swamp pop songs to do so, it peaked at number eighty-one. Three subsequent Nasco releases, however, failed to achieve the same success, although "Troubles Troubles (Troubles on My Mind)," "So Long So Long (Good Bye Good Bye)" (both Miller compositions) and "Birmingham Jail" (the country and western standard popularized in the late 1920s by Darby and Tarlton) sold moderately well. Storm left Nasco after the expiration of his contract and recorded for Miller's own Rocko and Zynn labels, as well as for major labels like Top Rank and Dot. "I Want to Thank You So Much" on Rocko sold well in south Louisiana and southeast Texas, but the 1960 session for Top Rank resulted in an unsuccessful single, "Bohawk Georgia Grind"/"No No," released around 1961. The lackluster Top Rank sides no doubt suffered largely from their reliance on a team of Nashville session artists and arrangers—the same team that participated in colorless sessions for Mercury swamp pop artists like Jivin' Gene and Rod Bernard.

> **SB:** [The Nashville session] didn't turn out too well. When I listen to the stuff . . . [that Rod Bernard and others] did there, they took all the swamp pop sound out of it.
>
> **WS:** Oh, yeah. It wasn't swamp pop. It was more pop than anything else. . . . It was the Nashville sound, that's what it was. Nashville.
>
> **SB:** But it was overproduced in a way. . . . It's so slick, it kinda loses its edge.
>
> **WS:** Yeah. It was mechanical because it was the Nashville sound. All the records that came out of there, it was the same music background.
>
> **SB:** So you didn't like that sound either, that you came out with there?
>
> **WS:** I thought it was good. I liked it.
>
> **SB:** Did you notice that it was different from what you were doing back home at Miller's?
>
> **WS:** Oh, definitely.
>
> **SB:** Which did you prefer?
>
> **WS:** Well, we were trying to upgrade our sound, is what we were doing. We got away from the swamp pop thing. . . . Like everybody tries to do, they try to cross over different fields of music.[7]

In the early 1960s Storm founded a new group, the Wanderers, but in 1963 he teamed up with Rod Bernard and Skip Stewart to form the Shondells, performing with them throughout south Louisiana until the group disbanded around 1970. Storm also recorded for the La Louisianne label from 1963 to around '66, appearing not only on releases with the Shondells but with Cajun musician Doc Guidry, country musicians Al Terry and Eddy Raven, and swamp poppers Jewel and the Rubies, Bobby Charles, and Dale and Grace. Storm even provides the drumming on Dale and Grace's number-one hit "I'm Leaving It Up to You." In 1964, however, he took a job at a Lafayette print shop to supplement his musical earnings. (Storm maintained this job until 1980, when he returned to music as his sole profession.) Around 1966 he appeared with Huey Meaux's assistance (albeit without much success) on the ATCO label and Meaux's own Sincere and Teardrop labels. These sessions yielded only two notable tracks, "Tennessee Waltz" and "The Gypsy." Years later Meaux issued two albums of material from this period, including *Warren Storm and Johnny Allen* [sic], dividing the album's sides between the two swamp poppers.[8]

According to Storm in Broven's *South to Louisiana,* Meaux "had a misfortune with his business" in the late 1960s, leaving Storm without a label from 1969 to '73, when he returned to Crowley to record for Miller's new Premier and Showtime labels. Backed by another new band, Bad Weather, Storm recorded two regional hits, "Lord I Need Somebody Bad Tonight" and "My House of Memories," both of which became mid-1970s swamp pop classics. He also recorded an album for Miller entitled *At Last Warren Storm.* Storm continued to perform with Bad Weather throughout the '70s, and in 1979 he and the group joined up for a brief period with former Shondells member Rod Bernard (for whom Storm played drums on *Boogie in Black & White* in 1976).[9]

In 1980 Storm formed yet another group, Cypress, and recorded for Meaux's new Starflite label. In 1984 CBS distributed one Starflite single, "Things Have Gone to Pieces"/"Please Mr. Sandman," but it failed to make the charts. That same year Storm recorded the *Heart and Soul* album on South Star, a label formed especially for him by Bob Hendricks, an art and Indian artifact dealer from Hendersonville, Tennessee, and a Warren Storm devotee since the 1950s. In fact, Hendricks had attempted to locate Storm for over twenty years, advertising for information about the swamp popper in music-oriented magazines. Around the mid-1980s a chance encounter with Eddy Raven revealed not only that Storm had played drums on Raven's first record, but that Storm resided in Raven's hometown of Lafayette. Traveling to Louisiana, Hendricks met Storm and offered to finance an album—Storm accepted the offer, went to Nashville and recorded the *Heart and Soul* album with backing by local studio musicians (who apparently this time had been coached on the swamp pop sound).[10]

Although a South Star single, "Seven Letters"/"I Need Somebody Bad" sold promisingly, the album failed to impact the national charts. (Floyd Soileau eventually leased the album for distribution on Jin and since then "Seven Letters" has become a regional swamp pop favorite.) During the mid-1980s Storm continued to perform in Lafayette area nightclubs and occasionally to back other artists in the studio. In fact, he played drums at Miller's studio for former Creedence Clearwater Revival member John Fogerty, who had traveled to south Louisiana to record a cover of Rockin' Sidney's 1985 zydeco hit "My Toot Toot." Storm appeared in a documentary about the session (shown on the Showtime cable channel), and around this time he also hosted his own TV program on Lafayette's KADN, which sporadically aired his videotaped performances with Cypress at all hours of the early morning. Around 1985 Storm left Cypress and joined the Yesterday's Band (house band for the now defunct Yesterday's swamp pop club in Lafayette). In 1989 he recorded *Cajun Born* for La Louisianne with Rufus Thibodeaux's Cajun Born group, a swamp pop/Cajun music ensemble also featuring Clint West and Johnnie Allan. Storm recorded the aptly titled *Night after Night* album for Floyd Soileau in 1991 and toured overseas with Allan in 1991 and '93. Around early 1995 he joined Kenny and the Jokers, which eventually became Warren Storm and Bad Weather, Storm's current group. Storm remains one of the most active swamp pop artists, appearing to the present almost nightly in south Louisiana nightclubs, particularly the Back to Back and Four Seasons in Lafayette.[11]

Rod Bernard

Although today he performs in public only sporadically, Rod Bernard remains a notable figure in swamp pop's history. Recording his first hit at age eighteen, he went on to release a series of classic swamp pop songs, including "Colinda," "One More Chance," "Pardon Mr. Gordon," and most notably "This Should Go On Forever"—a slow, plaintive ballad considered by some the model swamp pop recording after Cookie and the Cupcakes' "Mathilda." Backed by his own small-town band, Bernard's recording of "This Should Go On Forever" pushed him into the national spotlight and inspired other budding swamp pop artists to cut records of their own. "By hitting the charts," observes Broven in *South to Louisiana,* "Bernard had fulfilled every dream in the Bayou country."[1]

Born in Opelousas on August 12, 1940, Bernard (whose surname is of Acadian origin) grew up in an ordinary working-class Cajun family. His father held a variety of jobs, including oil field and postal worker, and his mother found employment as a telephone operator. Although both parents were bilingual, the younger Bernard—whose generation was punished by educators for speaking French—never learned the Cajun dialect. He notes, however, that "I was raised with Cajun music from the time I was a kid." Although he knows of no musical forebears, Bernard always was attracted to music, particularly Cajun and country and western music, and often heard live performances at his grandfather's dance hall.

> ***Shane Bernard:*** So you don't know of anyone in . . . [your] family who used to play music?
>
> ***Rod Bernard:*** No. My grandfather had a big nightclub in Port Barre and it was a French nightclub where bands like Aldus Roger [and] Papa Cairo . . . played.

We used to go over there and I'd just hang on the bandstand and watch the musicians the whole time. . . .

SB: What was the name of the nightclub?

RB: Courtableau Inn, in Port Barre. It was right on the bayou. Huge, big old building.

SB: Was it a fais do-do place?

RB: Yeah. The old mamas would bring their daughters and the mamas would sit at the back along the wall while their daughters danced. And then they'd wait till the dance was over and take their daughters home. And they had slot machines [in the club] and all that . . . even when it was illegal.

Bernard also recalls hearing Cajun/country musician Jimmy C. Newman and zydeco pioneer Clifton Chenier perform at the Courtableau.[2]

Picking pecans in his backyard, Bernard accrued enough money around age eight to purchase his first guitar, a Gene Autry box-type model, from a local pharmacy. His younger brother, Oscar "Ric" Bernard—who soon would learn to outplay the elder Bernard—helped to purchase the instrument. Bernard quickly mastered the basic chords and advanced to a more professional Harmony model, which he played on local merchant Felix Dezauche's early morning radio programs, broadcast live on KSLO from Dezauche's Feed Store in Opelousas. "[Mr. Dezauche] played the harmonica," recalls Bernard. "He would play a song or two and then [he and his daughter,] they'd talk about how many people came in the store and who bought what and Aldus Joubert came in and bought a hundred pounds of Texo Feed for his horses and stuff like that."[3]

Around 1950 Dezauche began to sponsor a live thirty-minute program on Saturday mornings featuring the Blue Room Gang, a troupe of young local musicians. Bernard joined the group as a rhythm guitarist and vocalist noted for his yodeling. During this period Bernard approached the music director of KSLO about hosting his own live music program. Agreeing to give the ten-year-old a show if he obtained a sponsor, Bernard returned with the backing of the local Lincoln-Mercury dealership, which previously had ignored overtures from the station's sales department. Strumming his guitar, Bernard sang for listeners every Saturday afternoon for fifteen minutes and often invited other young musicians to perform on his program. Around 1952 he began to deejay on KSLO, playing country and western music for an hour every Tuesday night.[4]

Accompanying the Blue Room Gang on a tour of the South and Midwest to promote Dezauche's Red Bird brand sweet potatoes, Bernard, backed by the group, cut his first record around age thirteen in a Waterloo, Indiana, studio.

Rod Bernard (at center) with the Cajun/country group the Blue Room Gang, rodeo, Church Point, La., 1950. Back row, left to right: Rene Fontenot, Johnny Badeaux, Nolan Badeaux, Felix Dezauche, and Pee Wee McCauley. (Photo courtesy of Rod Bernard)

The record was a 78 rpm extended-play custom acetate of Hank Williams, Sr.'s "Jambalaya." Bernard idolized Williams, whom he once met backstage before an Opelousas show.

> **SB:** Tell me about meeting Hank Williams.
>
> **RB:** I met Hank Williams, Sr., when I was about eight years old, I guess . . . no, I was probably about nine, 'cause he died, what, 1950? [Williams died in 1953.] It was probably about a year before he died. He played at the Opelousas High School gym. Back then they played in gyms because they didn't have places like they have now. . . . Mr. Dezauche took me backstage and Hank Williams was standing there in his underwear. I'll never forget that. And I walked up to him and that was my god at the time—or a god, it was like Elvis later on. Man, to see Hank Williams, Sr., in person standing there! And he shook hands with me and I had an autograph book and he signed my autograph book and I found out later that he never signed many autographs, that he didn't really like to sign autographs. . . . He

had a doctor traveling with him and I stayed backstage and about every twenty
minutes a doctor would come and give him a shot and I kept thinking . . . "Poor
guy, he's really sick." I didn't realize that it was drugs—they would give him shots
to wake him up and drugs to put him to sleep.[5]

Around 1953–54 Bernard left KSLO and the Blue Room Gang to accom-
pany his family to Winnie, Texas, where his father labored in nearby oil fields.
(Coincidentally, at the time Bernard often visited the Winnie barber shop of
Huey Meaux, who later would break into the music business and represent
Bernard as a manager and producer.) The young musician continued to perform,
however, entertaining enough southeast Texas audiences to grab the attention
of the *Beaumont Enterprise*: "Rodney Bernard, 14, Plays Guitar, Sings 'Cajun'
Tunes" reads the article's heading. "He doesn't want to become a professional
musician," noted his interviewer. "He wants to be a doctor."[6]

Bernard continued to move in a musical direction, however, returning to
Opelousas in 1956 to work as a full-time deejay at KSLO. By this time a change
had swept over popular music: Teenagers were demanding rhythm and blues
music and KSLO responded with "Boogie Time," a program featuring "race music" (rhythm and blues) for an hour each evening. Bernard hosted the program
as "Hot Rod" in imitation of J. P. Richardson's "Big Bopper" character, whom he
often heard on Beaumont's KTRM radio. Playing records by local black artists
like King Karl, Guitar Gable, and Lonesome Sundown, Bernard began to incor-
porate the new sounds into his own musical performances and soon helped to
organize the Twisters (as in "tornado," not the dance), a group composed of
fellow high school students, including his brother Oscar.[7]

Performing at teen center dances, high school hops and various civic functions, the seven- to eight-member group approached local music shop owner
Jake Graffagnino in 1957 about producing two 45 rpm singles. They recorded
their first single, "Linda Gail"/"Little Bitty Mama," in the Southern Club's empty
dance hall with one microphone and a portable tape recorder. The Twisters
employed an identical setup when they recorded their second single, "All Night
in Jail"/"Set Me Free" around the counter of Jake's Music Shop. They pressed
five hundred copies of each single on Graffagnino's Carl label and distributed
the records themselves. Today these collectors items capture the simplicity
of early swamp pop, but at the time the Carl releases garnered little attention
except from the musicians' families and classmates. In 1958, however, Ville Platte
producer Floyd Soileau approached Bernard and the Twisters about recording a
single for his fledgling Jin label.

RB: [Soileau] said, "You want to cut a record? I'm starting a record company." And
I said, "Yeah, sure, why not." And he said, "Well, find a couple of songs." When
I got off of work at ten o'clock, I'd go listen to Guitar Gable and King Karl
and those guys and I went to the Moonlight Inn in Opelousas, which was the
nightclub that they played in. When I walked in [one night] Karl said something
about that Rod Bernard from KSLO had just come in and he said, "Rod, we want
to play our next record, a song I wrote called 'This Should Go On Forever.'"
And he sang it and when I heard it, man, it just hit me like "Boy—what a hit
song!" When Floyd called me and said to find a couple of songs, I wrote one
called "Pardon Mr. Gordon" and then I thought about that song. So I went to
meet Karl at his house and I said, "Look, you think it'd be okay if I recorded that
song I like?" And he said, "Sure, they're never going to release it anyway." So he
taught it to me and I learned it. We sat on his front porch. I don't know how
to read music and write any music or anything and I didn't have a tape recorder.
I mean, we had big ones at the radio station. So he'd sing it and I'd sing it, he'd
sing it, I'd sing it and then I started humming it and singing and I jumped in my
car and I drove to the radio station and I put it on tape and I didn't realize I had
changed it a little bit.[8]

Bernard's version of "This Should Go On Forever," recorded at J. D. Miller's
studio in Crowley, appeared in October 1958 and immediately received airplay
throughout south Louisiana and southeast Texas. Record shops began to order
the single for eager listeners and soon Soileau no longer could meet demand,
prompting other local artists—such as the Boogie Kings and the Down Beats—
to record rival versions for larger labels. Soileau finally leased "This Should Go
On Forever" to Leonard Chess's Argo label of Chicago, which distributed the
record nationwide. By the spring of 1959 it had reached number eight in *Hit
Parade* and the Top 20 in *Billboard* and *Cashbox*, propelling Bernard onto road
shows with Chuck Berry, Jerry Lee Lewis, B. B. King, Roy Orbison, and Frankie
Avalon, and onto TV programs like the "Alan Freed Show" and Dick Clark's
"American Bandstand."[9]

A follow-up Argo single, "You're on My Mind" (written by Roy Perkins),
backed with "My Life Is a Mystery" (written by King Karl), failed to achieve
the success of "This Should Go On Forever." In late 1959 Bernard signed with
producer Bill Hall of Beaumont, who switched the artist to the Mercury label.
As it would do with other swamp pop artists, Mercury replaced swamp pop
elements with the slick Nashville sound, complete with female choruses and

lush violin sections. Only one minor hit, "One More Chance," emerged from these sessions, which mainly yielded what Broven calls "vacuous teen ballads, more 'pop' than 'swamp.'" Owing the label thousands of dollars for production costs, Bernard left Mercury after the expiration of his two-year contract and signed with Bill Hall's own Hall-Way label of Beaumont. Recording with local artists Johnny and Edgar Winter, he released several notable tunes, including "Fais Do Do," "Who's Gonna Rock My Baby" and one of his nightclub standards, "Colinda" (a song Bernard at first declined to record because he could not imagine it a pop success).[10]

Leaving for Marine Corps boot camp the day after recording "Colinda," Bernard returned in late summer 1962 to form the Shondells with fellow swamp poppers Warren Storm and Skip Stewart. (Also known as Skip Morris, Stewart formerly played with the Boogie Kings and the Twisters and in 1962 worked with Bernard at KVOL radio in Lafayette.) During the mid-1960s the group recorded several singles and an album, *The Shondells at the Saturday Hop,* for La Louisianne records of Lafayette. Bernard also recorded for Huey Meaux's Teardrop and Copyright labels and Soileau's familiar Jin label. Isolated singles appeared on the Scepter and SSS International labels. In 1965 Bernard even formed his own short-lived label with producer Carol Rachou (of La Louisiane) called Arbee—as in Rachou-Bernard. Notable songs issuing from this period include "Recorded in England" for Arbee, "Papa Thibodeaux" for Copyright, and "Congratulations to You Darling" for Jin.[11]

Bernard played infrequently during the 1970s, but released several country and western–influenced swamp pop albums and most notably the *Boogie in Black & White* LP, recorded for Jin in 1976 with legendary black Creole musician Clifton Chenier. Music writers continue to praise this unaffected swamp pop–zydeco jam. Bill Millar, for instance, describes it as "a wild and woolly rock 'n' roll set with spontaneity one normally only dreams about," and Larry Benicewicz even claims, "such a masterpiece, no doubt, spawned other 'experiments' like Wayne Toups' 'ZydeCajun' style or, perhaps, a Zachary Richard 'Zack Attack,' a similar fusion of Cajun, zydeco, and R&B."[12]

Around 1980 Bernard overcame a chronic addiction to alcohol and prescription drugs, and for years avoided the nightclub scene except to attend semiannual Shondells reunions at the Southern Club. These days he appears almost weekly in central Acadiana swamp pop clubs, yet in general the music business no longer appeals to him. "If you have to force yourself to smile and perform when it's not fun," he says, "then it's not worth it. And it got to that point."

He recorded his last album, *A Lot of Dominoes*—a collection of his favorite Fats Domino compositions—around 1980 for Jin. The masters disappeared until 1991, however, when Soileau finally released the material on audio cassette. Several of Bernard's tracks recently appeared on various artists releases on the Ace compact disc label of England, which in 1994 issued a twenty-eight track compilation of his best recordings entitled *Swamp Rock 'n' Roller*. Bernard works today as an advertising salesman at KLFY-TV in Lafayette, a position he has held since 1965.[13]

Johnnie Allan

Although his records never appeared on U.S. charts, Johnnie Allan is the top-selling artist on Floyd Soileau's swamp pop–heavy Jin label, a standing in part achieved through the sheer volume of Allan's recordings. Appearing on roughly sixty singles, thirty long-playing albums, and twenty-five compact discs, Allan has scored numerous hits (regional and otherwise) over the years, including "Lonely Days, Lonely Nights," "South to Louisiana," "Your Picture," "Family Rules," "Somewhere on Skid Row," and "Promised Land." He remains the most visible and perhaps best-known swamp popper, appearing on stage at swamp pop shows throughout south Louisiana and even Europe. He also has promoted the genre (and other local genres) through his collection of vintage photographs called *Memories: A Pictorial History of South Louisiana Music* and through his former swamp pop program on KRVS, the University of Southwestern Louisiana's public radio station in Lafayette.[1]

Allan was born John Allen Guillot (a Cajun name of French Creole origin) on March 10, 1938, in Rayne, to poor Cajun sharecroppers. His mother pawned her guitar for three dollars to hire a midwife for his delivery. Reared on the prairie around Bosco, near the intersection of Acadia, Lafayette, and St. Landry parishes, Allan worked with his family in the fields, growing cotton, sweet potatoes, Irish potatoes, corn, and hay. His parents spoke only Cajun French, and by age six Allan knew only a few words of English. As an infant, however, he memorized the English lyrics of a few popular bluegrass tunes.

> ***Shane Bernard:*** That's something that your mom told you, but you really don't remember, because you were so young, or do you definitely remember it?
>
> ***Johnnie Allan:*** See, my mother played guitar and sang and she used to sing those songs, so I would imagine—I'm like three years old—I would imagine listening to

her and my uncles and aunts, they were six—three boys and three girls in the family—whenever they'd come visiting, they'd bring the guitar and the fiddle and they'd sit outside on the steps or the porch and play music. And these are some of the songs that they sang.

SB: This is in Rayne?

JA: No, this is back in the country by Bosco, not far from here, by the Bosco oil field. . . .

SB: How many people in your family played music?

JA: Well, all of them did. Like I say, they were three brothers and three sisters and all of them sang and played instruments. And, of course, my grandfather played music. He played with his brother, with [celebrated Cajun accordionist] Joe Falcon. He played fiddle with Uncle Joe. A lot of people don't know this, my grandfather played a hell of a better accordion than Uncle Joe did, a lot better. And my mother [Helen Falcon Guillot] played guitar with Uncle Joe, as did my aunt, her sister, Marie Falcon. She later recorded. She played Cajun music and recorded Cajun songs. And Uncle Joe's first wife [Cléoma Breaux Falcon] also played in the band.[2]

At about age six Allan acquired his first guitar—probably a Harmony brand box-type model—with money he and his brother earned by selling vegetable seeds. "One day my brother and I were out in the fields and my mummy and daddy came back from Lafayette in the horse and buggy," he says, recalling that his parents emerged from the vehicle only to explain they could not find an affordable guitar. "I went back in and there was the guitar on the bed." Allan's mother taught him to play the instrument and he soon joined in at family gatherings, where he sang Cajun, country and western, and bluegrass tunes. Though his family was too poor to afford a radio throughout most of the 1940s, Allan regularly gained access to a neighbor's set. "When I did, I glued my ears to it," he reminisces. Allan tuned in to popular country and western stations like WSM in Nashville (which featured "The Grand Ole Opry") and XERF (located in Del Rio, Texas, across the border from its powerful transmitter in nearby Villa Acuna, Mexico).[3]

Around 1951 at age thirteen, Allan and schoolmate Walter Mouton, a skillful accordionist, formed Walter Mouton and the Scott Playboys, a group specializing in traditional Cajun music. After about two years, however, renowned Cajun musician Lawrence Walker invited Allan to join his troupe, the Wandering Aces. Allan accepted and Walker switched him from rhythm guitar to drums and steel guitar.

SB: I saw that when you first joined Walter Mouton and the Scott Playboys you played rhythm guitar?

JA: Yeah.

SB: And then when you joined Lawrence Walker's band you played steel guitar?

JA: I started out playing the drums for a very short period of time with him because his drum player—

SB: With Lawrence Walker?

JA: Yeah. His drum player had gotten sick or something and [so I] played drums and then in the interim his steel player quit or he got fired or something and then . . . let me put it this way, with Walter I went from rhythm guitar to drums and then Rodney Miller was playing steel, then he left to go with Aldus Roger and I took over on steel. So Lawrence knew that I could play drums and steel guitar, both . . . . I enjoyed playing steel guitar more than the drums, so when the steel player quit, [I said,] "Let me try on the steel."

In addition to playing rhythm guitar, steel guitar and drums, Allan dabbled on the tenor saxophone.[4]

Around 1958 Allan played on his first recording session, held for Walker, he recalls, at KEUN radio in Eunice. The session yielded "Bon Ton Rouley" and "Osson Two-Step" for Floyd Soileau's short-lived Vee-Pee label (as in Ville Platte). By that time Allan already had noticed Cajun music's decline in popularity, a condition he attributed to the rise of rock 'n' roll and rhythm and blues. "Landry's Palladium in Lafayette would bring in guys like Earl King and Gatemouth Brown," he remembers. "I went there one night and both of them were on the bill and I was so impressed. It was so packed in there you could hardly move—I could see the trend was moving away from Cajun music to that type of music. And our crowds when we played were getting smaller and smaller with the Cajun music, while the crowds at the clubs with the rock 'n' roll bill were getting bigger and bigger."[5]

Although as a teenager he listened to little popular music other than country and western, Allan experienced a musical awakening in January 1956 when he witnessed a live performance by an up-and-coming Elvis Presley at Shreveport's "Louisiana Hayride." The event, acknowledges Allan, eventually altered the course of his musical career.

JA: It was my senior year in high school and I was in the Future Farmers of America, the FFA, and our old ag[riculture] teacher, Mr. Claude Hebert, as a treat for putting up—I don't know if it was with him or with us for four years—he brought us to a convention in Shreveport and that was a treat. After the convention was over he brought us to the "Louisiana Hayride" that Saturday night. You could wring my neck right now but I don't believe I could remember who else was on that show except Elvis Presley, because he just stole the show from everybody. I mean, it was just unreal. I was eighteen years old and this is thirty-five years ago—I still remember what he wore that night. That's how much of an impression he made on me. But he just stole, he just blew everybody off of the stage. And he was leaving that night, he had to catch a plane that night, to go to Nashville, he sang "Heartbreak Hotel" that night, before it was cut . . . . He was going to record it, he had to leave that night to go cut the session the next morning.

Charles "C. C." Adcock: What was he wearing?

JA: He had on pink shoes, he had on light green pants with a shirt to match, chartreuse coat, and a tie to match the coat! [*laughs*] Wow! . . .

CA: But that had to influence—

JA: Oh, yes! I was still playing Cajun music, but, oh, within three or four months after that we broke away from Cajun music and went to playing rock 'n' roll and believe you me, Elvis Presley's songs were in the repertoire.[6]

Allan's departure from Cajun music required a break with Walker, a break hastened by the Wandering Aces' wish to leave with Allan. The group attempted to perform in secret without Walker, but the veteran performer found them out, forcing the group reluctantly to confess their decision. "So that's what happens when you put an old horse out to grass," lamented Walker on learning that his Wandering Aces were becoming the Rhythm Rockers, soon to be renamed the Krazy Kats—a group Allan modeled after southeast Texas swamp pop band Gene Terry and the Down Beats. (Allan notes, however, that the Krazy Kats' name only coincidentally resembles the Down Beats' original name, the Kool Kats.) A change of instruments, of course, accompanied the group's reorganization: Allan gave up steel guitar to sing and play rhythm guitar; rhythm guitarist Al Foreman changed to electric lead; fiddler U. J. Meaux switched to upright piano; and while Bhuel Hoffpauir remained on drums, the group hired Ashton Langlinais on sax.[7]

After a few additional changes in personnel, such as switching Hoffpauir to bass, putting Austin Broussard on drums, and replacing Langlinais with saxophonist Leroy Castille, the group finally was outfitted to play the music later dubbed *swamp pop*. Although Allan recalls switching to rhythm and blues only a

few months after witnessing Elvis's 1956 performance, he and the Aces still performed Cajun music as late as around 1958, when they recorded with Walker
at KEUN. Regardless, Allan's Elvis experience did, as he claims, partly inspire
the furtive Rhythm Kings performances and the group's eventual break with the
accordionist.[8]

By this time Allan, now an education major at the local university, was de-
vouring records by new favorites like Elvis Presley, Chuck Berry, and particularly
Fats Domino and other New Orleans rhythm and blues artists. He also listened
to records by local artists like Cookie and the Cupcakes, Warren Storm, Bobby
Charles, Rod Bernard, and Jimmy Clanton, who inspired the Krazy Kats to make
a recording of their own. "We could see that everybody else was recording.
So we just got to talking one night after a gig, 'Man, if we're ever going to get
this band off the ground the first thing we've got to do is have a record out.'
'Where're we going to get a song?' Nobody had any songs. And U. J. Meaux, the
keyboard player, he said, 'Why don't you sit down and try to write something?' I
did. I came back home and I wrote 'Lonely Days and Lonely Nights' . . . and 'My
Baby's Gone.' We went to [local big-band musician] Aaron Domingue's house
in Scott, he had one of those reel-to-reel tape recorders, put it on tape and
brought it to Floyd [Soileau] and Floyd liked it."[9]

Renting J. D. Miller's studio in Crowley, Soileau had the group rerecord
"Lonely Days, Lonely Nights," which he released in 1958 on his new Jin label.
The record sold exceptionally well along the Gulf Coast, says Allan, enticing
MGM to lease the single for nationwide distribution within three months of
its original issue. The record failed to break into the Top 100, however, a cir-
cumstance Allan blames on payola (the bribery of deejays to promote certain
records).

> *SB:* In Broven's book you mention something about payola and how you think it
> affected "Lonely Days and Lonely Nights."
> *JA:* Well, I saw Bill Hall, who was our manager after I got on MGM, when "Lonely
> Days and Lonely Nights" was leased off to MGM, I was in his office in Beaumont
> and I saw him write a check out to a deejay in Philadelphia, so, greedy little
> Cajun, [I asked,] "What'cha doin'?" "Well," he said, "we just taking some of that
> money from those records and putting it in the right place, trying to get it off
> the ground, getting it in the charts." And I didn't know too, too much about
> payola then, but then as time progressed and I started talking to other people
> I realized what he had done. That's exactly what it was. Well, the record never

really made enough money to send out as payola money and I guess they didn't want to sink any more money into it. So consequently it never did really get into the charts. It was just bubbling under the Top 100, it never made it.[10]

Yet the regional success of Allan's first release prompted Soileau to team up with Hall and fellow swamp pop producer Huey Meaux to promote Allan's next Jin recording, "Letter of Love." After a favorable start the trio leased the recording to Mercury Records, which eventually represented several swamp pop performers, including Johnny Preston, Jivin' Gene, Rod Bernard, Roy Perkins, and Elton Anderson. In typical fashion, the Mercury label failed to promote "Letter of Love," inducing Allan around 1960 to depart for Charles "Dago" Redlich's Viking label of Crowley. During a short but highly productive tenure with that label he recorded several swamp pop classics, including "Your Picture," "Family Rules" and "South to Louisiana." Viking eventually filed for bankruptcy, however, and after a brief sojourn with Huey Meaux's Pic-1 label Allan returned to Soileau around 1964. Their collaboration paid off in the early 1970s (around which time Allan formed a new group, the Memories) with two vital swamp pop recordings, "Promised Land" and its flip side "Somewhere on Skid Row," the former of which became an international hit with amazing longevity, eventually prompting Allan's first European performance in 1978.

SB: Tell me about "Promised Land," because I was reading in Broven, he made it sound like it was a hit twice, it was rereleased in '78—

JA: Four times . . . four times in Europe. . . .

SB: How did that happen?

JA: Well, it sold real good in England the first time it was released—. Let me go back from the start with it. A guy by the name of Charlie Gillett [author of *The Sound of the City: The Rise of Rock 'n' Roll*] released it on Oval label in 1974 and it was starting to climb up the charts. So they called me up and they wanted me to do a tour. And the school board told me, "Well, you can, but we can't promise you your job when you come back." I had fourteen years in the school business, I was an assistant principal. I said, "Man, I can't put all my eggs in one basket and do that," so I turned them down. Luck and fate was with me, I guess, because six weeks later when they saw that mine was making noise, Elvis Presley had a version of it. Well, they released it, sent it over out there and they took mine and put it in the trash can—goodbye! Then in 1978 Stiff record company merged with Oval record company . . . [they re-released it] and boom! Back up the charts again. Now this time I had a week off for Easter vacation and I went out there and it really helped it, I mean it helped push the record. Well, since then, Polydor released it, V.I.P. in the Benelux countries released it. That's four times—four different releases of it. The other three didn't do as good as the Oval/Stiff did in '78 in England, but it was still released four times, it still got me some other tours.[11]

Since 1978 Allan has conducted sixteen additional concert forays to Europe, often including other swamp pop artists in his entourage. In addition, his swamp pop radio program attracted fans throughout south Louisiana and southeast Texas, and his 1988 photo book, *Memories*—which documents several musical genres, including Cajun, zydeco, and swamp pop—continues to garner the attention of music enthusiasts and recently was reissued in a revised and expanded edition. Retiring in 1981 after twenty years in education, he supplements his pension by taking on odd jobs, like distributing records to local tourist spots and, of course, performing in south Louisiana nightclubs. In addition, Allan and a co-writer recently completed *Born to Be a Loser,* a biography of swamp popper Jimmy Donley. Rightly called both "the ambassador of swamp pop" and "the elder statesman of swamp pop," Allan continues to promote the genre and to labor for its acceptance as an indigenous form of south Louisiana music.[12]

Gene Terry

Although Gene Terry and the Down Beats never yielded a hit record, the group exerted a strong influence on the developing swamp pop genre. Terry's trademark—a highly disciplined stage band with a sizable horn section—evoked emulation by other swamp pop artists. For instance, swamp pop ambassador Johnnie Allan modeled his Krazy Kats on the Down Beats. Although Terry has been classified by some as a rockabilly artist, he clearly developed into a swamp popper by 1958, the midpoint of his brief musical career. In fact, Terry considers himself a swamp pop musician. Like numerous swamp poppers, however, he failed to achieve much celebrity beyond the Cajun communities of south Louisiana and southeast Texas. Nevertheless, he and the Down Beats recorded several vintage singles for Eddie Shuler's famed Goldband label of Lake Charles, including the notable "Cindy Lou," a high-strung rockabilly-ish tune now considered a swamp pop classic. Unconcerned about record sales, Terry worked to perfect his group's live performances, which often eclipsed those of rival swamp pop groups, such as the early Boogie Kings.[1]

Although his parents resided in Lake Charles, Terry was born in Lafayette on January 7, 1940, as Terry Gene DeRouen. (DeRouen is a common Cajun surname of French Creole origin.) In 1942 his family moved to Port Arthur, where Terry—like many other swamp pop artists—frequently was exposed to Cajun music by musically adept relatives.

> **Shane Bernard:** What about your family musical history?
>
> **Gene Terry:** I tell you, this is funny, because we just watched [a Cajun music documentary], my dad was at the house yesterday, we watched it and he was telling me that he played [guitar] with this guy and he played with that guy and he said that this guy—I forget his name—called him to sit in and daddy played piano and I didn't know that [he played piano]! And his dad played fiddle and accordion. They were DeRouens. They played house dances . . . . What happened is, I'd go back to Louisiana or the Lake Charles area, Bell City, every summer to spend time with my grandparents. And my uncle took me to a house dance—I didn't know what that was—one time and it pretty impressed me. My uncle at the time played guitar and sang. But that's how my dad started—barn dances, house dances. My dad was a pretty good musician . . . . I remember my grand dad, my dad's dad, sitting on the front porch in Bell City on a farm playing that fiddle. The kids would sit on the porch and he'd play that fiddle. He could play it good, man!

Terry believes that his great-grandfather DeRouen also played Cajun music.[2]

Growing up in Port Arthur, Terry became acquainted with several young musicians: For instance, he graduated from high school with future swamp poppers Jivin' Gene and Johnny Preston. But Terry's musical encouragement came primarily from his uncle, R. C. DeRouen, who often performed with local Cajun groups. DeRouen taught his nephew to play guitar and accompanied him to nightclubs in the Beaumont–Port Arthur and Lake Charles areas, where Terry sat in with Cajun/country musicians.

> **SB:** Do you think Cajun music influenced your music?
>
> **GT:** I think so . . . . I didn't stay with country and western. That's all that was being played when I started. I'd get up and sing with [Cajun/country performer] Jimmy Newman at the Lacassine Clover Club. But when Elvis and the rhythm and blues came out, I switched because that's what I liked. That's where my feet were.[3]

Around 1954 or '55 Terry formed his first group, the Kool Kats, consisting of Terry on vocals and rhythm guitar, an upright bass player, and Terry's uncle on drums. (Terry's uncle also acted as guardian of his underage nephew.) Originally the group performed only country and western tunes and a few early Elvis numbers, but it gradually included black rhythm and blues music, to which Terry listened intently during this period, running home after school to catch local deejay and future recording star J. P. "The Big Bopper" Richardson on Beaumont's KTRM radio. Richardson's program featured musicians like Elvis, Big Joe Turner, Fats Domino, Otis Williams and Little Richard, all regarded by Terry as his major influences. The new rhythm and blues sound, however, initially baffled the young performer: "I said 'Whoever would make a song like "Tutti Frutti"?' Now I was still balancing between country and rhythm and blues. But I'd find myself getting back from school and turning on the Big Bopper. [I thought] 'Well, you know, that's kind of good music there. I like the stuff.' I just crossed over. That's when I started gettin' to moving, man! I wanted to be like them guys."[4]

Introducing the rhythm and blues sound in local nightclubs around 1956, Terry and his group—now called the Down Beats—attracted an increasing number of followers. Clubgoers, says Terry, simply regarded them as "different." Wishing to better accommodate the popular rhythm and blues sound, the bandleader soon added a pianist, two sax players, and a trumpeter. Around 1957 the group was appearing not only in southeast Texas, but also across the Sabine River at the Big Oaks Club in Vinton. "We played under two big oak trees for a long time," recalls Terry, "packed that place—and it would hold over a thousand people." The band's reputation soon reached Lake Charles, sparking the interest of a local club owner.

> **GT:** In 1958, the year I graduated [from high school], I had a guy come over from the Moulin Rouge in Lake Charles to sign me to a contract. Now, I had army reserve duty to take care of before I could go over there. So I did that and I had this contract and I was eighteen years old and was guaranteed two [hundred] fifty a week to play at the Moulin Rouge, Tuesdays through Saturdays.
>
> **SB:** Back then I suppose that was pretty good?
>
> **GT:** That's big money . . . I was eighteen years old. Hell, I made more than an engineer. I'll never forget. We started on a Tuesday night. That was our opening night. We went on KPLC, the twelve o'clock show—
>
> **SB:** When it was radio still?
>
> **GT:** No, it was TV. The band set up and played "What Am I Living For?" on that twelve o'clock show. And my aunt, who lived in Westlake [near Lake Charles], she was my biggest critic, she said it was beautiful. So we got through with the

show and then we got ready to play the dance that night. Well, it was a Tuesday night—bad night. They had Frankie Lowery and the Golden Rockets [a swamp pop group] down the road. They'd been jam-packing their place for a year. I said, "I think they're going to do better than us." You know, little kid thinking, "We ain't gonna make it here!" I sat in the car that night—time to go play! And I got cold feet. I wouldn't go in the back door of the club, the Moulin Rouge. My uncle come out [and said], "C'mon, let's go! It's time to start!" I said, "Man, I don't want to go!" I said, "I think we made a big mistake! We should have stayed at the Big Oaks!" He says, "C'mon!" I walked in the back and there were over six hundred people in that place on a Tuesday night. *And we boogied, son. We boogied.*[5]

Terry and the Down Beats moved to Lake Charles and at this time began to perform in central Acadiana nightspots like the Pelican Club in Marksville, the Four Corners in Cecilia, and the Step Inn Club in Lawtell (where they competed for local audiences with the Boogie Kings, playing in the nearby Green Lantern). Shortly before the Down Beats left Beaumont–Port Arthur, however, producer Eddie Shuler approached the group about recording for his Goldband label. Signing a five-year contract with Shuler, Terry recalls the release of only three 45 singles: "Cindy Lou"/"Teardrops in My Eyes," "Never Let Her Go"/"No Mail Today," and "Guy with a Million Dreams"/"Cinderella Cinderella." In 1958 or '59, however, Shuler leased Gene Terry and the Down Beats' "Fine—Fine" to the Savoy label as a B-side. On the flip side Shuler placed a cover of "This Should Go On Forever," hoping to capitalize on the popularity of swamp popper Rod Bernard's then-current hit recording. Although Terry provides the vocals on "Fine—Fine," Shuler replaced Terry's vocal track on "This Should Go On Forever" with a new one by a certain Ronnie Dee, who to the producer must have sounded more like Bernard than the Down Beats' leader. (Shuler's efforts no doubt met with some success. The Savoy release appears on the *Billboard* charts as an alternative to Bernard's recording.)[6]

Shuler later reissued "Cindy Lou" with a different flip side, "What Can I Do I Still Love You," but mixed Terry's inspired "Cindy Lou" vocals with new vocals by young Jenny Scroggins, producing a horrible duet effect that obscured the original recording's integrity. Terry, who never met Scroggins, fails to comprehend Shuler's reasons for tampering with "Cindy Lou." (Fortunately, Ace Records of the UK uncovered the *original* version of "Cindy Lou" in Shuler's immense master tape library and released it on the recent CD compilation *Eddie's House of Hits: The Story of Goldband Records*.) As John Broven writes in *South to*

Louisiana, the song "was a wild, unforgettable sax-guitar-piano rocker that was a generation removed from the restrained bluesy original by Shelton Dunaway and the Boogie Ramblers. Nothing else Gene Terry recorded possessed the same supercharged energy—or magic."[7]

Although the Boogie Ramblers (later known as swamp pop group Cookie and the Cupcakes, of "Mathilda" fame) and the Down Beats often crossed paths in the Goldband studio, Terry recalls hearing "Cindy Lou" from a different source.

> *SB:* Let me ask you about "Cindy Lou." You got that song from Shelton Dunaway
> and the Boogie Ramblers, right? Didn't they do that first?
> *GT:* Shelton and Cookie and them, yeah.
> *SB:* I think at the time they were called the Boogie Ramblers.
> *GT:* Well, you know who we learned it from? Shelton made it, [but] I got a cousin
> that was going to McNeese [State University in Lake Charles] and he played
> drums . . . . He had a friend named Preston Vanicor and the Night Riders and
> he played a little bit with them. And I'd go with them when I'd go over there
> and I'd be off a night and I'd listen to 'em. Preston sang this song "Cindy Lou."
> That's where I learned it. I told . . . [my cousin] to either write the words down
> or something or I just sat there and memorized it. I had a pretty good memory
> back then . . . . I asked Eddie [Shuler], "I want to do this song, 'Cindy Lou.'" I
> said, "Can you get it for me?" He said, "That's my song—go for it."[8]

Recorded in 1958, "Cindy Lou" documents the genre's early rawness and mirrors its crude birth in the Cajun and black Creole nightclubs of rural south Louisiana and southeast Texas. Indeed, Terry recounts that he and the group "played like we played for a dance" during the "Cindy Lou" session. The recording's primitive sound also owes much to Shuler's sparse production efforts: He employed one or two microphones at most—probably two, says Terry, one in the center of the tiny studio for the Down Beats and another solely to pick up his vocals. A single-track recorder probably captured the music, which—judging from the ferocity with which the musicians perform over one another—resembles an unrestrained jam rather than a recording session. Interestingly, "Cindy Lou" features former Cajun string band musician Patrick "Pee Wee" Higginbotham on upright bass, an unusual instrument for a swamp pop group. "What we had him for was the slapping of the bass for the Elvis stuff," recalls Terry. (Moving from country and western and rockabilly to swamp pop, Higginbotham traded his upright bass for a standard electric bass shortly after recording "Cindy Lou.") The flip side, "Teardrops in My Eyes," was inspired by

Gene Terry, poster photo, shot at the home of Down Beats saxophonist Doug Dean, Nederland, Tex., 1958. (Photo courtesy of the Johnnie Allan Collection)

Bill Bodaford and the Rockets' original, which Terry first heard over Nashville's WLAC radio. Terry's rendition features heavy backing vocals—also an unusual element for swamp pop—with Charles "Dago" Redlich, owner of the Viking label of Crowley, singing bass.[9]

According to Terry, he and the Down Beats recorded little after 1959, focusing instead on their nightclub act. "The fact is," he says, "I wasn't into the records. I wanted the sound and the music." Terry admits his discontent with the Goldband releases, however, stating that in his opinion Shuler failed to issue the best material. In fact, Terry wanted to quit recording with Shuler and work instead with Redlich or fellow Crowley producer J. D. Miller, but his five-year contract prevented him from recording for another label. Remaining largely inactive with Shuler, Terry continued to appear in nightclubs, and by 1960 his interest in performing began to diminish.

SB: So you got out of the recording business around '60?

GT: Yeah. We probably didn't record much after '58, '59.

SB: And what about playing in clubs?

GT: Yeah, [we played in] clubs, club circuit.

SB: How long did that go on?

GT: Till the end of '60. I got married in '60 and I probably played a year . . . and then the jobs got so—you have to go so far to make so little. I said, "Man, I gotta get a job!" [*Laughs*] I quit playing in Bossier City [in northwest Louisiana]. Left everything, trailer and all, with the band and said, "I've had it. That's it." And I came back to Port Arthur and went to work for the city.

Without Terry's leadership the Down Beats soon disbanded. His guitarist and brass section, he claims, eventually merged with the formerly rival Boogie Kings.[10]

Terry worked for the city of Port Arthur until 1965, when he signed on with the local police department as a patrolman. During this period he joined a group featuring a local pianist and his percussionist uncle; Terry learned the electric bass for the occasion and sang harmony with the other two musicians in southeast Texas supper clubs. In 1969 he left the police department to work at a local Du Pont chemical plant, his current place of employment. Terry still performs the old Down Beats material, however, but only on special occasions, such as New Year's Eve dances at St. Peter's Catholic Church in Groves, Texas. As a member of the Du Pont safety committee, however, he occasionally sings at seminars for his fellow workers, changing the lyrics of popular songs to convey safety messages.[11]

Joe Barry

Joe Barry attained the status of swamp pop legend both through his music and his offstage antics. A versatile performer with wide appeal, he performed not only in south Louisiana and southeast Texas nightspots, but also in exclusive clubs in Las Vegas, Los Angeles, and New York. During the 1960s Barry often spent his earnings on wild parties and consumed huge amounts of drugs and liquor. Prone to violent mood swings—a symptom of his addictive habits—he wrecked numerous hotel rooms, once tossing a TV from his balcony into a swimming pool, a feat that helped earn the hotel a franchise award for "Most Destroyed Room." Despite the lore associated with Barry, his fame derives mainly from his recordings of mournful swamp pop ballads.[1]

Born Joseph Barrios on July 13, 1939, in Cut Off—a small bayou town in
Lafourche Parish, in eastern Acadiana—he grew up in a poor Cajun family. His
mother, Josephine, worked in the sugarcane fields and his father, Josef, piloted
boats, mainly on the Mississippi, and also trapped muskrat and hunted alligator
and wildfowl, often without regard for local game laws. Josef also possessed
an interest in music (he played the harmonica and Jew's harp), as did many of
Barry's relatives.

Shane Bernard: Your dad played a Jew's harp?

Joe Barry: [Yeah.]

SB: Is that the only thing he played?

JB: Harmonica. My uncles on my mama's side all played guitar and accordions and
fiddles.

SB: That's what I wanted to get into. How many people in your family played
musical instruments? I read your cousin and your father [did]—your cousin played
guitar, right?

JB: I've got more than one cousin that can play guitar. [Cajun string band musician]
Vin Bruce is my cousin . . . . He recorded for Columbia way before anybody ever
thought of it. It was French music back then. [Swamp pop producer/performer]
Lee Martin is my cousin. He played music all his life. He's the assessor of
Lafourche Parish right now. But before that, my mama's side alone, my
brothers—they had about, I guess, six or seven in the family who played musical
instruments. But none of those influenced me. My daddy influenced me because I
loved to hear him play. But what really influenced me back then was listening to
the radio, "Grand Ole Opry." And then when I was old enough—well, I was . . .
nine years old . . . I had to go with my sister to make sure she was all right. I
couldn't give a damn what she was doing. I wanted to hear the band.

SB: You mean at a fais do-do?

JB: Yeah. And so I'd stick myself in front of the bandstand. I don't know what she
did all night—I could care less. What I wanted was to watch the band. And Vin
Bruce was playing. He was my idol—still is.[2]

Barry first expressed an interest in music around age five, when he fashioned
a makeshift guitar from a cigar box and wire from a screen door. A brother
soon presented him with a neglected guitar, on which Barry taught himself to
play (in about two days, he says). His parents shortly bought him a new Stella
brand guitar and Barry began to pick up additional playing techniques from Vin
Bruce. At the time Barry was listening to Cajun and country and western music,

favoring the sounds of string artists like Ernest Tubb and south Louisiana's own Happy Fats, Doc Guidry and the Boys. He also developed an appreciation for black gospel music, furtively skipping his solemn Catholic Masses to attend high-spirited black services.[3]

Barry made his earliest public appearances around age eight, when his parents took him to fais do-dos at nightclubs around Cut Off. Some of these clubs lay in enclaves Barry calls "Indian parts" (Lafourche Parish contains a small native American population), noting that "it was pretty rough, they'd chop you to pieces in a second." Clubgoers, however, knew his father's reputation as a fighter, a reputation later inherited by Barry—a student, he claims, of *le sabot* or French kickfighting. Most fais do-dos occurred without violence, however, permitting Barry to perform all night with local Cajun bands in the rowdiest clubs. "And the music just went on, boy, that was it until daybreak," he recalls. "I was one of those that didn't want to sleep, I wanted to play!"[4]

During the late 1940s Barry often sat in with Cajun string musicians like cousin Vin Bruce and Blackie Dartez; on occasion he also played with country groups and even a few jazz bands. Years later he briefly studied music under New Orleans jazz musicians Al Hirt and Pete Fountain. Drawing on these diverse musical genres, Barry notes, "I listened to the black gospel and listened to Cajun, and I had a feeling that there's gotta be some way this can be put together." Adding a rhythm and blues element borrowed mainly from Ray Charles and Fats Domino, Barry began to perform around 1955 the hybrid musical style later called *swamp pop*. (The gospel music influence is rare among Cajun and black Creole swamp poppers: Both groups are almost exclusively Catholic in upbringing and—as south Louisiana lies outside the Protestant "Bible Belt" of the southern U.S.—few ever experienced the gospel tradition.) "I went into a fever, called the south Louisiana fever," he explains, "which had a little beat in the country songs which the country entertainers back then did not go for. So they said 'Well, Joe, you can sit in, but you gonna play that funny stuff?' And I said 'Yeah, I'm gonna sing that funny stuff.' And they'd laugh at me, poke fun. So I'd take an old Gene Autry song like 'I'm a Fool to Care' and I'd hit a little different note on it, you know, with the beat. And the kids started liking it, which was the new generation to come and some of the grown-ups started liking it. So finally all the guys that were the big stars in the local bayou country wouldn't let me sit in with their bands because I kept singing this funny stuff— the club owners were asking me to replace them!"[5]

During the late 1950s Barry often traveled to New Orleans to visit recording studios and nightclubs, sitting in with local rhythm and blues masters like Edgar

"Big Boy" Myles, Smiley Lewis, James "Sugar Boy" Crawford, and Tommy Ridgley, all of whom influenced his developing musical style. Around 1958 he formed his first group, a nine-piece swamp pop band called the Dukes of Rhythm (named after the renowned Dukes of Dixieland of New Orleans). He fronted the group as "Rockin' Roland," but exchanged the pseudonym for "Joe Barry" when he quit the Dukes following a dispute. (The group soon appointed swamp popper Joe Carl as their new leader.) Barry then formed the Delphis, borrowing the name from Greek mythology, a subject that always has interested the performer. The eight-piece group backed Barry on his first notable record, "Greatest Moment of My Life"/"Heartbroken Love," recorded for Jin in 1960. (Barry's earliest recording was "I'm Walking Behind You"/"My Shoes Keep Walking Back to You," issued around 1956–57 on the Houma label; he also recorded two singles in 1958 for Sho-Biz, owned by New Orleans deejay Jim Stewart.)[6]

After an unsuccessful session at KLFT radio in Golden Meadow, the group reassembled at swamp pop producer Floyd Soileau's tiny one-room studio in Ville Platte, where the Delphis finally recorded acceptable tracks. The ensuing single sold poorly, however—only about seven hundred to one thousand copies, according to Barry. A short time later, his cousin, Lee Martin, sent Soileau a demo of "I Got a Feeling," a composition by Barry. The song sounded so much like classic Ray Charles that Soileau scheduled a session for Barry at Cosimo Matassa's studio in New Orleans. Backed by his new band, the Vikings, a short-lived group composed of high school students, Barry recorded both "I Got a Feeling" and his nightclub standard "I'm a Fool to Care."

> *JB:* I think Floyd was kind of leery about putting a second one out. Then out of the blue, he said, "Okay, but this time instead of coming to Ville Platte . . . y'all go cut at Cosimo's [in New Orleans]." So we arranged it, cut it, sent it to him . . . . We all thought the other side was going to be a hit. I had wrote the other side.
>
> *SB:* That was "I Got a Feeling"?
>
> *JB:* Yeah . . . . Half of the band was partial to one side, the other half—. So [I said,] "Let's take it to some place that can really test it out." We went to this whorehouse, put it on the jukebox. They all liked "I'm a Fool to Care." I was pissed off, boy . . . . And I'll be doggone—first time I heard it on the radio, that's the side [they played. I thought,] "You're on the wrong side, stupid!" So I was the stupid one.[7]

Although the final cut of "I Got a Feeling" disappointed Soileau—it failed to recapture the Ray Charles sound, he thought—"I'm a Fool to Care" so impressed him that he formed a partnership with fellow swamp pop producer

Huey Meaux to promote Barry and his new recording. As predicted, the Jin single sold extremely well throughout south Louisiana and southeast Texas, and Soileau and Meaux soon leased "I'm a Fool to Care" to Mercury, which released it nationwide on its new subsidiary label, Smash. By April 1961 the song peaked in *Billboard* at number twenty-four, resulting in Barry's appearances on programs like Dick Clark's "American Bandstand"—an appearance that turned off black consumers, who suddenly realized Barry was white. Wishing to appeal to a broad audience, however, that same year he recorded a Cajun French version of "I'm a Fool to Care" (as Josef Barrios) called "Je suis bêt pour t'aimer," which he backed with another Cajun recording, "Oh Teet Fille" (unrelated, he claims, to Clifton Chenier's early zydeco recording "Ay-Tete-Fee"). This version attracted listeners not only in south Louisiana, but also in Canada and France.[8]

According to Barry, the original "Fool to Care" sold over a million copies, garnering the attention of booking agents across the country. As his career took off, Barry's act moved from Acadiana's largely rural dance halls to ritzy urban nightclubs on the East and West coasts, exposing the singer to promoters of dubious character.

SB: You performed in New York, too, didn't you?

JB: Oh, yeah. Performing, I covered twenty-six countries, all fifty states. . . .

SB: That's more than most . . . swamp pop singers.

JB: Well, to be honest, before 'Fool to Care' I was just to about a three-state area . . . but after 'Fool to Care' the bookings came in through a lot of—. I had made some good contacts with the Jewish Syndicate, Greek Syndicate, and Italian Syndicate and to play all these clubs all over and its like a clique, 'cause everybody knows everybody else and once you get in with them, the bookings run—

SB: You're talking about the Mafia?

JB: Yeah. They were great with me, man. So like [my contact would say,] "Hey—hey, man, Joe's playing for me this week. You got something open down the road?" "What days you want?" he'd ask me. "Well, I'm open this, this, this, and this." He says "Okay, you got 'em." . . .

SB: This is in New Orleans or New York or both?

JB: This is all over—this is all over. I can be in St. Louis . . . he'd tell me, "Okay, well, you're going to Kansas City" or "You're going to go to Chicago."

SB: It sounds like they almost managed you.

JB: No. You know, they tried one time to get into my contract—well, if I'd have been smart, I'd have let them, really, 'cause I don't think they'd have robbed me as bad as I did get robbed.[9]

After "Fool to Care" came a string of minor successes for Barry: Released on Jin and Smash, "Teardrops in My Heart"/"For You Sunshine" reached number sixty-three in *Billboard* in August 1961. Also on Jin and Smash was "You Don't Have to Be a Baby to Cry" and the flip side "Till the End of the World." "Little Papoose"/"Why Did You Say Goodbye" appeared on Smash and Meaux's own Princess label, which also issued his "Little Jewel of the Vieux Carre"/"Just Because." It was around this time that Barry appeared on the Jamie and SOM labels under the pseudonym "Roosevelt Jones," a disguise permitting him to dodge the terms of preexisting contracts and also to hide his race from black consumers (who otherwise might not purchase recordings by a white rhythm and blues performer). Barry left Smash in the mid-1960s to record exclusively for Princess, an arrangement that yielded about a dozen sides, including a version of the Cajun standard "Big Mamou" with Jin artist Mary McCoy.[10]

During this period Barry appeared frequently at the Esquire ballroom in Houston and, most notably, at Papa Joe's in New Orleans, where in 1965 he teamed up with swamp poppers Freddy Fender and Joey Long and New Orleans rhythm and blues artists Skip Easterling and Mac ("Dr. John") Rebennack.

SB: And you said Freddy Fender was in the band?

JB: Yeah. Freddy had just got out of Angola [State Penitentiary] . . . . We had the hottest thing in the Quarter going. The strippers at Papa Joe's, they used to dance—well, all day, really—but up till about three in the morning. And we'd start a jam session from three in the morning on. And when they say *on,* they mean *on* . . . . Sometimes we'd go till noon. But they wasn't stingy. They paid the money. But in those days we were so pilled up we could have went forty-eight hours. So the shows got bigger and bigger and drawing more and more people . . . and you got people fighting, I mean fistfighting to get in there . . . . [The club owner] got people just coming in at midnight and booing the strippers, that wanted the band. That's weird for New Orleans . . . . But it got so where we had to start playing at midnight. They'd knock the strippers off at midnight and sometimes we'd play till noon the next day. People coming home from church, when they were coming back was when we were knocking off.[11]

Drained by long hours on the road and stage, and disgruntled about the loss of royalties through fraud, Barry gave up music around 1967, returning to the Cut Off area to work as a roughneck on Louisiana's offshore oil platforms. A musician at heart, he soon returned to the studio to record an album for the Houma label—the same label for which he recorded around 1957–58—receiving as pay only a guitar and tape recorder. The master tapes were found to be flawed, however, and an attempt to salvage them ended when the tapes were destroyed by fire. In 1968 he found work as a Nashville session artist and shortly signed with the Nugget label. Barry recorded six tracks for Nugget, two of which, Merle Haggard's "Today I Started Loving You Again" and the Big Bopper's "Chantilly Lace," sold promisingly. Dismayed by squabbling among the label's management, Barry refused to record further for Nugget, and in turn Nugget declined to release Barry from his five-year contract. Unable to record for anyone, Barry went back to the Louisiana oil fields.[12]

During the early 1970s Barry abandoned his former wild lifestyle and embraced religion, a calling that would sustain him through approaching hard times. In 1976 he briefly renewed his musical efforts, recording the *Joe Barry* album in Houston with the assistance of Huey Meaux and Freddy Fender, both of whom were profiting hugely from Fender's record sales on ABC/Dot. Barry's album also appeared on ABC/Dot. Country ballads were not his specialty, however, and shortly after the album's release an internal shake-up at the label condemned the album to promotional limbo.[13]

By 1980 Barry was working as a used-car salesman in Cut Off, but he recorded an album of original gospel tunes, *Sweet Rose of Sharon,* in September of that year and shortly served a stint as a missionary preacher in Africa and the Caribbean. Discouraged by the corruption of certain "televangelists," Barry eventually returned in disgust to the Cut Off area and during the mid-to-late 1980s endured several shattering reverses. Ill health robbed him of strength and resources, forcing him to convalesce in a home without electricity, gas, or running water. He speculates that an overturned lantern touched off a fire that destroyed the house and most of his belongings, including an extensive record collection. Friends organized a benefit to defray some of Barry's losses.[14]

Barry continued to perform sporadically over the next several years, but worsening health now prevents him from taking the bandstand and has delayed the release of two albums on his own New Dawn label and a third on a Nashville label. He was honored in 1993 with a "Tribute to Joe Barry" concert in Lafayette, which featured performances by several fellow swamp poppers, including Jivin' Gene, Clint West, Grace Broussard (of Dale and Grace fame), John Fred, T. K. Hulin, Rod Bernard, Little Alfred, Lil' Bob, and Warren Storm.[15]

Benny Graeff

One of the most unconventional swamp pop artists, Benny Graeff and his "Cajun-hippie" group, known as Rufus or Rufus Jagneaux, recorded one of the latest but most popular swamp pop classics, the sing-along favorite "Opelousas Sostan." Labeled "a South Louisiana Mick Jagger" by John Broven, Graeff infused his swamp pop music not only with the familiar rhythm and blues sounds of performers like Fats Domino and Ray Charles, but also with the sound of more modern groups like the Animals and the Rolling Stones. Despite a long absence from south Louisiana during his youth, Graeff, like other swamp pop performers, also borrowed musical elements from traditional Cajun and black Creole sources, a fact overlooked by some critics who condemned his group's only hit song as an affront to south Louisiana's Cajun culture.[1]

Although his mother hailed from south Louisiana, Graeff was born on an army base in Aberdeen, Maryland, on February 24, 1948. When his father, a military officer from Pennsylvania, shipped off to serve in the Korean War, Graeff and his mother moved to Lake Arthur, where they resided with his grandmother, a Toups by marriage. (Toups is a Cajun surname of German Creole origin; in fact, "zydecajun" musician Wayne Toups is a close relative of Graeff.) Although he soon was to leave south Louisiana for about thirteen years, Graeff states that he absorbed much of his native culture while residing at his grandmother's house.

> *Benny Graeff:* My dad was in the service. My mom's from here. And when he
> would go off, we would stay here—when he would get stationed overseas. So
> I spent the first four or five years of my life living with my grandmother, who
> never wrote or spoke English. And I don't remember, but they tell me that that's
> what I did, was speak French 'cause I was with her. And then when they sent
> us to school, there was no more French. And then the [Korean] War was over,
> my dad came back, we left here. So the French I had was like a five-year-old
> vocabulary. But I grew up with all these [Cajun] people.
>
> *Shane Bernard:* So you don't speak French anymore?
>
> *BG:* I speak very little.[2]

Around 1954 Graeff moved with his parents to England, where he first discovered rhythm and blues on an officers' club jukebox. Accompanying his parents to the officers' club every Sunday—family day on the base—he listened intently to the strange new sounds of artists like Elvis Presley, Bill Haley, and Little Richard. Graeff's interest in music grew, spurred on in part by a two-year stay in Crowley during the early 1960s. At this time Graeff often visited his cousin, Charles Bailly, a young swamp pop drummer from nearby Lake Arthur, who introduced him to the music of many local swamp pop artists. In addition, Bailly's family owned a jukebox company, which ensured an endless supply of rhythm and blues records for Graeff.[3]

Moving with his family to Japan in 1964, Graeff—by this time in high school— joined a local band as lead singer. His parents supported his decision and encouraged his interest in music, which at the time included surf music (he admired the guitar work and the beat) and, of course, rhythm and blues.

> *BG:* When I was in Japan I was in my first real band in high school.
>
> *SB:* What was it called?
>
> *BG:* Japan has tidal waves and typhoons and volcanoes and earthquakes, so we called ourselves the Disasters.
>
> *SB:* Who'd you play for?
>
> *BG:* We'd play two nights a week for teen dances and two nights a week we played for a musical instrument company, the Japanese version of Fender . . . . They saw us and what they would do is they would pick us up twice a week. We would play wherever they told us to play. We'd showcase their equipment. They provided us with equipment. They transported us around. They took pictures of us. We played at all the biggest places in Tokyo. We opened for people—we opened for the Ventures, just 'cause it was their group. They were doing the sound. We didn't get billing a lot of times—we just got to open. Now, all the Caucasian groups over there were heavily into the Beatles and white rock 'n' roll. We played a lot of Fats Domino, a lot of Ray Charles, 'cause that's what I liked and that's the songs that I knew. And so we were different there and the Japanese just ate us up.

Graeff encountered at least a small amount of swamp pop while in Japan, hearing Rod Bernard's version of "Colinda" for the first time as he listened to the armed forces radio network.[4]

Graduating from high school in 1965, Graeff returned with his parents to the United States and settled in Virginia. Shortly after their arrival, Graeff and his father toured a Pennsylvania military college, where faculty interviewed the young musician as a prospective cadet. "My dad excused us halfway through the interview," recalls Graeff, "and said, 'It's not for you. I'm sending you down to Louisiana. There's something else in store for you.' I don't know what brought it on to him, but he just knew I needed to come back here [to Louisiana]."

Moving to Lake Charles, Graeff resided with his cousin, Bailly, who by now was drumming with several south Louisiana artists, including Tommy McLain and the Boogie Kings.[5]

Graeff traveled with his cousin to swamp pop clubs throughout south Louisiana and southeast Texas, working as a "roadie" while soaking up the local sounds. He soon purchased a bass guitar and began to study the techniques of acclaimed bass players like Bill Wyman of the Rolling Stones, Chas Chandler of the Animals, and Donald "Duck" Dunn of Booker T. and the MGs. Graeff also studied swamp pop music, often hearing it performed live in the nightclubs by local favorites like Cookie and the Cupcakes and Lil' Bob and the Lollipops. In fact, Graeff expresses a strong appreciation for swamp popper Clint West, whose performances with the Boogie Kings he often witnessed at the Bamboo Club in Lake Charles. He cites West's "Mr. Jeweler" as one of his favorite swamp pop songs.[6]

Mastering the bass guitar, Graeff joined several south Louisiana groups during the late 1960s. Around 1970, however, he formed Rufus, later called Rufus Jagneaux, a group that featured other young local musicians, including his brother, Gary. Performing an unusual strain of swamp pop music, they combined the usual rhythm and blues, country and western, and Cajun and black Creole elements with sounds borrowed from folk rock and hard rock music—sounds that appeared too late to influence other swamp poppers. The group attracted a large following throughout south Louisiana and southeast Texas. Rufus even opened for ZZ Top at the Texas trio's first concert, having already shared a stage at a Lafayette nightclub.[7]

Graeff maintains that his group's popularity derived largely from its reliance on original material. "We didn't do cover tunes," he says. "We just said, 'We're jumping in and swimming—we're writing all our own songs.' And that's what we did." One of their original songs, of course, was "Opelousas Sostan," which the group recorded as Rufus (Jagneaux) [sic]. A source of much confusion over the years, Graeff explains the origin of the group's name and the process by which it became his pseudonym.

SB: Rufus Jagneaux . . . is that a group or is that your stage name?

BG: There was a girl in the band named Carla . . . and we'd do these little duets. We'd do some pop and soul stuff. And Leon Medica, [of local rock band] LeRoux, when he'd see us coming, he'd call us Rufus and Carla [after soul singers Rufus and Carla Thomas] . . . . And so he started nicknaming me Rufus and when we started the band, the guys in the band said "Let's just call it Rufus." . . . And there was a guy at work that . . . used to call me Mr. Jagneaux. Simple as that. So we called the band Rufus and then when we went to record we didn't want to be confused with Rufus Thibodeaux, the fiddler, so we put Jagneaux on there. . . .

SB: So the guy [at work] . . . just called you Jagneaux, just for a joke? It really didn't have anything to do with you, really?

BG: No. A lot of the stuff we did before we did that was Rolling Stones and rock 'n' roll. . . .

SB: So it's a Jagger joke?

BG: Yeah, it's a takeoff. We had a band one time called the *Jagged* Edge. You know, one of these garage bands, a rock 'n' roll band. But we've always been into the Stones. . . .

SB: There's still something I don't understand. Did you yourself ever use the name Rufus Jagneaux, or was that the group?

BG: That started off as a group name and then it got pegged into me as being Rufus. People would come up . . . and they would say, "I want to talk to Rufus." And everybody just after a while knew they wanted to talk to the guy with the voice that was on that record.[8]

Like the name Rufus Jagneaux, the origin of "Opelousas Sostan" also has confounded music researchers. (*Opelousas* is the name of a town bordering the northern prairie region of central Acadiana; *Sostan* is merely an archaic Cajun first name.) John Broven and fellow music writer Macon Fry, for instance, report that Graeff wrote the song during a sojourn at a Tennessee hippie commune. Graeff dismisses the story, however, stating that he and fellow band member Victor Palmer actually wrote the song during a rehearsal break in Lafayette. In fact, "Sostan" was merely the second of three songs they composed on a piece of scrap paper. Graeff identifies one of the other songs as "Colorado," a country-rock tune the group often played on stage; he cannot recall the third.[9]

After live audiences reacted positively to "Opelousas Sostan" Graeff played a demo of the song for producer Floyd Soileau, who approved and recorded the group in his Ville Platte studio. The resulting track, appearing with the more upbeat "Port Barre" in 1971 on the Jin label, is performed to the easy rhythm and melody of an old-time Cajun waltz and features a harmonica imitating the diatonic accordion. An instant regional hit, it sold over 30,000 copies in the first month of its release. Rejoicing in their success, Graeff and his fellow band members soon encountered a few unexpected problems.[10] Several radio stations, for instance, refused to play the record. One music director rejected it simply because he feared his deejays would be deluged by requests for the tune. "God bless, what are you supposed to do," wondered Soileau, "you are supposed to be doing what your audience wants!" One station, however—Lafayette's KVOL—refused to play the record for a different reason.

> **BG:** A lot of stations wouldn't deal with it.
>
> **SB:** Soileau just mentioned one that wouldn't play "Opelousas Sostan" because they thought it would catch on so much that it would just be kinda a pain. . . .
>
> **BG:** KVOL wouldn't play it. The disk jockey said he didn't think it was representative of the band and that we didn't want to get tagged as that being our identity . . . . All we wanted was something to help us get more jobs. When he said he didn't want to play it, when [deejay] Buddy King said he didn't want to play it, it didn't bother us.
>
> **SB:** Really? Buddy King didn't want to play it?
>
> **BG:** Yeah. Well, in a way he had a protective attitude about it. He'd seen the band a lot, he'd come and seen the band. We were friends. And he was afraid that we'd get pegged as a novelty band . . . . And I think he was trying to do us a favor. When the song hit, oh, he played it as much as anybody after he talked to me about it and we told him, "Look, it's just a song that's in our repertoire that everybody liked. So we decided to put it out to get some jobs, just to get more work." It's what you did in those days.[11]

More than the refusal of some radio stations to play "Sostan," however, Graeff resented the angry reaction of some listeners. According to him, a small faction of local cultural activists denounced "Opelousas Sostan" as an offensive parody of Cajun music and culture. Although popular among the general public, Graeff and his band suddenly found themselves ostracized from several cultural events by certain music enthusiasts and festival organizers. Ironically, the group had drawn on the region's traditional music with a strong sense of ethnic pride—only to be assailed by those struggling to restore pride to the Cajun inhabitants of south Louisiana. (Stressing his admiration for traditional music, Graeff takes partial credit for introducing zydeco pioneer Clifton Chenier to white audiences in south Louisiana.) Sadly, the same misconceptions that plagued other swamp pop artists also hounded Rufus Jagneaux.

> **BG:** People also thought, like some of the more-Cajun-than-thou people, thought we were ridiculing Cajuns and that we were prostituting it [Cajun culture] and

all this stuff. And that couldn't be further from the truth. The songs that my grandmother taught me, one of them was [*sings*] *"Oh, Madame Sosthène—"* And I'm a kid. When I left here, there were certain memories that I had about Louisiana from the pictures and the sounds and stuff that I retained in my head. And that was one of the things. And when I'd think of grandma . . . that little song, I could see her sing it and the little tunes—she taught me "Colinda." I had an aunt that played "Colinda" on harmonica all the time. These things stuck with me. And "Jolie blonde." Just these things a five-year-old would leave with . . . . [But] there was a lot of negative backwash to us that was really kind of unjust. Some of it was probably jealousy. Some of it was they just didn't understand what was fixing to happen. We played all over and people were booking us for the uniqueness of being from Louisiana. There's people out there now making big bucks 'cause they're from Louisiana. Well, we went out there and got our faces dirty. We basically went down and kicked down doors in universities and places. And they were booking us as being "From Louisiana!" We were bringing them the best representation of our culture. We didn't ridicule Louisiana music. We didn't put on overalls and go *"Mais,* dis and dat, *cher!"* . . . We played original music and people started seeing that there's something really good from Louisiana. We played as much Cajun-oriented [music]—We took a bunch of 'em and did 'em instrumental, we converted some of 'em to English so that we could really sing 'em instead of being up there faking that we could speak French . . . And there were a lot of the holier-than-thou people that were killing us.[12]

Ignoring their detractors, Graeff and his group released an admirable follow-up single, "Downhome Music," but the record fared poorly compared to "Opelousas Sostan." Other tracks issued during this period include "Dr. Juban Le-Le," "Quadroon," "Ridin'," "Sha T Babe" (a play on the Cajun phrase *cher 'tit babe,* "dear little babe"), "Carry On," and the belated swamp pop classic "The Back Door," a bilingual cover of Cajun musician D. L. Menard's renowned "La porte d'en arrière." Unable to repeat their past success, however, Rufus Jagneaux split up around 1974 or '75 and Graeff formed a new group called PoBoy Rufus and the Sostan Band. (Of its members only Graeff's brother, Gary, had performed with the previous group.) An ensuing self-titled album sold relatively well—about 16,000 copies—despite the absence of familiar songs like "Opelousas Sostan" and "Downhome Music." Yet the group failed to capture the attention of south Louisiana audiences and soon disbanded. In the meantime, former Rufus Jagneaux members joined or founded a number of highly influential south Louisiana groups: Coteau, Beausoleil, Red Beans and Rice Revue, and even Zachary Richard's band. Graeff himself performed with several groups before focusing on a more stable career as a commercial artist. (He found time in the late 1960s to study advertising design.) In fact, Graeff has created numerous album jackets and cassette packages for Floyd Soileau's various labels. With "Opelousas Sostan" co-writer Victor Palmer, however, he now records other south Louisiana artists, such as Cajun groups Tasso and the Mamou Prairie Band, at Dockside Studio near Milton. Graeff also plays bass with the local rhythm and blues group Walter Jr. and the Juice.[13]

SWAMP POP TIMELINE AND DISCOGRAPHY

In addition to important musical events, this timeline lists notable releases in swamp pop's history as determined by regional popularity or national chart rankings. It also includes other, more obscure compositions cited in the text. I have altered certain artists' credits for the sake of clarity or brevity, and in general I cite original labels, record numbers, and release dates instead of those of licensed or reissued tracks. As precise release dates often are impossible to obtain, in some cases I have given approximate ones.

1944 Prior to swamp pop's advent, Eddie Shuler founds Goldband records of Lake Charles—in coming years a major swamp pop label.

Early 1950s Teenage Cajuns and black Creoles from Acadiana and southeast Texas begin to experiment with big-city rhythm and blues (especially the New Orleans variety), combining it unwittingly with country and western and Cajun and black Creole elements to create swamp pop music.

1950 George Khoury founds the Lyric and Khoury labels of Lake Charles.

1952 Eddie Shuler signs swamp pop group the Boogie Ramblers (later known as Cookie and the Cupcakes) to his Goldband label. New Orleans rhythm and blues artist Lloyd Price records "Lawdy Miss Clawdy" (Specialty 428), greatly influencing the budding swamp pop sound. Founded in 1951, big band group Phillip Comeaux and the Modernaires—spurred by its pianist, Roy Perkins—begins to include rhythm and blues in its repertoire, introducing Cajun audiences to the genre and contributing to the rise of swamp pop.

1953   New Orleans rhythm and blues artist Guitar Slim records the influential "The Things That I Used to Do" (Specialty 482).

1955   New Orleans rhythm and blues artist Earl King releases "Those Lonely Lonely Nights" (Ace 509), a quasi–swamp pop song inspired by his encounters with the developing genre in Acadiana. Appearance of the earliest swamp pop recordings: The Boogie Ramblers, "Cindy Lou"/"Such as Love" (Goldband 1030); Roy Perkins, "You're on My Mind" (Meladee 111); and Bobby Charles, "Later Alligator"/"On Bended Knee" (Chess 1609) and "Why Did You Leave"/ "Don't You Know I Love You" (Chess 1617).

1956   New Orleans rhythm and blues artist Fats Domino records the influential "Blueberry Hill" (Imperial 5407). Black Creole swamp pop saxophonist Gabriel King is found guilty of indecent behavior with a juvenile Cajun female. The Southern Club, a swamp pop nightspot, opens in Opelousas. Swamp pop releases include: King Karl and Guitar Gable, "Life Problem"/"Congo Mombo" (Excello 2082) and "Irene" (Excello 2094); and Bobby Charles, "Take It Easy Greasy" (Chess 1628), "No Use Knockin'" (Chess 1638), and "Why Can't You" (Chess 1647).

1957   Swamp bluesman Joe Hudson and His Rockin' Dukes—with Lester Robertson on vocals—record the swamp pop–influenced "Baby Give Me a Chance" (Excello 2112) at J. D. Miller's studio. Other swamp pop releases include: King Karl and Guitar Gable, "It's Hard but It's Fair" (Excello 2108); Guitar Jr., "Family Rules" (Goldband 1058); and Bobby Charles, "You Can Suit Yourself" (Chess 1658) and "One-Eyed Jack" (Chess 1670).

1958   Dawn of swamp pop's golden age. Floyd Soileau forms the swamp pop–oriented Jin label of Ville Platte. Robert Thibodeaux founds the L. K. label of St. Martinville to promote T. K. Hulin. Jimmy Clanton becomes the first swamp popper to break into the *Billboard Hot 100* as "Just a Dream" (Ace 546) reaches No. 4 nationally. Swamp pop releases include: Cookie and the Cupcakes, "Mathilda"/"I'm Twisted" (Lyric 1003); Doug Ardoin and the Boogie Kings, "Southland"/"Lost

Love" (Jin 101); Rod Bernard, "This Should Go On Forever"/"Pardon Mr. Gordon" (Jin 105); Jivin' Gene, "Going Out with the Tide" (Jin 109); Johnnie Allan, "Lonely Days, Lonely Nights" (Jin 111); Red Smiley and the Vel-Tones, "Jailbird" (Jin 115); King Karl and Guitar Gable, "Walking in the Park" (Excello 2140); Warren Storm, "Prisoner's Song"/"Mama Mama Mama" (Nasco 6015); Gene Terry, "Cindy Lou" (Goldband 1066); Jimmy Wilson, "Please Accept My Love" (Goldband 1074); Guitar Jr., "The Crawl" (Goldband 1076); Bobby Page and the Riff Raffs, "Loneliness"/"Hippy-Ti-Yo" (Ram 1338); Roy Perkins, "Drop Top" (Mercury 71278); and Jimmy Donley, "Born to Be a Loser" (Decca 9-30574).

1959 Although an atypical swamp pop recording, Johnny Preston's "Running Bear" (Mercury 71474) becomes the genre's first number one national hit. S. J. Montalbano founds the Montel label of Baton Rouge. Carol Rachou founds the La Louisianne label of Lafayette. J. D. Miller's Rocko (originally Rocket) and Zynn labels of Crowley are operational. Charles "Dago" Redlich founds the Viking label of Crowley. Swamp pop releases include: Phil Phillips, "Sea of Love" (Khoury 711); Rod Bernard, "One More Chance" (Mercury 71507); Jivin' Gene, "Breaking Up Is Hard to Do" (Jin 116); Elton Anderson, "Secret of Love" (Trey 1011); King Karl and Guitar Gable, "This Should Go On Forever" (Excello 2153); Warren Storm, "In My Moments of Sorrow" (Nasco 6025) and "So Long So Long" (Nasco 6028); John Fred and the Playboys, "Shirley" (Montel 1002); Buck Rogers, "Crazy Baby" (Montel 2002); and Randy and the Rockets, "Genevieve" (Viking 1000).

1960 Fats Domino begins to record songs composed by swamp poppers Bobby Charles and Jimmy Donley. Lee Lavergne establishes the Lanor label of Church Point. Joe Carl and the Rhythm Kings record their nightclub act at the College Inn in Thibodaux—the only known sample of live swamp pop from the genre's golden age. Releases include: Jimmy Clanton, "Another Sleepless Night" (Ace 585); Prince Charles, "Cheryl Ann" (Jin 127); Rockin' Dave Allen, "Shirley Jean" (Jin 136); Joe Barry, "I'm a Fool to Care" (Jin 144), "Je suis bêt pour t'aimer"/"Oh Teet Fille" (Jin 150), and "Teardrops in My Heart" (Jin 152); Phil Bo, "Don't Take It So Hard," (Jin 151); John Fred and the Playboys, "Good Lovin'" (Montel 1007); Johnnie Allan, "Cry Foolish Heart" (Viking 1006); Little

Alfred, "Walking Down the Aisle" (Lyric 1016); Johnny Preston, "Cradle of Love" (Mercury 71598) and "Feel So Fine" (Mercury 71651); and Gabe Dean, "Slop And Stroll Jolie Blonde" (Goldband 1108).

1961   Swamp bluesman Slim Harpo records the swamp pop–influenced "Rainin' in My Heart" (Excello 2194) at J. D. Miller's studio. Releases include: Johnnie Allan, "Your Picture" (Viking 1008) and "Family Rules" (Viking 1010); Gene King, "Little Cajun Girl" (Rod 5806); Elton Anderson, "Please Accept My Love," (Mercury 71778); Jerry Raines, "Our Teenage Love" (Drew-Blan 1001); and Cookie and the Cupcakes, "Betty and Dupree" (Lyric 1010).

1962   Swamp pop releases include: Rod Bernard, "Colinda" (Hall-Way 1902), "Fais Do Do" (Hall-Way 1906) and "Diggy Liggy Lo" (Hall 1917); Johnnie Allan, "South to Louisiana" (Viking 1015); Rockin' Sidney, "No Good Woman"/"You Ain't Nothing but Fine" (Jin 156); Randy and the Rockets, "Let's Do the Cajun Twist" (Jin 161); Elton Anderson, "Life Problem" (Lanor 509); Barbara Lynn, "You'll Lose a Good Thing" (Jamie 1220); Warren Storm, "I Want to Thank You So Much" (Rocko 512); and Jimmy Donley, "Please Mr. Sandman" (Teardrop 3002), "Think It Over" (Teardrop 3007), and "Lovin' Cajun Style" (Teardrop 3009).

1963   Influential swamp pop songwriter and performer Jimmy Donley commits suicide. Swamp pop releases include: Dale and Grace, "I'm Leaving It Up to You" (Montel 921) and "Stop and Think It Over" (Montel 922); Cookie and the Cupcakes, "Got You On My Mind" (Lyric 1004) and "Belinda" (Lyric 1020); T. K. Hulin, "I'm Not a Fool Anymore" (LK 1112); The Shondells (Rod Bernard, Warren Storm, and Skip Stewart), "A-2-Fay" (La Louisianne 8038); Jewel and the Rubies, "Kidnapper" (La Louisianne 8041); Elton Anderson, "The Crawl" (Lanor 516); and Huey Darby, "Rockin' Robin" (N-Joy 1008).

1964   The Beatles phenomenon spreads to the U.S. It and the ensuing British Invasion bring to a close swamp pop's golden age, and the genre begins a slow decline. Swamp bluesman Silas Hogan records the swamp pop–influenced "Everybody Needs Somebody" (Excello 2255) at J. D. Miller's studio. Rod Bernard hosts "Saturday Hop" dance program on KLFY-TV in Lafayette, lip-syncing to tracks recorded by the Shondells. The group records *The Shondells at the Saturday Hop* (La Louisianne

LL-109). Other swamp pop releases include: Clint West, "Twelfth of Never" (Jin 186); Jay Randall, "Cherry Pie" (Jin 189); T. K. Hulin, "(As You Pass Me By) Graduation Night" (L&K 1118).

1965 The Rolling Stones cover Barbara Lynn's "Oh Baby (We Got a Good Thing Goin')" (Jamie 1277) for the *Rolling Stones, Now!* album (London 3420). Floyd Soileau issues the first swamp pop compilation album, *A Rockin' Date with South Louisiana Stars* (Jin LP 4002). Releases include: Rod Bernard, "Somebody Wrote That Song for Me"/"Recorded in England" (Arbee 101); Lil' Bob and the Lollipops, "I Got Loaded" (La Louisianne 8067); Tommy McLain and Clint West, "Try to Find Another Man" (Jin 191); Clint West, "Mr. Jeweler" (Jin 191) and "Big Blue Diamonds" (Jin 196).

1966 Swamp pop releases include: Tommy McLain, "Sweet Dreams" (Jin 197) and "Think It Over" (Jin 209); Clint West, "Try Me" (Jin 199) and "Another Saturday Night" (Jin 212); Johnnie Allan, "Cajun Man" (Jin 207) and "You Got Me Whistling" (Jin 215); Charles Mann, "Keep Your Arms around Me" (Lanor 524).

1967 The "Rod Bernard" music program appears Saturday afternoons on KLFY-TV. Former swamp pop group John Fred and the Playboys hit internationally with the Beatlesesque "Judy in Disguise (with Glasses)" (Paula 282). Tommy McLain records "I'd Be a Legend in My Time" (Jin 221).

1968 "The Shondells" music program appears Saturday afternoons on KLFY-TV. Swamp pop releases include: Tommy McLain, "Before I Grow Too Old" (Jin 228) and "Tender Years" (Jin 230); Rod Bernard, "Congratulations to You Darling" (Jin 232) and "Papa Thibodeaux"/"Play a Song for My Baby" (Copyright 2316).

1969 The Beatles record the swamp pop-ish "Oh! Darling" for the *Abbey Road* album (Apple PCS 7088). The "Lil' Bob" music program appears Saturday afternoons on KLFY-TV. Releases include: Charles Mann, "Red Red Wine" (Lanor 543); Tommy McLain, "After Loving You" (Jin 235).

1970 Swamp pop releases include: Jay Randall, "Oh! Darling" (Lanor 548); Johnnie Allan, "I'll Never Love Again" (Jin 233); and Belton Richard, "Un autre soir d'ennui" (Swallow 10187).

1971   Swamp pop releases include: Rufus (Jagneaux), "Opelousas Sostan" (Jin 242) and "Downhome Music" (Jin 245) and Johnnie Allan, "Promised Land"/"Somewhere on Skid Row" (Jin 244).

1972   The *Bobby Charles* album (Bearsville 2104) is issued to poor sales but critical acclaim. Releases include: Clint West, "Sweet Suzannah" (Jin 249) and "Shelly's Winter Love" (Jin 257); Tommy McLain, "(If You Don't Love Me) Why Don't You Just Leave Me Alone Babe" (American Pla-boy 1987); and Belton Richard, "Give Me Another Chance" (Swallow 10192), "J'ai pleurer pour toi" (Swallow 10200), and "I'm Not a Fool Anymore" (Swallow 10205).

1973   Swamp pop releases include: Johnnie Allan, "I Wonder Where You Are Tonight" (Jin 275); Clint West, "Bayou Pon Pon" (Jin 279); and Blackie Forestier, "What's Her Name" ["Please Accept My Love"] (La Louisianne LP 135).

1974   J. D. Miller founds the Showtime label of Crowley. Charlie Gillett issues the U.K. album *Another Saturday Night* (Oval 3001), a compilation of vintage swamp pop and Cajun recordings, including Johnnie Allan's "Promised Land" (Oval 1001), which becomes a hit in the U.K. Warren Storm records, "Lord I Need Somebody Bad" (Showtime 1000) and "My House of Memories" (Showtime 1001); Freddy Fender, "Before the Next Teardrop Falls" (ABC/Dot 17540) and "Wasted Days, Wasted Nights" (ABC/Dot 17558); Rod Bernard, "Sometimes I Talk in My Sleep" (Jin 325); Tommy McLain, "Dim Lights, Thick Smoke" (American Pla-boy 1996); and Belton Richard, "Lord I Need Somebody Bad" (Swallow 10237).

1975   Swamp pop releases include: Johnnie Allan, "Before the Next Teardrop Falls" (Jin 331) and Rufus Jagneaux, "The Back Door" (Jin 332).

1976   The Flyright label of England begins issuing LPs of vintage swamp pop from J. D. Miller's master tape library. Swamp pop releases include: Rod Bernard and Clifton Chenier, *Boogie in Black & White* (Jin LP 9014) and T. K. Hulin, "Alligator Bayou" (Booray 1005).

1977   Swamp pop releases include: Van Broussard, "I Need Somebody Bad" (Bayou Boogie 144) and Tommy McLain, "Juke Box Songs" (Crazy Cajun 2027).

1978   Johnnie Allan's "Promised Land" (OvalStiff LOT 1) is reissued in the U.K., spurring his first overseas performance.

1979   Accompanied by other British swamp pop enthusiasts, John Broven conducts a fact-finding tour of the genre's homeland to research his forthcoming *South to Louisiana: The Music of the Cajun Bayous,* introducing the term *swamp pop* to its originators. Johnnie Allan records "I Cried" (Jin 372).

1981   Johnnie Allan organizes the First South Louisiana All-Star Music Show in Thibodaux, a tribute to swamp pop featuring Allan, T. K. Hulin, Warren Storm, Grace and Van Broussard, Rod Bernard, Charles Mann, Clint West, Tommy McLain, and Jivin' Gene.

1982   British artists Chas and Dave record the swamp pop-ish U.K. hit "Ain't No Pleasing You" (Rockney KOR 14).

1983   Publication of John Broven's *South to Louisiana* helps to revitalize swamp pop and prompts a greater appreciation of the genre. *Swamp pop* begins to replace *south Louisiana music* as the term of preference used to describe the sound in its homeland. Releases include: Johnnie Allan, "I'm Missing You" (Jin 388) and Darby Douget, "Mathilda Finally Came Back Home" (Jin 392).

1984   Johnnie Allan performs at the World's Fair and Exposition in New Orleans. Allan, Warren Storm, and Rod Bernard make an initial and rare appearance at the New Orleans Jazz and Heritage Festival at the invitation of New Orleans rhythm and blues artist Frankie Ford. Allan promotes the genre through his "Swamp Pop Music Show" on KRVS public radio, Lafayette, La.

1985   Swamp pop releases include: Tommy McLain, "Baby Dolls" (Crazy Cajun 2074) and "I'll Change My Style" (Crazy Cajun 2083).

1986   Tommy McLain records "Roses Don't Grow Here Anymore" (Crazy Cajun 2087).

1987   Warren Storm records "Seven Letters" (South Star 1001).

1988   Johnnie Allan publishes *Memories: A Pictorial History of South Louisiana Music,* preserving photographic, discographic, and biographic data on

Cajun, zydeco, swamp pop, and other south Louisiana and southeast Texas genres. Swamp pop releases include: Cypress City, "Cajun Rap Song" (Jin 409) and Charles Mann, "Walk of Life" (Lanor 621).

1 9 8 9 Performing mostly Cajun tunes, Johnnie Allan, Warren Storm, and Clint West record the *Cajun Born* album (La Louisianne 147). Lafayette's entertainment-heavy *Times of Acadiana* weekly newspaper establishes the South Louisiana Hall of Fame and inducts several swamp poppers in following years.

1 9 9 0 The Ace label of England begins to reissue vintage swamp pop on CDs aimed at serious enthusiasts. Regularly honoring swamp pop performers, the Louisiana Hall of Fame is established at Acadian Village in Lafayette.

1 9 9 1 Floyd Soileau begins to reissue vintage swamp pop recordings on the Jin CD label. Johnnie Allan and Warren Storm appear at the Utrecht Blues Festival in the Netherlands. Kenny Thibodeaux and the Jokers record "Holly Beach (Under the Boardwalk)" (Jin 417).

1 9 9 2 Johnnie Allan and Bernice Larson Webb publish *Born to Be a Loser: The Jimmy Donley Story.*

1 9 9 3 Swamp poppers-turned-soulmen the Boogie Kings record "I Love That Swamp Pop Music," a tribute to the genre and its pioneers (Jin 9038-2). Johnnie Allan, Warren Storm, and Tommy McLain appear at the Another Saturday Night concert in London.

1 9 9 4 Ignored by U.S. festival organizers, swamp poppers stage their own Swamp Pop Music Festival at the Acadian Village in Lafayette—the only festival dedicated to the genre since the First South Louisiana All-Star Music Show (1981). Charles "C. C." Adcock records his self-titled, swamp pop–influenced debut album (314–518 840-2) for the major Island label with cameos by Warren Storm, Tommy McLain, and Clarence "Jockey" Etienne. Bobby Charles's composition "I Don't Know Why but I Do" appears on the *Forrest Gump* motion picture soundtrack (Epic Soundtrax E2K 66329).

1 9 9 5 Forty years after its birth swamp pop persists. In fact, 1995 is a banner year despite the genre's continuing decline: By popular demand Johnnie

Allan reissues his *Memories* book in a revised and expanded edition. Spurred by the success of their 1993 swamp pop tribute song "I Love That Swamp Pop Music," the Boogie Kings record the *Swamp Boogie Blues* CD, (Jin 9046) featuring swamp pop cover tunes with cameo vocals by the original artists. Bobby Charles releases his first domestic album in almost a quarter-century, *Wish You Were Here Right Now* (Rice & Gravy/Stoney Plain 1203) and reissues on CD his 1972 *Bobby Charles* album (Rice & Gravy/Stoney Plain 1202). Urged largely by swamp pop deejay Mark Layne of KVPI radio, the Louisiana state legislature proclaims Ville Platte the "Swamp Pop Capital of the World." It also proclaims Church Point the "official home of Cajun, zydeco, and swamp pop" in conjunction with the birth of the Acadian Music Heritage Association—based in Church Point—which aims to equally promote and preserve Cajun, zydeco and swamp pop music. At the invitation of Charles "C. C." Adcock, King Karl and Guitar Gable reunite at the ninth annual *Festival International de Louisiane* (their first reunion since breaking up in the late 1960s), where Karl also duets for the first time with Rod Bernard on "This Should Go On Forever." "Saturday Hop" dance program reunion airs on KLFY TV-10 in Lafayette thirty years after its cancellation.

This timeline was compiled with the assistance of Johnnie Allan; Larry Benicewicz; Rod Bernard; John Broven of Ace Records (UK); Huey Darby of KROF radio; Butch Landry; Lee Lavergne of Lanor Records; Tommy McLain; Keith Manuel of KKAY radio; Dennis Norris; Floyd Soileau and Mona Ortego of Flat Town Music Co.; Joanne Reeves; Steve Rodolfiche of Ace video and music (Biloxi, Miss.); Eddie Shuler of Goldband Records; Warren Storm; Pat Strazza; and Clint West. SOURCES: Johnnie Allan, comp., "Johnnie Allan Discography," ed. Shane K. Bernard (Lafayette, La.: Privately published, 1994), 1–9; Allan and Bernice Larson Webb, *Born to Be a Loser: The Jimmy Donley Story* (Lafayette, La.: JADFEL, 1992), Appendix F (Jimmy Donley discography); Shane K. Bernard, "Joe Barry: Swamp Popper from Cut Off," *Now Dig This,* March 1995, 12; Bernard, comp. and ed., "Rod Bernard Discography," (Lafayette, La.: Privately published, 1994), 1–7; Bernard Boyat, "Swamp Pop," *Musiques et collections* [France], November 1994, n.p.; John Broven, *South to Louisiana: The Music of the Cajun Bayous* (Gretna, La.: Pelican, 1983), 46, 263, 276, 318–21, 335–37; Broven, *Rhythm and Blues in New Orleans* [*Walking to New Orleans: The Story of New Orleans Rhythm and Blues*] (Gretna, La.: Pelican, 1988), 113–14, 229; Contract between Goldband Records and the Boogie Ramblers, 19 July 1952, signed by Simon Lubin, Ernest Jacobs, Shelton Dunaway, and Marshall LeDee, original in the possession of Eddie Shuler, Lake Charles, La.; Goldband label discography, original in the possession of Eddie Shuler, Lake Charles, La.; Jin and Swallow labels discographies, originals in the possession of Floyd Soileau, Ville Platte, La.; La Louisianne label discography, original in the possession of David Rachou, Lafayette, La.; Lanor label discography, original in the possession of Lee Lavergne, Church Point, La.; Mike Leadbitter and Eddie Shuler, *From the Bayou: The Story of Goldband Records* (Bexhill-on-Sea, U.K.: Blues Unlimited, 1969), 35; Leadbitter and Neil Slaven, *Blues Records, 1943–1970,* vol. 1, A–K, 2d ed. (London: Record Information Services, 1987), 278, 502–3; Personal record collection of Butch Landry, Bayou Vista, La.; Personal record collection of Johnnie Allan, Lafayette, La.; Personal record collection of Larry Benicewicz, Baltimore, Md.; Personal record collection of Pat Strazza, New Iberia, La.; Personal record collection of Rod Bernard, Lafayette, La.; Swamp pop TV program listings, *Lafayette (La.) Daily Advertiser,* 23 October 1964, 20; 24 September 1965, 8; 22 April 1967, 6; 2 March 1968, 10; 16 November 1968, 10; 24 May 1969, 10; 20 December 1969, 8; 17 January 1970, 10; Warren Storm discography, original in the possession of Larry Benicewicz, Baltimore, Md.

SUGGESTED LISTENING ON COMPACT DISC*

Allan, Johnnie. *Promised Land.* CDCHD 380. Ace (UK), 1992.
Promised Land; South to Louisiana; She's Gone; Let's Do It; Cry Foolish Heart; What'cha Do; Your Picture; Somebody Else; Please Accept My Love; You Got Me Whistling; I'll Never Love Again; Secret of Love; Nights of Misery; Cajun Man; (As You Pass Me By) Graduation Night; Please Help Me I'm Falling; Somewhere on Skid Row; Isle of Capri; Sweet Dreams; I Cried; A Stranger to You; I Can't Wait; I'm Missing You; Little Fat Man; Today I Started Loving You Again; Homebound Train; Let's Go Get Drunk; Tennessee Blues.

————. *Swamp Pop Legend: Johnnie Allan—The Essential Collection.* Compact disc 9044. Jin, 1995.
Just Remember; Your Picture; Angel Love; Heaven Sent; Family Rule; Lonely Days, Lonely Nights; South to Louisiana; Cry Foolish Heart; What'cha Do; Somewhere on Skid Row; Promised Land; I'm Missing You; I Cried; You Got Me Whistlin'; Let's Do It; Please Accept My Love; Let's Go Get Drunk; Today I Started Loving You Again; Little White Cloud; Do You Love Me So; One More Chance; Whispering Wind; Mama and Daddy; I Wonder Where You Are Tonight; Unfaithful One.

*For a more extensive discography of swamp pop music, see Shane K. Bernard, comp. and ed., *Bernard's Swamp Pop Music Source Book: A Semi-Official and Highly Incomplete Bibliography and Compact Disc-ography of South Louisiana Swamp Pop Music,* No. 3 (January 1995), privately published, 28 pp., on file in the author's collection in the Southwestern Archives, University of Southwestern Louisiana, Lafayette, La.

Bernard, Rod. *Swamp Rock 'n' Roller*. CDCHD 488. Ace (UK), 1994.
   Pardon Mr. Gordon; Recorded in England; Memphis; Gimme Back My Cadillac; Who's Gonna Rock My Baby; Forgive; My Old Mother in Law; I Might as Well; Boss Man's Son; Fais Do Do; Loneliness; Colinda; I Want Somebody; Diggy Liggy Lo; Lawdy Miss Clawdy; The Prisoner's Song; Thirty Days; That's Alright Mama; Lover's Blues; Maybellene; Midnight Special; My Babe; Jambalaya; Big Mamou; New Orleans Jail; Give Me Love; Shake Rattle and Roll (with Clifton Chenier); This Should Go On Forever.

Boogie Kings, The. *Swamp Boogie Blues*. CD 9045. Jin, 1995. (Newly arranged covers of swamp pop classics with guest vocals.)
   Boil the Crawfish (Duane Yates and Everett Brady); I'm Not a Fool Anymore (Wayne Toups); Ça Fait Chaud (Pat Strazza); Mathilda (Cookie); Promised Land (Johnnie Allan); Red Red Wine (Charles Mann); I Got Loaded (Lil' Bob); Sweet Dreams (Tommy McLain); Kidnapper (Warren Storm, Willie Tee, John Smith); This Should Go On Forever (Rod Bernard); The Cajun Twist (Dennis Norris); Don't Take It So Hard (Willie Tee); Madame René (Willie Tee); It's Raining (Pat Strazza); Eight Nights a Week (Willie Tee); Opelousas Sostan (Willie Tee and Jon Smith); Cherry Pie (Duane Yates and Everett Brady); Hey Baby (Everett Brady); No More Troubles (Warren Storm); I'm Leaving It Up to You (Dale and Grace).

Broussard, Van. *"Bayou Boogie Fever."* CSP 1004-CD. CSP Records, 1991.
   Lord I Need Somebody Bad Tonight; I Got Loaded; Lost World for Love; Old Time Rock 'n' Roll; Got You on My Mind; Your Picture; If You Don't Want Me To (The Freeze); Please Say You're Fooling; Then You Can Tell Me Goodbye; Jambalaya; To Love and Be Loved; Red Red Wine; Kidnapper; That's My Desire; Mojo; Why Can't You; Record Machine; Mathilda; Feed the Flame; Crazy Baby.

———. *The Early Years*. CSP 1007–2. CSP Records, 1993.
   Pledging My Love (Van and Grace Broussard); Feels So Good (Van and Grace Broussard); When It Rains It Pours (Van Broussard); In Real Life (Van Broussard); Young Girls (Grace Broussard); Hot Nuts (Van Broussard); Your Picture (Van Broussard); My Girl across Town (Van Broussard); Everything's Gonna Be Alright (Van and Grace Broussard); My Ting-A-Ling (Van Broussard); I'm Asking Forgiveness (Van Broussard); Hold My Hand (Van Broussard); Baby Please (Van Broussard); By the Light of the Silvery Moon (Grace Broussard); Crying to See You (Van Broussard); Miss You So (Inst.).

Cookie and the Cupcakes. *By Request.* Compact disc 9037–2. Jin, 1993.
  Belinda (Cookie); Got You on My Mind (Cookie and Shelton Dunaway);
  Mathilda (Cookie); Walking Down the Aisle (Little Alfred); Even Though (Lit-
  tle Alfred); I Almost Lost My Mind (Little Alfred); Just One Kiss (Dunaway);
  Honey Hush (Dunaway); Sea of Love (Cookie); Betty and Dupree (Dunaway);
  Shake 'Em Up (Dunaway); Breaking Up Is Hard to Do (Cookie and Dunaway);
  I Cried (Cookie); Long Time Ago (Cookie); Trouble in My Life (Cookie); Feel
  So Good (Little Alfred); The Peanut (Instr.); Charged with Cheating (Little
  Alfred); I've Been So Lonely (Cookie); The Duck (Dunaway).

McLain, Tommy. *Sweet Dreams.* CDCH 285. Ace (UK), 1990.
  Sweet Dreams; Before I Grow Too Old; Think It Over; Barefootin'; I Can't
  Take It No More; Try to Find Another Man (with Clint West); When a Man
  Loves a Woman; After Loving You; A Tribute to Fats Domino (Medley):
  Goin' Home/Poor Me/Going to the River; Just Because; I'd Be a Legend in
  My Time; Together Again; I Thought I'd Never Fall in Love Again; So Sad (To
  Watch Good Love Go Bad); Sticks and Stones; My Heart Remembers; I'll
  Miss You; I Need You So; Am I That Easy to Forget; Tender Years.

Storm, Warren. *Night After Night.* Compact disc 9036–2. Jin, 1992.
  If You Don't Want Me To (The Freeze); I Need Somebody Bad Tonight; Send
  Me Some Lovin'; My House of Memories; I'm a Fool to Care; Prisoner's
  Song; What Am I Living For; Those Eyes; I Got Loaded; Those Lonely Lonely
  Nights; These Arms of Mine; Bad Moon Rising; Touch Me; Slowdown; Don't
  Toss Us Away; I Almost Called Your Name.

Various Artists. *Another Saturday Night.* CDCH 288. Ace (UK), 1990.
  Before I Grow Too Old (Tommy McLain); Sweet Dreams (Tommy McLain);
  Another Sleepless Night (Belton Richard); Try to Find Another Man (Tommy
  McLain and Clint West); I Cried (Cookie and the Cupcakes); Breaking Up Is
  Hard to Do (Cookie and the Cupcakes); Opelousas Sostan (Rufus Jagneaux);
  Downhome Music (Rufus Jagneaux); Another Saturday Night (Clint West);
  Promised Land (Johnnie Allan).

Various Artists. *Eddie's House of Hits: The Story of Goldband Records.* CDCHD
424. Ace (UK), 1992.
  Stormy Weather (Phil Phillips); The Crawl (Guitar Jr.); Cindy Lou (Gene
  Terry and the Down Beats); Please Accept My Love (Jimmy Wilson); Blue
  Bayou Shuffle (Cookie and the Cupcakes); Teenage Baby (Sticks Herman);

Secret of Love (Elton Anderson); Teardrops in My Eyes (Gene Terry and the Down Beats); Don't Leave Me (Phil Phillips).

Various Artists. *Lafayette Saturday Night.* CDCHD 371. Ace (UK), 1992.
Recorded in England (Rod Bernard); Kidnapper (Jewel and the Rubies); Memphis (Shondells [Rod Bernard, Warren Storm, and Skip Stewart]) I Got Loaded (Lil' Bob and the Lollipops); A 2 Fee [i.e., A-2-Fay] (Shondells); Come On Over (Gee Gee Shinn); What's Her Name [Please Accept My Love] (Blackie Forestier); Slow Down (Shondells); Domino (Rodney Miller); Just Because (King Karl); Before I Grow Too Old (Rodney Miller); I'm Cajun Cool (Cajun Born); Candy Ann (Jewel and the Rubies); Everybody's Feeling Good (King Karl).

Various Artists. *Lafayette Soul Show.* CDKEND 101. Kent (UK), 1993.
I Stand Accused (Don Fredericks); A Little Bit of Soap (Fredericks); Big Boys Cry (Fredericks); Everybody's Feeling Good (King Karl); Blues for Men (Karl); Got the Fever Child (Karl); Do You Like to See Me Cry (Karl); Burghers Beat (John Hart with Lil' Bob and the Lollipops); I Need Your Love (Jewel and the Rubies); Candy Ann (Jewel); Days Go By (Jewel); Kidnapper (Jewel); Agent Double O Soul (Lil' Bob and the Lollipops); Stop (Lil' Bob); Nobody but You (Lil' Bob); Out of Sight (Lil' Bob); Cry Cry Cry (Lil' Bob); Mule Train (Lil' Bob); I Got Loaded (Lil' Bob).

Various Artists. *Louisiana Rockers.* CDCHD 491. Ace (UK), 1994.
Cindy Lou (Gene Terry and the Down Beats); Come Along with Me (Charles Perrywell); Yankee Danky Doodle (Jimmy Wilson); Baby You've Been to School (Charles Page); Bye Bye Baby (Ray Gerdson with the Yellow Jackets); Catch That Train (Elton Anderson); Chickee Town Rock (The Yellow Jackets); Clemae (Jerry Morris); I Keep Cryin' (Cookie and the Cupcakes); Why Did You Leave Me (Frankie Lowery); Wiggle Rock (Jay Richards); I Love You (Elton Anderson); Orelia (Ivory Jackson); Flim Flam (Lionel Prevost); No Mail Today (Gene Terry and the Down Beats); Emmagene (Duke Stevens); Slop and Stroll Jolie Blonde (Gabe Dean); Fattie Hattie (Ray Gerdson with the Yellow Jackets); Do You Take Me for a Fool (Chuck Hillier).

Various Artists. *Louisiana Saturday Night.* CDCHD 490. Ace (UK), 1993.
Louisiana Man (Rusty and Doug Kershaw); I Cried (Johnnie Allan); Mathilda (Cookie and the Cupcakes); My Jolie Blonde (Rod Bernard with Clifton Chenier); She Wears My Ring (Phil Bo); Feed the Flame (Van Broussard);

Little Cajun Girl (Gene King); Big Boys Cry (Bobby Charles); Sugar Bee
(Cleveland Crochet); Jailbird (Bob Shurley and the Vel-Tones); I'd Be a Legend
in My Time (Tommy McLain); Diggy Liggy Lo (Rusty and Doug Kershaw);
You Ain't Nothin' but Fine (Rockin' Sidney); Big Blue Diamonds (Clint West);
Rubber Dolly (Johnnie Allan); There Goes That Train (Lee Martin); Let's Do
the Cajun Twist (Randy and the Rockets); Crazy Baby (Buck Rogers); Can't
Stand to See You Go (Rockin' Dave Allen); Whole Lotta Shakin' Goin' On
(Prentice Thomas); I'm Not a Fool Anymore (Van Broussard); The Back
Door (Rufus Jagneaux); Seven Letters (Warren Storm); I Love My Saturday
Night (Herbie Stutes).

Various Artists. *Louisiana Swamp Pop*. FLY CD 21. Flyright (UK), 1990.
  You're on My Mind (Doug Charles); Prisoner's Song (Warren Storm); Irene
  (King Karl and Guitar Gable); Teenagers (Bobby Charles); Sea of Love (Katie
  Webster); The Snake (Merton Thibodeaux); Lonely Lonely Heart (Tommy
  Strange); Kissin' Kin (Tony Perreau); This Life I Live (Rocket Morgan); Talk
  to Your Daughter (Doug Charles); Eternally (Everette Daigle); Lonely Street
  (Everette Daigle); Mama Mama Mama (Warren Storm); Won't You Believe
  Me (Dale Houston); Puppy Love (Guitar Jeff); My Man Treats Me So Nice
  (unknown); Hold My Hand (Joe Rich); This Should Go On Forever (King Karl
  and Guitar Gable).

Various Artists. *Sea of Love: Louisiana Bayou Hits 1950's to 1960's*. PCD-2137.
Blues Interactions (Japan), 1990.
  Sea of Love (Cookie and the Cupcakes); Shirley Jean (Rockin' Dave Allen);
  Sweet Dreams (Tommy McLain); South to Louisiana (Johnnie Allan); Promised
  Land (Johnnie Allan); This Should Go On Forever (Rod Bernard); Breaking
  Up Is Hard to Do (Jivin' Gene); Lover's Blues (Red Smiley and the Vel-Tones);
  You Belong to My Heart (Joe Barry); Sweet Soul Music (Lil' Bob and the
  Lollipops); She Wears My Ring (Phil Bo).

Various Artists. *Shreveport Stomp, Vol. 1*. CDCHD 495. Ace (UK), 1994.
  Ba Da (Roy "Boogie Boy" Perkins); Red Beans and Rice (Scatman Patin
  with Linda Brannon); Bow Wow Puppy Love (Jimmy Bonin); Drop Top (Roy
  "Boogie Boy" Perkins); Hippy Ti Yo [Hippy-Ti-Yo] (Bobby Page [and the Riff
  Raffs]); Ginning (Scatman Patin); Baby Please Forgive Me (Troy Webb); What
  Did You Do Last Night (Rocky Robin and the Riff Raffs).

Various Artists. *Swamp Gold, Vol. 1.* CD-106. Jin, 1991.

This Should Go On Forever (Rod Bernard); Breaking Up Is Hard to Do (Jivin' Gene); Mathilda (Cookie and the Cupcakes); Lonely Days, Lonely Nights (Johnnie Allan); Let's Do the Cajun Twist (Randy and the Rockets); Our Love (Clint West); Born to Be a Loser (Lee Martin); Don't Take It So Hard (Phil Bo); Opelousas Sostan (Rufus Jagneaux); Sweet Dreams (Tommy McLain); I Got Loaded (Lil' Bob and the Lollipops); I'm Leaving It Up to You (Dale and Grace); Shirley Jean (Rockin' Sidney); Diggy Liggy Lo (Rod Bernard); Prisoner's Song [rerecording] (Warren Storm).

Various Artists. *Swamp Gold, Vol. 2.* CD-107. Jin, 1991.

Got You On My Mind (Cookie and the Cupcakes); Your Picture (Johnnie Allan); Colinda (Rod Bernard); Feed the Flame (Van Broussard); Before I Grow Too Old (Tommy McLain); All These Things (The Uniques); Red Red Wine (Charles Mann); Promised Land (Johnnie Allan); I Can't Sleep If I Can't Sleep With You (Floyd Brown); Try to Find Another Man (Tommy McLain and Clint West); Cherry Pie (Jay Randall); Betty and Dupree (Shelton Dunaway and the Cupcakes); Big Blue Diamonds (Clint West); My Toot Toot (Rockin' Sidney); Lord I Need Somebody Bad Tonight (Warren Storm); Cajun Rap Song (Cypress City).

Various Artists. *Swamp Gold, Vol. 3.* CD-108. Jin, 1994.

Don't You Think I've Paid Enough? (Rod Bernard); You're Pouring Water (Lil' Bob and the Lollipops); (As You Pass Me By) Graduation Night (T.K. Hulin); A Stranger to You (Johnnie Allan); Send Me Some Lovin' (Warren Storm); Sea of Love (Cookie and the Cupcakes); Try Me (Clint West); Jailbird (Red Smiley and the Vel-tones); Just Because (Tommy McLain); The Back Door (Rufus Jagneaux); I Love That Swamp Pop Music (The Boogie Kings); Mathilda Finally Came Back Home (Darby Douget); Holly Beach (Under the Boardwalk) (Kenny Tibbs and the Jokers); Hope You Have a Merry Christmas (Kane Glaze).

Various Artists. *Swamp Gold, Vol. 4.* CD-109. Jin, 1994.

Congratulations to You Darling (Rod Bernard); Time and Time Again (Gary T. and Deuce of Hearts); Nobody but You (Lil' Bob and the Lollipops); Those Lonely Lonely Nights (Warren Storm); Down on the Corner (Gary Walker); Stop and Think It Over (Dale and Grace); Today I Started Loving You Again

(Johnnie Allan); Don't Let Me Cross Over (Johnny Koonse); Belinda (Cookie and the Cupcakes); Another Saturday Night (Clint West); No Good Woman (Rockin' Sidney); Sixteen Candles (Skip Stewart); Sea Cruise (Van Broussard); Seven Letters (Warren Storm); Shake Rattle and Roll (Rod Bernard with Clifton Chenier).

NOTES

Louisiana Saturday Night: An Introduction

1. Gene King, "Little Cajun Girl," on Various Artists, *Louisiana Saturday Night,* compact disc CDCHD 490, Ace (UK), 1993; Cookie and the Cupcakes, "Mathilda," on Various Artists, *Louisiana Saturday Night,* compact disc.

2. John Broven, *South to Louisiana: The Music of the Cajun Bayous* (Gretna, La.: Pelican, 1983), 335–37.

3. Broven, *South to Louisiana,* 180–81; Bill C. Malone, *Southern Music/American Music* (Lexington: University Press of Kentucky, 1979), 101–5; Robert Palmer, *A Tale of Two Cities: Memphis Rock and New Orleans Roll* (New York: Institute for Studies in American Music/Brooklyn College of the City University of New York, 1979), 27, 32; Colin Escott with Martin Hawkins, *Good Rockin' Tonight: Sun Records and the Birth of Rock 'n' Roll* (New York: St. Martin's Press, 1991), 116–19, 125–29, 145–48, 169–87, 190–92.

4. Johnnie Allan, comp. and ed., *Memories: A Pictorial History of South Louisiana Music, 1920s–1980s,* Vol. 1, *South Louisiana and East Texas Musicians* (Lafayette, La.: Johnnie Allan/JADFEL, 1988), 207, 217; Broven, *South to Louisiana,* 153–54, 155–56, 159; Escott with Hawkins, *Good Rockin' Tonight,* 251; Palmer, *Tale of Two Cities,* 25; Charlie Gillett, *The Sound of the City: The Rise of Rock 'n' Roll* (New York: Dell, 1972), 23, 26, 131, 311; Malone, *Southern Music/American Music,* 74, 97.

5. Trent Angers, *The Truth about the Cajuns* (Lafayette, La.: Acadian House, 1989), 13–15, 93–102; Carl A. Brasseaux, *The Founding of New Acadia: The Beginnings of Acadian Life in Louisiana, 1765–1803* (Baton Rouge: Louisiana State University Press, 1987), 90–91; "Cajuns Get New Respect from [Census] Bureau," *Lafayette (La.) Daily Advertiser,* 1 August 1991, A-12; Dick Blackburn, liner notes for *Sound of the Swamp: The Best of Excello Records,* vol. 1, compact disc R2 70896, Rhino, 1990.

6. *American Heritage Dictionary,* 2d college ed., and *Webster's New Collegiate Dictionary* (1981) s.v. "Cajun"; Barry Jean Ancelet, *Cajun Music: Its Origins and Development* (Lafayette: Center for Louisiana Studies/University of Southwestern Louisiana, 1989), 5,

7, 17; Ancelet, Jay Edwards, Glen Pitre et al., *Cajun Country* (Jackson: University Press of Mississippi, 1991), xv–xvi, 3–4, 36; Ancelet and Elemore Morgan, Jr., *The Makers of Cajun Music (Musiciens cadiens et créoles)* (Austin: University of Texas Press, 1984), 20; Brasseaux, *Founding of New Acadia,* 8; Brasseaux, interview by author, 13 July 1992, Lafayette, La., interview notes; James H. Dormon, *The People Called Cajuns: An Introduction to an Ethnohistory* (Lafayette: Center for Louisiana Studies/University of Southwestern Louisiana, 1983), 8–9, 44–47.

7. Ancelet et al., *Cajun Country,* xiii–xiv, 34–36, 37; Dormon, *People Called Cajuns,* 20; Dormon, "Louisiana's 'Creoles of Color': Ethnicity, Marginality, and Identity," *Social Science Quarterly* 73 (September 1992): 616, 621–22; Joseph G. Tregle, Jr., "On That Word 'Creole' Again: A Note," *Louisiana History* 23 (Spring 1982): 193–98. For additional data on Creoles see Carl A. Brasseaux, Keith P. Fontenot, and Claude F. Oubre, *Creoles of Color in the Bayou Country* (Jackson: University Press of Mississippi, 1994).

8. Ancelet et al., *Cajun Country,* xv–xvi, 37, 150; Ancelet, *Cajun Music,* 19; Ancelet and Morgan, *Makers of Cajun Music,* 22, 23; Dormon, "Creoles of Color," 621–22; Ann Allen Savoy, comp. and ed., *Cajun Music: A Reflection of a People,* 3d ed., vol. 1 (Eunice, La.: Bluebird, 1988), 13, 55, 67, 68.

9. Ancelet, *Cajun Music,* 35; Broven, *South to Louisiana,* 6.

10. Broven, *South to Louisiana,* 101–2; Barry Jean Ancelet, introduction to Philip Gould, *Cajun Music and Zydeco* (Baton Rouge: Louisiana State University Press, 1992), x; Savoy, *Cajun Music,* 305.

1. Who Named It Swamp Pop and What Is It?

1. Charles "C. C." Adcock, interview by author, 15 September 1992, Lafayette, La., interview notes; Bill Millar, "Johnnie Allan: A Swamp-Pop Special," *New Kommotion,* Summer 1978, 15; Millar, "Rockin' on the Bayou," *Melody Maker,* 17 February 1979, 51; Millar, "Sounds of the Swamp: Local Heroes Who Rocked the Everglades," *The History of Rock* 7 (1983): 1455; Huey Darby, telephone interview by author, 16 January 1992, interview notes; Broven, *South to Louisiana,* xi, 179; Grace Broussard, telephone interview by author, 2 October 1991, Lafayette, La., to Prairieville, La., tape recording; Van Broussard, telephone interview by author, 8 January 1992, Lafayette, La., to Prairieville, La., tape recording; Kurt Loder, "Sound of the Swamp," *Esquire,* November 1991, 64; Bruce Bastin, liner notes for *Louisiana "High School Hop,"* The Legendary Jay Miller Sessions, vol. 51, long-playing record FLY 616, Flyright, 1988; Johnnie Allan, "With Johnnie Allan in the Promised Land," interview by Ken Weir (Lafayette, La., March 1990), *Big Beat of the Fifties,* March 1991, 38, 39; Harry Simoneaux, interview by author, 3 May 1992, Lafayette, La., tape recording.

2. Broven, *South to Louisiana,* 179; Broven to the author, 18 November 1991, typewritten letter signed (hereinafter TLS), original in the possession of the author; Millar, "Johnnie Allan," 15; Millar, "Rockin' on the Bayou," 51.

3. Bill Millar, telephone interview by author, 24 February 1992, Lafayette, La., to London, England, interview notes; Millar to the author, 14 August 1995, autograph letter signed (hereinafter ALS), original in the possession of the author; Millar to John Broven, 12 November 1991, ALS, original in the possession of the author; Millar, "Swamp Pop-Music from Cajun Country," *Record Mirror*, 12 June 1971, n.p.; Broven to the author.

4. John Broven, interview by author, 1 May 1992, Lafayette, La., tape recording; Broven, *South to Louisiana*, ix, xiii. For more information on Broven, see Vincent Fumar, "A Blues Lover from Britain," *Dixie (New Orleans Times-Picayune)*, 20 November 1983, 12–20.

5. Broven interview; Broven to the author; Broven, *South to Louisiana*, ix–x.

6. Broven interview; Broven to the author; Broven, *South to Louisiana*, x, xi.

7. Larry Benicewicz, "Johnnie Allan: Cajun Chronicler," *Newsletter of the Baltimore Blues Society*, February 1989, n.p.; Broven, *South to Louisiana*, 214; Joe Sasfy, "The Bayou Beat," *Washington, D.C., City Paper*, 15 June 1984, 17; Rod Bernard, interview by author, 18 October 1991, Lafayette, La., tape recording; Roy Perkins, interview by author, 22 October 1991, Lafayette, La., tape recording; Bobby Charles, interview by author, 3 August 1991, Abbeville, La., tape recording.

8. Mirek Kocandrle, *The History of Rock and Roll: A Selective Discography* (Boston: G. K. Hall, 1988), 82–87; Robert Sacré, *Musiques cajun, créole et zydeco* (Paris: Presses Universitaires de France, 1995), 60–61; *Guinness Encyclopedia of Popular Music*, 1st ed., s.v. "Bernard, Rod"; Gillett, *Sound of the City* (1972), 190; Gillett, *The Sound of the City: The Rise of Rock 'n' Roll* (New York: Pantheon, 1983), 175.

9. Dr. John [Mac Rebennack], liner notes for Dr. John, *Dr. John's Gumbo*, long-playing record SD 7006, Atco 1972; see also Dr. John, liner notes for Dr. John, *Dr. John's Gumbo*, compact disc 7006–2, Atco n.d.; Larry Benicewicz, "Rod Bernard and Swamp Pop," *Newsletter of the Baltimore Blues Society*, February 1992, 2; Broven, *South to Louisiana*, 180; Millar, "Rockin' on the Bayou," 51; Millar, "Sounds of the Swamp," 1455; Millar to the author, 9 January 1995, ALS, original in the possession of the author; Simoneaux interview.

10. Broven, *South to Louisiana*, 179; Jeff Hannusch to the author, 21? January 1992, ALS, original in the possession of the author; Benicewicz, "Rod Bernard and Swamp Pop," 2; Sasfy, "Bayou Beat," 17; Sasfy, "Swamp Pop: This Should Go On Forever," *Washington, D.C., Unicorn Times*, August 1982, 12; Macon Fry and Julie Posner, *Cajun Country Guide* (Gretna, La.: Pelican, 1992), 75; Millar, "Rockin' on the Bayou," 51; Millar, "Sounds of the Swamp," 1455; Millar, "Johnnie Allan," 15; Rico [Rick Olivier], "Putting the Fizz in Swamp Pop," *Wavelength*, April 1984, 22.

11. Dennis McGee, "O malheureuse," *J'ai été au bal (I Went to the Dance): The Cajun and Zydeco Music of Louisiana*, vol. 1, compact disc CD-331, Arhoolie, 1990; McGee, "Happy One-Step," *J'ai été au bal*, vol. 1, compact disc; Doc Guidry, "La valse d'amitié," *The Best of La Louisianne Records*, compact disc LLCD-1001, La Louisianne, 1990; Guidry, "Colinda," *Best of La Louisianne Records*, compact disc.

12. Lawrence N. Redd, "Rock! It's Still Rhythm and Blues," *Black Perspective in Music* 13 (Spring 1985): 31.

13. Ibid., 31, 40–42, 46; Broven, *South to Louisiana*, 181–82.

14. Millar, "Swamp-Pop Music from Cajun Country," n.p.; Millar to the author, 25 February 1992, ALS, original in the possession of the author.

15. Broven, *South to Louisiana*, 180, 215; Broven to the author; Broven, liner notes for Rod Bernard, *Rod Bernard,* long-playing record CH 143, Ace (UK), 1985; Jeff Hannusch, liner notes for Various Artists, *Swamp Gold,* vol. 2, compact disc CD-107, Jin, 1991.

16. Ancelet et al., *Cajun Country,* 15; *American Heritage Dictionary,* 2d college ed., and *Webster's New Collegiate Dictionary* (1981), s.v. "pop," "popular"; Jon Pareles and Patricia Romanowski, eds., *The Rolling Stone Encyclopedia of Rock & Roll* (New York: Rolling Stone/Summit, 1983), s.v. "pop."

2. The Sound of Swamp Pop

1. Lyrics to Dennis McGee's "Mon chère bébé créole" appear in Raymond E. François, comp. and anno., *Yé Yaille, Chère! Traditional Cajun Dance Music* (Lafayette, La.: Thunderstone Press, 1990), 43–46; and Savoy, *Cajun Music,* 57–58 (see also discography on 54). Balfa is quoted in Broven, *South to Louisiana,* 8; Jimmy Wilson, "Please Accept My Love," on Various Artists, *Eddie's House of Hits: The Story of Goldband Records,* compact disc CDCHD 424, Ace (UK), 1992.

2. Musical transcriptions in this chapter are by Anne K. Simpson with assistance from David Evans and Arthur E. Riedel.

3. Johnnie Allan, "South to Louisiana," *Promised Land,* compact disc CDCHD 380, Ace (UK), 1992; Johnnie Allan, interview by author, 12 June 1991, Lafayette, La., tape recording; Mike Leadbitter, *Crowley, Louisiana, Blues* (Bexhill-on-Sea, England: Blues Unlimited, 1968), 9.

4. Cookie and the Cupcakes, "Mathilda," 45 rpm single 1003, Lyric [recorded in Lake Charles, La.], 1958. The recording is available on Various Artists, *Louisiana Saturday Night,* compact disc; Broven, *South to Louisiana,* 187–89.

5. Guitar Gable and the Musical Kings featuring King Karl, "Irene," 45 rpm single 2094, Excello [recorded in Crowley, La.], 1956. The recording is available on *Guitar Gable with King Karl: Cool, Calm, Collected,* long-playing album FLY 599, Flyright, 1984; Broven, *South to Louisiana,* 154.

6. Rod Bernard, "This Should Go On Forever," 45 rpm single 105, Jin [recorded in Crowley, La.], 1958. The recording is available on *Swamp Rock 'n' Roller,* compact disc CDCHD 488, Ace (UK), 1994; Shane K. Bernard, "A Swamp Rock 'n' Roller Remembers: Rod Bernard and *American Bandstand,"* *Now Dig This,* June 1994, 5–8; Bernard, "A Swamp Rock 'n' Roller Remembers: Rod Bernard and *American Bandstand,"* *Goldmine* (31 March 1995), 64, 66, 129, 132, 138; Broven, *South to Louisiana,* 204.

7. Pareles and Romanowski, *Rolling Stone Encyclopedia,* s.v. "Neil Sedaka."

8. Jivin' Gene, "Breaking Up Is Hard To Do," 45 rpm single 116, Jin [recorded in Crowley, La.], 1959. The recording is available on Various Artists, *Swamp Gold,* vol. 1, compact disc CD-106, Jin, 1991.

9. Johnnie Allan, "Lonely Days, Lonely Nights," 45 rpm single 111, Jin [recorded in Crowley, La.], 1958; the recording is available on Various Artists, *Swamp Gold,* vol. 1, compact disc.

10. Clint West, "Big Blue Diamonds," 45 rpm single 196, Jin [recorded in Ville Platte, La.], 1965. The recording is available on Various Artists, *Swamp Gold,* vol. 2, compact disc; Clint West, interview by author, 4 August 1991, Opelousas, La., tape recording; Broven, *South to Louisiana,* 231; Mike Leadbitter and Neil Slaven, comps., *Blues Records, 1943–1970,* vol. 1 (A–K), 2d ed. (London: Record Information Services, 1987), 689.

11. Tommy McLain, "Sweet Dreams," 45 rpm single 197, Jin [recorded in Ville Platte, La.], 1966. The recording is available on *Sweet Dreams,* compact disc CDCH 285, Ace, 1990; Tommy McLain, telephone interview by author, 18 September 1991, Lafayette, La., to Alexandria, La., tape recording; Robert Lissauer, comp. and ed., *Lissauer's Encyclopedia of Popular Music in America, 1888 to the Present* (New York: Paragon House, 1991), s.v. "Sweet Dreams."

12. Tommy McLain, "Before I Grow Too Old," 45 rpm single 228, Jin [recorded in Ville Platte, La.], 1968. The recording is available on *Sweet Dreams,* compact disc; C. C. Adcock, "Done Most Everything," *C. C. Adcock,* compact disc 314–518 840–2, Island, 1994; McLain interview; Broven, *South to Louisiana,* 183, 185, 231; Larry Benicewicz, "Poet of the Bayou: Bobby Charles," *Newsletter of the Baltimore Blues Society,* November 1988, 2.

13. Johnnie Allan, "Your Picture," 45 rpm single 1008, Viking [recorded in Crowley, La.], 1961. The recording is available on Various Artists, *Swamp Gold,* vol. 2, compact disc; Broven, *South to Louisiana,* 215, 237.

14. Dale and Grace, "I'm Leaving It Up to You," 45 rpm single 921, Montel [recorded in Lafayette, La.], 1963; the recording is available on Various Artists, *Swamp Gold,* vol. 1, compact disc; Leadbitter and Slaven, *Blues Records,* vol. 1, 523; Broven, *South to Louisiana,* 265.

15. Rod Bernard, "Pardon Mr. Gordon," 45 rpm single 105, Jin [recorded in Crowley, La.], 1958. The recording is available on *Swamp Rock 'n' Roller,* compact disc; Broven, *South to Louisiana,* 199, 200.

16. Johnnie Allan, "Promised Land," 45 rpm single 244, Jin [recorded in Ville Platte, La.], 1971. The recording is available on *Promised Land,* compact disc; Allan, "Promised Land," the Boogie Kings, *Swamp Boogie Blues,* compact disc CD 9045, Jin, 1995; Allan interview, 12 June 1991; Allan, "South Louisiana—The Promised Land: Johnnie Allan," interview by Paul Harris, part 2 (England, 1986), *Now Dig This,* April 1987, 9–10; Benicewicz,

"Cajun Chronicler," n.p.; Broven, *South to Louisiana,* 215–16; Martha Aycock, "Johnny Allen [sic] Single English 'Pick Hit,' " *Lafayette (La.) Daily Advertiser,* 2 April 1978, 62; Bill Millar, "Cajun and Proud of It: Bill Millar Talks to Johnnie Allan, the Louisiana Swamp Fox," *Goldmine,* June 1982, 14; Millar, "Johnnie Allan," *New Kommotion,* 16.

17. Bobby Charles, "Later Alligator," 45 rpm single 1609, Chess [recorded in New Orleans, La.], 1955. The recording is available on Various Artists, *Rock & Roll Originators,* compact disc TSD-3706, Tel-Star, 1991; Bobby Charles, "Later Alligator," *Wish You Were Here Right Now,* compact disc 1203, Rice & Gravy/Stoney Plain, 1995; Charles interview; Broven, *South to Louisiana,* 183–84; Benicewicz, "Poet of the Bayou," 2.

18. Charles interview; Clarence Major, ed. and intro., *Juba to Jive: A Dictionary of African-American Slang* (New York: Penguin, 1994), s.v. "Alligator," "Gate," "Gator"; Robert L. Chapman, ed., *The New Dictionary of American Slang* (New York: Harper and Row, 1986), s.v., "Alligator"; Eric Partridge, *A Dictionary of Slang and Unconventional English,* 8th ed. (New York: Macmillan, 1984), s.v. "See you later—alligator!"; Stuart Berg Flexner, *Listening to America: An Illustrated History of Words and Phrases from Our Lively and Splendid Past* (New York: Touchstone, 1982), s.v. "Alligators and crocodiles."

19. Charles is quoted in Broven, *South to Louisiana,* 183.

20. Guitar Gable and the Musical Kings, "Congo Mombo," 45 rpm single 2082, Excello [recorded in Crowley, La.], 1956. The recording is available on Various Artists, *Sound of the Swamp,* vol. 1, compact disc; The Boogie Ramblers, "Such as Love," 45 rpm single, Goldband 1030, ca. 1955; King Karl, interview by author, 11 December 1991, Scott, La., tape recording; Guitar Gable, interview by author, 1 November 1991, Bellevue, La., tape recording; Broven, *South to Louisiana,* 154; Shane K. Bernard, "Creole Swamp Poppers: King Karl and Guitar Gable," *Now Dig This,* January 1995, 28.

21. Cookie and His Cupcakes [sic], "I'm Twisted," 45 rpm single 1003, Lyric [recorded in Lake Charles, La.], 1958; Leadbitter and Slaven, *Blues Records,* vol. 1, 278; Huey "Cookie" Thierry and Ernest Jacobs, interview by author, 19 July 1995, Lake Charles, La., tape recording; Tim Riley, *Tell Me Why: A Beatles Commentary* (New York: Vintage, 1989), xvii, xviii.

3. The Birth of Swamp Pop Music

1. Allan provides biographical data for seventy-one swamp pop artists, but to his list I have added seven additional artists whom Allan regards as mainstream rhythm and blues performers, namely, Doug Ardoin, Guitar Gable, Guitar Jr., King Karl, Lil' Bob, Bert Miller, and Sticks Herman. The cumulative list includes Johnnie Allan, Rockin' Dave Allen, Vince Anthony, Bruce Austin, Doug Ardoin, Joe Barry, Bobby B., Rod Bernard, Wade Bernard, V. J. "Boo" Boulet, Grace Broussard, Van Broussard, Danny Brown, Joe Carl, Lee Castle, Bobby Charles, Charles "Charlo" Guilbeau, Jr., Ike Clanton, Jimmy Clanton,

Jay Collins, Huey Darby, Jimmy Donley, *Shelton Dunaway,* Elton Hargrave, Freddy Fender, Rick Fontaine, John Fred, Benny Graeff, Terry "Gilroy" Guillory, *Guitar Gable,* Guitar Jeff, *Guitar Jr.,* Steve Hebert, Dale Houston, T. K. Hulin, Bobby James, Danny James, Jivin' Gene, Billy John, *King Karl, Lil' Bob, Little Alfred,* Little Robert, Joey Long, Bobby Lovelace, Frankie Lowery, *Barbara Lynn,* Tommy McLain, Charles Mann, Lee Martin, Paul Marx, Bert Miller, Dennis Norris, Bobby Page, Victor Palmer, Roy Perkins, *Phil Phillips,* Johnny Preston, Van Preston, Jay Randall, *Sidney Reynaud,* Jerry Scott, G. G. Shinn, Johnny Spain, Joe Stampley, Jerry Starr, Skip Stewart, *Sticks Herman,* Warren Storm, Jesse Stuart, Willie Tee, Gene Terry, *Huey "Cookie" Thierry,* Kenny Tibbs, *Lionel Torrence,* Glenn Wells, Clint West, and Mike Young. One important black swamp pop artist, however, is missing from Allan's list and understandably so: talented Elton Anderson, about whom practically nothing is known. (The names of black swamp pop artists are *italicized* in the above list.)

Statistics on Cajun and black Creole musicians derive from Allan's data for 240 artists (207 Cajun and 33 black Creole musicians).

These and other figures based on Allan's data offer an approximate, somewhat less-than-scientific survey of south Louisiana and southeast Texas musical demographics. Although Allan never intended his biographical listings to serve as a database for scholarly study, his extensive research represents the only such database presently in existence; his findings have been verified when possible and found to be extremely accurate. Allan, *Memories,* 2–7, 84, 89, 102–3, 160–61, 202, 207, 232.

Regarding the musical importance of the northern prairie region, see Ancelet and Morgan, *Makers of Cajun Music,* 21; Brasseaux interview; Alan Lomax, prod. and dir., *Cajun Country: Don't Drop the Potato,* American Patchwork: Songs and Stories about America, 60 min. (New York: Pacific Arts Video/PBS Home Video/Association for Cultural Equity, Hunter College, Columbia University, 1990), videocassette; Lauren C. Post, *Cajun Sketches: From the Prairies of Southwest Louisiana* (Baton Rouge, La.: Louisiana State University Press, 1990), 159.

2. Ancelet, *Cajun Music,* 1–7, 15, 16; Ancelet, interview by author, 29 October 1992, Lafayette, La., interview notes; Ancelet et al., *Cajun Country,* xv, 9, 12, 151–54, 164; Ancelet and Morgan, Jr., *Makers of Cajun Music,* 20, 21–22; Brasseaux, *Founding of New Acadia,* 21, 91–92, 93, 97, 102, 147; Brasseaux, *"Scattered to the Wind": Dispersal and Wanderings of the Acadians, 1755–1809* (Lafayette: Center for Louisiana Studies/University of Southwestern Louisiana, 1991), 4, 62, 63, 67, 69; Savoy, *Cajun Music,* 13.

3. Ancelet, *Cajun Music,* 16–17; Ancelet et al., *Cajun Country,* 12–14; Ancelet and Morgan, *Makers of Cajun Music,* 20–22; Brasseaux, *Founding of New Acadia,* 93–94, 95, 98–100, 112–14.

4. Ancelet, *Cajun Music,* 1, 15, 16–17, 19; Ancelet et al., *Cajun Country,* xv, 22–24, 26, 28, 34–36; Ancelet and Morgan, *Makers of Cajun Music,* 20, 22–23; Dormon, *People Called Cajuns,* 44–47; Lawrence E. Estaville, Jr., "Changeless Cajuns: Nineteenth-Century Reality

or Myth?" *Louisiana History* 28 (Spring 1987): 126–30, 139–40; Post, *Cajun Sketches*, 8–11, 71, 79.

5. Ancelet, *Cajun Music*, 1, 15, 17, 19; Ancelet et al., *Cajun Country*, xv–xvi, 34–37, 149–50; Ancelet and Morgan, *Makers of Cajun Music*, 20, 22–23; Ancelet, introduction to *Cajun Music and Zydeco*, ix; Brasseaux, *Founding of New Acadia*, 135; Dormon, "Louisiana's 'Creoles of Color,' " 616–17; Dormon, *People Called Cajuns*, 44–47; Savoy, *Cajun Music*, 13, 304.

6. Ancelet, *Cajun Music*, 17, 19–26; Ancelet interview; Ancelet et al., *Cajun Country*, 150–51; Ancelet and Morgan, *Makers of Cajun Music*, 23–24; Savoy, *Cajun Music*, 13–14, 82, 103.

7. Ancelet, *Cajun Music*, 26–31; Ancelet et al., *Cajun Country*, 151, 157–58, see also map on 27; Ancelet and Morgan, *Makers of Cajun Music*, 24; Savoy, *Cajun Music*, 14.

8. Ancelet, *Cajun Music*, 26–31; Ancelet et al., *Cajun Country*, 151, 157–58; Ancelet and Morgan, *Makers of Cajun Music*, 25–27; Savoy, *Cajun Music*, 14.

9. Ancelet, *Cajun Music*, 31–36; Ancelet et al., *Cajun Country*, 158–60; Ancelet and Morgan, *Makers of Cajun Music*, 27–28; Broven, *South to Louisiana*, 79; Savoy, *Cajun Music*, 14.

10. Gene Terry, telephone interview by author, 20 October 1992, Lafayette, La., to Port Arthur, Tex., interview notes.

11. Although one source states that Allan's first group initially was called the Rhythm Kings, Allan confirms it actually was called the Rhythm Rockers. Allan, "South to Louisiana—The Promised Land: Johnnie Allan," interview by Paul Harris, part 1 (England, 1986), *Now Dig This*, March 1987, 11; Allan, telephone interview by author, 20 October 1992, Lafayette, La., interview notes; Broven, *South to Louisiana*, 214; Benicewicz, "Johnnie Allan: Cajun Chronicler," n.p.; Millar, "Cajun and Proud of It," 14; Millar, "Johnnie Allan," 15.

12. Broven, *South to Louisiana*, 179.

13. Benicewicz, "Rod Bernard and Swamp Pop," 2; Broven, *South to Louisiana*, 180; Simoneaux interview.

14. Belton Richard, "Un autre soir d'ennui (Another Sleepless Night)," "I'm Not a Fool Anymore," "J'ai pleurer pour toi," "Give Me Another Chance," *Belton Richard: Modern Sounds in Cajun Music*, compact disc CDCHD 378, Ace (UK), 1993; Richard, "Lord I Need Somebody Bad Tonight," *Good n' Cajun*, long-playing record 6021, Swallow, 1974; Jimmy Clanton, "Another Sleepless Night," "Just a Dream," on Various Artists, *The Best of Ace Records—The Pop Hits*, compact disc 72392–75266-2, Rock 'n' Roll/Scotti Bros., 1992; Blackie Forestier, "What's Her Name," on Various Artists, *Lafayette Saturday Night*, compact disc CDCHD 371, Ace (UK), 1992; Elton Anderson, "Please Accept My Love," 45 rpm single 71778, Mercury, 1961; Johnnie Allan, "Please Accept My Love,"

Promised Land, compact disc CDCHD 380, Ace (UK), 1992; Broven, *South to Louisiana,* 159, 181, 237–38, 272; Savoy, *Cajun Music,* 292.

15. Allan, "Promised Land," *Promised Land,* compact disc; Wilson, "Please Accept My Love," on Various Artists, *Eddie's House of Hits,* compact disc; Charles Mann, "Walk of Life," *Walk of Life,* compact disc 002, Gumbo/Cooking Vinyl, 1990; Mann, telephone interview by author, 12 September 1991, Lafayette, La., to Lake Charles, La., tape recording; Gene Terry and the Down Beats, "Cindy Lou," on Various Artists, *Eddie's House of Hits,* compact disc; C. C. Adcock, "Cindy Lou," *C. C. Adcock,* compact disc; Darby Douget, "Mathilda Finally Came Back Home," on Various Artists, *Swamp Gold,* vol. 3, compact disc 9041–2, Jin, 1994; Broven, *South to Louisiana,* 216; Loder, "Sound of the Swamp," 64.

16. The average is rounded off from the actual figure (1939.1) and is based on biographical data for 77 swamp pop performers. (Allan does not record a date of birth for one of the 78 swamp pop artists listed in n. 1 of this chapter.) Allan, *Memories,* 160–61, 202, 207, 232; Allan interview, 12 June 1991; Ancelet, *Cajun Music,* 28–32; Ancelet interview; Ancelet et al., *Cajun Country,* 151, 158–59; Ancelet and Morgan, *Makers of Cajun Music,* 25–27; Savoy, *Cajun Music,* 14; Broven, *South to Louisiana,* 197, 214, 218–19, 231, 246–47; Rod Bernard interview, 18 October 1991; Oscar "Ric" Bernard, interview by author, 28 November 1991, Opelousas, La., tape recording; Warren Storm, interview by author, 13 June 1991, Lafayette, La., tape recording; Joe Barry, interview by author, 26 June 1991, Lafayette, La., tape recording; Barry, telephone interview by author, 3 July 1992, Lafayette, La., to Galliano, La., interview notes; Shane K. Bernard, "Joe Barry: A Swamp Popper from Cut Off," *Now Dig This,* March 1995, 10; West interview.

17. Thierry and Jacobs interview; Little Alfred, interview by author, 8 September 1991, Lafayette, La., tape recording; Lil' Bob, interview by author, 9 July 1991, Opelousas, La., tape recording; Karl interview; Gable interview, 1 November 1991; Bernard, "Creole Swamp Poppers," 27.

18. Karl interview; Bernard, "Creole Swamp Poppers," 27.

19. Gable interview, 1 November 1991; Bernard, "Creole Swamp Poppers," 27.

20. Charles interview; Rod Bernard interview, 18 October 1991; Gene Terry, telephone interview by author, 8 January 1992, Lafayette, La., to Port Arthur, Tex., tape recording; Shane K. Bernard, "A Swamp Pop–Rockabilly Collision: Gene Terry and the Down Beats," *Now Dig This,* September 1994, 5.

21. Storm interview, 13 June 1991; Storm, telephone interview by author, 5 October 1992, Lafayette, La., interview notes; Bernard, "Warren Storm: The Workhorse of Swamp Pop," *Now Dig This,* July 1995, 29; Barry interview, 26 June 1991; Bernard, "Joe Barry," 10; Broven, *South to Louisiana,* 219, 246–47.

22. Allan interview, 12 June 1991; Allan, interview by Harris, part 1, 10–11; Benicewicz, "Johnnie Allan: Cajun Chronicler," n.p.; Millar, "Cajun and Proud of It," 14; Millar, "Johnnie Allan," 15.

23. Based on Allan's biographical data for 240 Cajun and black Creole performers and 78 swamp pop performers. Allan, *Memories,* 2–7, 84, 89, 102–3, 160–61, 202, 207, 232; Ancelet and Morgan, *Makers of Cajun Music,* 21; Brasseaux interview; Lomax, *Cajun Country,* videocassette; Post, *Cajun Sketches,* 159.

24. Benicewicz, "Rod Bernard and Swamp Pop," 2; John Broven, *Rhythm and Blues in New Orleans* [*Walking to New Orleans: The Story of New Orleans Rhythm and Blues*] (Gretna, La.: Pelican, 1988), 118; John Fred, telephone interview by author, 18 September 1991, Lafayette, La., to Baton Rouge, La., tape recording; Millar, "Rockin' on the Bayou," 51; Millar, "Sounds of the Swamp," 1455; Jeff Hannusch [Almost Slim], *I Hear You Knockin': The Sound of New Orleans Rhythm and Blues* (Ville Platte, La.: Swallow, 1989), 190, 197; Earl King, "Those Lonely Lonely Nights," 45 rpm single 509, Ace (USA), 1955 (see also King, "There's Been Some Lonely Lonely Nights [Those Lonely Lonely Nights]," *Glazed,* compact disc CD-BT-1035, Black Top, 1986).

25. Hannusch, *I Hear You Knockin',* 132; Buddy King, interview by author, 22 July 1991, Lafayette, La., tape recording.

26. Shuler informed Mike Leadbitter in the late 1960s that the Boogie Ramblers' "Cindy Lou"/"Such as Love" was issued in 1954. Most discographies, however (including Leadbitter and Slaven's *Blues Records*), list the single as a 1955 release. Mike Leadbitter and Eddie Shuler, *From the Bayou (The Story of Goldband Records)* (Bexhill-on-Sea, England: Blues Unlimited, 1969), 33–34; Leadbitter and Slaven, *Blues Records,* vol. 1, 278; Contract between Goldband Records and the Boogie Ramblers, 19 July 1952, signed by Simon Lubin, Ernest Jacobs, Shelton Dunaway, and Marshall LeDee, original in the possession of Eddie Shuler, Lake Charles, La.; Gable interview, 1 November 1991; Gable, telephone interview by author, 20 March 1995, Lafayette, La., to Bellevue, La., interview notes; Lil' Bob interview; The Boogie Ramblers, "Cindy Lou"/"Such as Love," 45 rpm single, Goldband 1030, ca. 1955.

27. Statistics on the median year of birth for swamp pop musicians are based on Allan's biographical data for 65 white and 12 black swamp pop performers. The relatively small number of black swamp pop performers included in Allan's survey reflects their paucity—see italicized names in n. 1 of this chapter for a listing of black swamp poppers. Lil' Bob's date of birth has been corrected from 1937 to 1938, and averages are rounded off from the actual figures (1939.8 and 1935.9). Allan, *Memories,* 160–61, 202, 207, 232; Lil' Bob interview; Benicewicz, "Rod Bernard and Swamp Pop," 2; Benicewicz, "Guitar Gable and King Karl: A New Brand of Blues," *Newsletter of the Baltimore Blues Society,* March 1994, 4–9; Gable interview, 1 November 1991; Gable interview, 20 March 1995; Karl interview; Little Alfred interview.

28. Roy Perkins, interview by author, 22 January 1995, Lafayette, La., tape recording; Phillip Comeaux, interview by author, 22 January 1995, Lafayette, La., tape recording; Little Alfred interview.

29. Lionel "Chick" Vidrine, interview by author, 5 February 1991, Opelousas, La., tape recording; Letter regarding Chick Vidrine and the Southern Club, *Opelousas (La.) Daily World,* 21 July 1991, n.p.; Judy Green, "Be There, Honey, Or Be Square," *Opelousas (La.) Daily World,* 25 July 1991, 6. For more information on the St. Landry Parish swamp pop nightclub scene in the 1950s and early '60s see Herman Fuselier, "[Southern] Club Fades, Not Memories," *Opelousas (La.) Daily World,* 12 October 1995, 1, 8, and idem, "Time for Step Inn Club to Bow Out," *Opelousas (La.) Daily World,* 20 July 1995, 1, 8; David Kurtz, "Devilish Politics in St. Landry Parish," *Lafayette (La.) Times of Acadiana,* 4 October 1995, 15.

30. Vidrine interview; Obituary of Lionel "Chick" Vidrine, *Opelousas (La.) Daily World,* 24 January 1994, 4; Ned Theall, interview by author, 3 July 1991, Lafayette, La., tape recording. For examples of early Boogie Kings swamp pop see Doug Ardoin and the Boogie Kings, "Lost Love," 45 rpm single 101, Jin, 1958; see also several Boogie Kings cuts on Various Artists, *Rockin' Fever,* the Legendary Jay Miller Sessions, vol. 15, long-playing record FLY 540, Flyright, 1978; and Various Artists, *Bayou Beat,* the Legendary Jay Miller Sessions, vol. 26, long-playing record FLY 581, Flyright, 1981. For additional information on the Boogie Kings, see Ned Theall, *Living Like a King* ([New Iberia, La.]: privately published, 1993); and Katrinna Huggs, "The Boogie Kings Are Back," *Lafayette (La.) Times of Acadiana,* 2 October 1991, 28–30. See also the Boogie Kings, "I Love That Swamp Pop Music," *Louisiana Country Soul,* compact disc 9038–2, Jin, 1993.

31. Eddie Shuler, telephone interview by author, 25 September 1991, Lafayette, La., to Lake Charles, La., tape recording; Shuler, telephone interview by author, 7 April 1993, Lafayette, La., to Lake Charles, La., tape recording; Shuler, telephone interview by author, 12 April 1993, Lafayette, La., to Lake Charles, La., interview notes; Shuler to the author, 10 July 1993, TLS, original in the possession of the author; Manny Warner to Eddie Shuler, 26 March 1945, typewritten letter, original in the possession of Eddie Shuler; Notarized document concerning the founding of Eddie Shuler's Goldband Records, 18 May 1993, original registered with the Calcasieu Parish clerk of court's office, Lake Charles, La.; Goldband label promotional discography, original in the possession of Eddie Shuler, Lake Charles, La.; George Khoury, telephone interview by author, 25 September 1991, Lake Charles, La., tape recording; J. D. Miller, interview by author, 21 February 1991, Crowley, La., tape recording; Broven, *South to Louisiana,* 36, 48, 78, 154, 158, 189, 199, 201, 246–48, 270; Shane K. Bernard, "J. D. Miller and Floyd Soileau: A Comparison of Two Small-Town Recordmen of Acadiana," *Louisiana Folklife* 25 (December 1991): 16. For more information on Shuler and Miller, see Leadbitter and Shuler, *From the Bayou;* Leadbitter, *Crowley, Louisiana, Blues;* and Mike Leadbitter, ed., *Nothing But the Blues* (London: Hanover, 1971).

32. Shuler interview, 25 September 1991; Miller interview; Obituary of J. D. Miller, *LaFayette (La.) Daily Advertiser,* 24 March 1996, A-14. Floyd Soileau, interview by au-

thor, 15 February 1991, Ville Platte, La., tape recording; Bernard, "J. D. Miller and Floyd Soileau," 12–13; Broven, *South to Louisiana,* 36–39, 48–49, 51–54, 211–12.

33. Broven, *Rhythm and Blues in New Orleans,* 104–5; Hannusch, *I Hear You Knockin',* 139, 283–84; Carol Rachou, interview by author, 24 October 1991, Lafayette, La., tape recording; Stan Lewis, telephone interview by author, 25 September 1991, Lafayette, La., to Shreveport, La., tape recording; Roland Robin, interview by author, 2 January 1992, Lafayette, La., tape recording; Lee Lavergne, interview by author, 30 January 1991, Church Point, La., tape recording; Khoury interview; S. J. Montalbano, telephone interview by author, 2 October 1991, Lafayette, La., to Baton Rouge, La., tape recording; King interview; Dave Miller, "Local Musicians Swing on the 45's," *Lafayette (La.) Daily Advertiser,* 30 January 1963, B-8; Allan, interview by Harris, part 1, 12.

34. Surname statistics are based on Allan's biographical data for 68 white and 15 black swamp pop performers. These figures should be considered rough (and conservative) estimates, as analysis of surname origins often fails to determine accurately a subject's ethnicity. A person bearing an Anglo-American surname, for instance, might descend from Cajuns through maternal lines, a fact demonstrated by Cajun musicians like Dennis McGee and Lawrence Walker—both of whom possess Anglo-American surnames. In addition, names like Martin or Bernard could represent Cajun, French Creole, or Anglo-American ancestry. Allan, *Memories,* 160–61, 202, 207, 232, 263–68; Glenn R. Conrad, interview by author, 20 July 1992, Lafayette, La., interview notes; Charles Mann, telephone interview by author, 12 September 1991, Lafayette, La., to Lake Charles, La., tape recording; Bobby Page, interview by author, 12 December 1991, Lafayette, La., tape recording; Barry interview, 26 June 1991; Little Alfred interview; Terry interview, 8 January 1992; Johnny Preston, telephone interview by author, 9 October 1991, Lafayette, La., to Nederland, Tex., interview transcript; Jivin' Gene, telephone interview by author, 9 October 1991, Lafayette, La., to Texas City, Tex., interview transcript; Charles interview; Fred interview; Barbara Lynn, interview by author, 31 August 1991, St. Martinville, La., tape recording; Broven, *South to Louisiana,* 183, 187, 190, 207, 212–13, 218, 264, 274, 351, 352, 354, 355, 356, 357, 358.

35. Allan, *Memories,* 160–61; Larry Benicewicz, "Warren and Tommy: Still Crazy after All These Years," *Newsletter of the Baltimore Blues Society,* January 1990, 2; Broven, *South to Louisiana,* 181, 187, 228–31, 263, 265–66; Dale Houston, telephone interview by author, 15 February 1995, Lafayette, La., to Knoxville, Tenn., tape recording; Montalbano interview; Mason McClain, "The Reunion of Dale and Grace," *Gonzales (La.) Jambalaya,* January 1995, 33–35; McLain interview; Katrinna Huggs, "Sweet Dreams," *Lafayette (La.) Times of Acadiana,* 17 April 1991, 12.

36. Allan, *Memories,* 160–61; Broven, *South to Louisiana,* 225–26; Johnnie Allan and Bernice Larson Webb, *Born to Be a Loser: The Jimmy Donley Story* (Lafayette, La.: JADFEL, 1992), xv.

37. Allan, *Memories*, 160–61; Broven, *South to Louisiana*, 281–85; Pareles and Romanowski, *Rolling Stone Encyclopedia*, s.v. "Freddy Fender"; Bill C. Malone, *Country Music, U.S.A.*, rev. ed. (Austin: University of Texas Press, 1991), 312; Joe Carl and the Dukes of Rhythm, *Everybody's Rockin' with the Dukes of Rhythm featuring Joe Carl and Harry Simoneaux*, compact disc RUN CD 7, Rundell (Germany), 1994; Barry interview, 26 June 1991; Bernard, "Joe Barry," 11; Freddy Fender, "Go On Go On" [ca. 1986], demo recording in the possession of Rod Bernard, original in the possession of Huey Meaux.

38. Broven, *South to Louisiana*, 181; Dormon, *People Called Cajuns*, 54.

39. Broven, *South to Louisiana*, 102–3; Lomax, *Cajun Country*, videocassette; Savoy, *Cajun Music*, 66–67.

40. Gable interview, 1 November 1991; Karl interview.

41. Little Alfred interview; Gable interview, 1 November 1991; Vidrine interview.

42. Lil' Bob interview; Karl interview.

43. Gable interview, 1 November 1991; Little Alfred interview; Vidrine interview; Johnnie Allan, "South to Louisiana—The Promised Land," interview by Paul Harris, part 4 (England, 1986), *Now Dig This*, June 1987, 28–29.

44. Thierry and Jacobs interview.

45. Lil' Bob interview; Karl interview; Gable interview, 1 November 1991; "Colored Band Man Faces 'Indecency' Trial over White Evangeline Girl," *Ville Platte (La.) Gazette*, 7 February 1957, front page; "Jail Sentence of Year Imposed on Colored Band Man for 'Indecent Act,'" *Ville Platte (La.) Gazette*, 14 March 1957, front and back pages; Various court documents regarding the arrest and trial of Gabriel King, December 1956–March 1957, originals in the possession of the Evangeline Parish clerk of court's office, Ville Platte, La.; Letter from Gabriel King to his admirer, 13 September 1956, original in the possession of the Evangeline Parish clerk of court's office, Ville Platte, La.

46. "Colored Band Man," front page; "Jail Sentence," front and last page.

47. "Jail Sentence," front and back pages; Obituary of Gabriel King, *Opelousas (La.) Daily World*, 30 December 1988.

48. Dormon, *People Called Cajuns*, 54; "Area Talent Featured at Benefit," undated newspaper clipping from an unidentified source, possibly the *Lafayette (La.) Daily Advertiser*, ca. 1960 [May 1961?], original in the possession of Johnnie Allan, Lafayette, La.; Lil' Bob interview.

49. Karl interview; Rod Bernard interview, 18 October 1991; Bernard, "(I Have a Vow) To Have and Hold," 45 rpm single 237, Jin, 1968; Bernard, "Gimme Back My Cadillac," *Swamp Rock 'n' Roller*, compact disc; Bernard, "My Life Is a Mystery," 45 rpm single 5338, Argo, 1959; Ray Topping, "Rod Bernard Discography," *Goldmine*, 6 July 1984, 46; Bo Berglind and Claes-Håkan Olofsson, "Rod Bernard," *American Music Magazine*, June 1995, 11, 13; Benicewicz, "Rod Bernard and Swamp Pop," 4, 5; Benicewicz, "Guitar Gable and King Karl," 6, 8; Benicewicz, "Clarence 'Jockey' Etienne," 6; Broven, *South to*

Louisiana, 155, 195, 198–99, 206; Katrinna Huggs, "Thirty Years of 'Forever,'" *Lafayette (La.) Times of Acadiana*, 23 November 1988, 40; Bill Millar, "Hot Rod from the Bayou," *Melody Maker*, 4 August 1979, 37; Millar, "Rod Bernard: Hot Rod," *Goldmine*, 6 July 1984, 40, 43.

50. Vidrine interview; Little Alfred interview; Theall interview; Huggs, "Boogie Kings Are Back," 29; *Random House Dictionary of the English Language*, 8th ed., s.v. "boogie."

51. Larry Benicewicz, "Allons à Lafayette," *Newsletter of the Baltimore Blues Society*, April 1988, n.p.; Benicewicz, "Warren and Tommy," 3; Bernard, "Warren Storm," 29, 30; Broven, *South to Louisiana*, 137, 155, 247, 248–49; Broven, *Rhythm and Blues in New Orleans*, 128–30; Hannusch, *I Hear You Knockin'*, 114–15, 132, 199, 310–11; Gillett, *Sound of the City* (1972), 248–49, 258, 262; Peter Guralnick, liner notes for Elvis Presley, *Elvis Presley: The Memphis Record*, compact disc 6221-2-R, RCA, 1987; Pareles and Romanowski, *Rolling Stone Encyclopedia*, s.v. "Booker T. and the MGs"; Rico, "Putting the Fizz in Swamp Pop," 22; Sasfy, "Bayou Beat," 17; Allan interview, 12 June 1991; Bastin, liner notes for *Louisiana "High School Hop"*; Gable interview, 1 November 1991. For additional information on J. D. Miller's session artists, see Larry Benicewicz, "Clarence 'Jockey' Etienne and the Crowley Staff Musicians," *The Newsletter of the Baltimore Blues Society*, January 1994, 4–8.

52. Allan interview, 12 June 1991; Broven, *South to Louisiana*, 182.

53. Allan interview, 12 June 1991.

4. Cajun and Black Creole Elements in Swamp Pop Music

1. Ancelet, *Cajun Music*, 40; Ancelet et al., *Cajun Country*, xvi–xvii, xxi; Ancelet and Morgan, *Makers of Cajun Music*, 31–32; Broven, *South to Louisiana*, 289–90, 292, 293; Dormon, *People Called Cajuns*, 82–87, 88; Dormon, "Louisiana's 'Creoles of Color,'" 622–24.

2. The photograph of Terry appears in Allan, *Memories*, 187; a similar picture (apparently from the same photo session) appears in Broven, *South to Louisiana*, 97. Les Blank and Chris Strachwitz, prods., *J'ai été au bal (I Went to the Dance): The Cajun and Zydeco Music of Louisiana*, 84 min. (Brazos Films, 1990), videocassette; Blank and Strachwitz, *French Dance Tonight: The Cajun and Zydeco Music of Louisiana*, 53 min. (Brazos Films, 1990), videocassette; Chris Strachwitz, "Cajun Country," *The American Folk Music Occasional* 2 (1970): 14. Strachwitz also is quoted in Millar, "Johnnie Allan," 15; and Millar, "Rockin' on the Bayou," 51.

3. D. L. Menard, telephone interview by author, 31 March 1994, Baton Rouge, La., to Erath, La., interview notes; Ancelet, *Cajun Music*, 41–42; Ancelet et al., *Cajun Country*, 159; Ancelet and Morgan, *Makers of Cajun Music*, 50–54; Broven, *South to Louisiana*, 235–37; Savoy, *Cajun Music*, 272; Dormon, *People Called Cajuns*, 76, 77.

4. Rod Bernard interview, 18 October 1991; Rod Bernard, interview by Louis Coco, KLIL radio, Moreauville, La., 23 July 1994, tape recording in the author's possession; Benicewicz, "Rod Bernard and Swamp Pop," 5; Broven, *South to Louisiana*, 208; Millar, "Hot Rod from the Bayou," 37; Millar, "Rod Bernard," 44.

5. French lyrics transcribed and translated by Carl A. Brasseaux. For the phonetic spelling of "Fais Do Do," see record label for Rod Bernard, "Fais Do Do (Fay Doe Doe)," 45 rpm single 1906, Hall-Way, 1962. Rod Bernard, "Fais Do Do," *Swamp Rock 'n' Roller*, compact disc.

6. Brasseaux, *Founding of New Acadia*, 73; Brasseaux, "Scattered to the Wind," 65–67.

7. Gillett, *Sound of the City* (1972), 220–21; Pareles and Romanowski, *Rolling Stone Encyclopedia*, s.v. "Hank Ballard," "Chubby Checker."

8. Angers, *Truth about the Cajuns*, 50–54; Dormon, *People Called Cajuns*, 34–39, 57–63, 72–73; Johnnie Allan, "Cajun Man," *Promised Land*, compact disc CDCHD 380, Ace (UK), 1992.

9. Allan, interview by Harris, part 1, 10.

10. Allan interview, 12 June 1991; Ancelet et al., *Cajun Country*, 22, 24, 27; Post, *Cajun Sketches*, 15, 81.

11. Eddy Raven, "Crawfish Festival Time" and "Alligator Bayou," on Various Artists, *Best of La Louisianne Records*, compact disc; T. K. Hulin, "Alligator Bayou," 45 rpm single 1005, Booray, 1976; Broven, *South to Louisiana*, 277, 278.

12. Allan interview, 12 June 1991; Allan, "South to Louisiana"; Ancelet et al., *Cajun Country*, 160; Broven, *South to Louisiana*, 215; Benicewicz, "Johnnie Allan: Cajun Chronicler," n.p.; Millar, "Cajun and Proud of It," 14; Millar, "Johnnie Allan," 16.

13. Allan interview, 12 June 1991; Broven, *South to Louisiana*, 5, 215.

14. Broven, *South to Louisiana*, 67, 197, 251; Rod Bernard, "Diggy Liggy Lo," *Swamp Rock 'n' Roller*, compact disc; Randy and the Rockets, "Let's Do the Cajun Twist," on Various Artists, *Swamp Gold*, vol. 1, compact disc.

15. Broven, *South to Louisiana*, 18, 237, 333; Gabe Dean, "Slop and Stroll Jolie Blonde," on Various Artists, *Louisiana Rockers*, compact disc CDCHD 491, Ace (UK), 1994.

16. Ancelet, *Cajun Music*, 41; Broven, *South to Louisiana*, 235–36; Cypress City, "Cajun Rap Song," on Various Artists, *Swamp Gold*, vol. 2, compact disc.

17. Hannusch, liner notes for *Swamp Gold*, vol. 2; Angers, *Truth about the Cajuns*, 14–15, 94–102; Dormon, *People Called Cajuns*, 34–35, 60–63, 72–73; Rufus Jagneaux, "The Back Door," on Various Artists, *Swamp Gold*, vol. 3, compact disc 9041–2, Jin, 1994.

18. Ancelet et al., *Cajun Country*, 160; Josef Barrios [Joe Barry], "Je suis bêt pour t'aimer," 45 rpm single 150, Jin, 1961; Johnnie Allan, "Before the Next Teardrop Falls," *Johnnie Allan's Greatest Hits*, long-playing record LP 9017, Jin, 1977; Allan, "Promised Land," *Promised Land*, compact disc; Allan, "Today I Started Loving You Again," *Promised Land*,

compact disc; Broven, *South to Louisiana,* 215, 216, 281–82, 285; Malone, *Country Music, U.S.A.,* 295, 312; Charles Mann, "Walk of Life"; Mann interview.

19. Compare Randy and the Rockets, "Let's Do the Cajun Twist" and Joseph Falcon and Cléoma Breaux, "Allons à Lafayette," on Various Artists, *J'ai été au bal,* vol. 1, compact disc. Also compare the Shondells, "A-2-Fay" [mistakenly listed as Rod Bernard, "A-2-Fee"], on Various Artists, *Lafayette Saturday Night,* compact disc CDCHD 371, Ace (UK), 1992, and Lawrence Walker, "Mamou Two-Step," on Various Artists, *Best of La Louisianne Records,* compact disc. Ancelet, *Cajun Music,* 19–20, 21; Ancelet et al., *Cajun Country,* 150, 157, 167; Broven, *South to Louisiana,* 15, 16–17; Broven, liner notes for Various Artists, *Lafayette Saturday Night,* compact disc; François, *Yé Yaille, Chère!* 13–15, 175–76, 410, 411; Macon Fry, liner notes for Various Artists, *Swamp Gold,* vol. 1, compact disc; Savoy, *Cajun Music,* 91, 103, 106–7, 207, 208; Rachou interview; Rufus Jagneaux, "Opelousas Sostan," on Various Artists, *Swamp Gold,* vol. 1, compact disc; Rufus Jagneaux, "The Back Door"; Rufus (Jagneaux), "Port Barre," 45 rpm single 242, Jin, 1973; Rockin' Sidney, "You Ain't Nothin' but Fine," on Various Artists, *Louisiana Saturday Night,* compact disc.

20. Musical transcriptions in this chapter are by Anne K. Simpson with assistance from David Evans and Arthur E. Riedel. French lyrics were transcribed and translated by Carl A. Brasseaux. Bobby Page and the Riff Raffs, "Hippy-Ti-Yo," 45 rpm single 1338, Ram, 1958. A slightly less rambunctious (and thus somewhat inferior) alternate take, probably recorded during the same session as the version on the original 45 single, appears as Bobby Page [and the Riff Raffs], "Hippy Ti Yo" ["Hippy-Ti-Yo"], on Various Artists, *Shreveport Stomp: Ram Records, Volume 1,* compact disc CDCHD 495, Ace (UK), 1994. Compare the lyrics of "Les haricots sont pas salés" and "Les Huppés Taïaut" in François, *Yé Yaille, Chère!* 160–62, 164–65; and "Ils ont volé mon traîneau" ("Il la volés mon trancas") and "Les haricots sont pas salés" ("Zydeco est pas salé") in Savoy, *Cajun Music,* 108, 392–93. Numerous versions of "Hip et Taïaut" and related songs appear on compact disc, but for comparison see Jimmy "C" Newman, "Hippy Tai Yo," on Various Artists, *Lafayette Saturday Night,* compact disc; Clifton Chenier, "Zydeco Sont Pas Salés," on Various Artists, *J'ai été au bal (I Went to the Dance: The Cajun and Zydeco Music of Louisiana,* vol. 2, compact disc CD-332, Arhoolie, 1990; and Breaux Frères, "T'as volé mon chapeau," on Various Artists, *Cajun, Volume 1: Abbeville Breakdown, 1929–1939,* Roots N' Blues series, compact disc CK 46220, Columbia, 1990. Broven, *South to Louisiana,* 186–87; Page interview; Perkins interview, 22 October 1991.

21. Post's interview with Joseph Falcon is adapted from Savoy, *Cajun Music,* 95–96. Brasseaux interview; Broven, *South to Louisiana,* 20, 75, 187, 261; François, *Yé Yaille, Chère!* 160–62, 164–65; Savoy, *Cajun Music,* 108, 122, 392–93; Breaux Frères, "T'as volé mon chapeau."

22. Lomax, *Cajun Country,* videocassette; John I. White, *Git Along, Little Dogies: Songs and Songmakers of the American West* (Urbana: University Press of Illinois, 1975), 16–26;

Ancelet et al., *Cajun Country,* xiv, 35; Brasseaux, *Founding of New Acadia,* 148; Tissa Porter, "Creole Trailrides . . . A Zydeco What?" *Creole Culture Magazine,* September 1991, 5–8; François, *Yé Yaille, Chère!* 164; *Oxford English Dictionary,* 2d ed., s.v. "tallyho"; Savoy, *Cajun Music,* 103.

23. Paul Tate, "The Cajuns of Louisiana," *American Folk Music Occasional* 2 (1970): 12; François, *Yé Yaille, Chère!* 28–30, 127–29, 130–31, 164–65; Barry Jean Ancelet, "Zydeco/Zarico: Beans, Blues and Beyond," *Black Music Research Journal* 8, no. 1 (1988): 45–47.

24. For additional data on "Colinda," see Shane K. Bernard and Julia Girouard, "'Colinda': Mysterious Origins of a Cajun Folksong," *Journal of Folklore Research,* 29 (January–April 1992): 37–52; and John Houlston Cowley, "Music and Migration: Aspects of Black Music in the British Caribbean, the United States, and Britain, before the Independence of Jamaica and Trinidad and Tobago" (Ph.D. diss., University of Warwick, Coventry, England, 1992), 71–94, 555–58. Rod Bernard interview, 18 October 1991; Broven, *South to Louisiana,* 208–9.

25. French lyrics transcribed and translated by Carl A. Brasseaux; Rod Bernard's version of "Colinda" is available on *Swamp Rock 'n' Roller,* compact disc; Rod Bernard interview, 18 October 1991.

26. Bernard Grun and Werner Stein, *The Timetables of History: A Horizontal Linkage of People and Events,* 3d rev. ed. (New York: Simon and Shuster/Touchstone, 1991), 70, 170, 249; Lee Warren, *The Dance of Africa: An Introduction* (Englewood Cliffs, N.J.: Prentice-Hall, 1972), 45–46; Dena J. Epstein, *Sinful Tunes and Spirituals: Black Folk Music to the Civil War* (Urbana: University of Illinois Press, 1977), 27–28.

27. R. Nettel, "Historical Introduction to 'La Calinda,'" *Music and Letters* 27 (January 1946): 60; Epstein, *Sinful Tunes,* 31–32, 135; George Washington Cable, "Creole Slave Songs," *Century Magazine* 31 (April 1886): 815–17; Harold Courlander, *Haiti Singing* (Chapel Hill: University of North Carolina, 1939), 71–72, 88; Courlander, *The Drum and the Hoe: Life and Lore of the Haitian People* (Berkeley: University of California Press, 1960), 132–33.

28. Mina Monroe, comp. and ed., *Bayou Ballads: Twelve Folk-Songs from Louisiana,* Schirmer's American Folk-Songs Series, set 2 (New York: G. Schirmer, 1921), vii; J. D. Elder, "*Kalinda*—Song of the Battling Troubadours of Trinidad," *Journal of the Folklore Institute* 3 (August 1966): 192–203.

29. Translated by Richard Guidry. Quoted in Epstein, *Sinful Tunes,* 94.

30. Monroe, *Bayou Ballads,* 40–55; Irène Thérèse Whitfield, *Louisiana French Folk Songs* (Baton Rouge: Louisiana State University Press, 1939), 135–37; George Washington Cable, "The Dance in Place Congo," *Century Magazine* 31 (February 1886): 528; Glenn R. Conrad, ed., *A Dictionary of Louisiana Biography* (Lafayette: University of Southwestern Louisiana, Center for Louisiana Studies/Louisiana Historical Association, 1988), s.v. "Mazureau, Etienne."

31. Performed by Godar Chalvin, 1956, Abbeville, La., field recording in the possession of Michael Doucet, Lafayette, La. This translation is based closely on Doucet's. The song also appears in Harry Oster, *Living Country Blues* (Detroit: Folklore Associates, 1969), 417–18.

32. Broven, *South to Louisiana,* 33; François, *Yé Yaille, Chère!* 443–45.

33. Savoy, *Cajun Music,* 95–96.

34. Ibid., 54, 62–63, 96; François, *Yé Yaille, Chère!* 209–11; Dennis McGee, "Madame Young donnez moi votre plus jolie blonde," on Various Artists, *Louisiana Cajun Music, Volume Five, The Early Years, 1928–1938,* long-playing record OTR 114, Old Timey Records, 1973; Broven, *South to Louisiana,* 39; Oran "Doc" Guidry, Sr., interview by author, 2 November 1991, Lafayette, La., tape recording; Miller interview; Jimmie Davis, "Colinda," 78 rpm single 28748, Decca 1953.

35. Rod Bernard interview, 18 October 1991.

36. Allan, "With Johnnie Allan," 39; Savoy, *Cajun Music,* 194, 202–3; François, *Yé Yaille, Chère!* 334; Broven, *South to Louisiana,* 210; Jay Randall, telephone interview by author, 8 January 1992, Lafayette, La., to Opelousas, La., tape recording; Rod Bernard and Clifton Chenier, *Boogie in Black & White,* long-playing record LP 9014, Jin, 1976.

5. The Future of Swamp Pop

1. Palmer, *Tale of Two Cities,* 1.

2. Palmer, *Tale of Two Cities,* 1; Allan, "With Johnnie Allan," 38; Storm interview, 13 June 1991.

3. Broven, *South to Louisiana,* 179, 281; Malone, *Southern Music/American Music,* 106–7; Rod Bernard, "Recorded in England," *Swamp Rock 'n' Roller,* compact disc.

4. Broven, *South to Louisiana,* 225, 228–31, 265; Fred interview; Pareles and Romanowski, *Rolling Stone Encyclopedia,* s.v. "John Fred and His Playboy Band"; McLain interview: see also McLain, "Tommy McLain Interviewed," telephone interview by Shane K. Bernard (Lafayette, La., to Alexandria, La., 18 September 1991), transcribed by John Stafford, *Now Dig This,* September 1993, 26.

5. Karl interview; Gable interview, 1 November 1991; Storm interview, 13 June 1991; Mann interview; Perkins interview, 22 October 1991; Page interview; Jivin' Gene interview; Preston interview; West interview; Little Alfred interview; McLain interview.

6. Skip Stewart, interview by author, 4 August 1991, Opelousas, La., tape recording.

7. Barry interview, 26 June 1991; Bernard, "Joe Barry," 10; Allan, interview by Harris, part 4, 28–30; Allan and Webb, *Born to Be a Loser,* 287, 289, 293, 298; Rod Bernard, interview by author, 9 September 1992, Lafayette, La., interview notes; Benicewicz, "Rod Bernard and Swamp Pop," 6; Herman Fuselier, "This Couldn't Go On Forever: Rod Bernard Recalls Roots of Swamp Pop," *Opelousas (La.) Daily World,* TV & Entertainment

section, 7 April 1994, 1, 26; McLain interview; Page interview; Broven, *South to Louisiana,* 223–24.

8. Huggs, "Thirty Years of 'Forever,'" 40.

9. KLOU radio station (Lake Charles, La.) playlist dated 13 July 1968, original in the possession of Rod Bernard; Broven, *South to Louisiana,* 191.

10. Ancelet, *Cajun Music,* 44–50; Ancelet et al., *Cajun Country,* 161–63; Broven, *South to Louisiana,* 232–33.

11. Ancelet, *Cajun Music,* 44–50; Ancelet et al., *Cajun Country,* 161–63; Ancelet and Morgan, *Makers of Cajun Music,* 93–94, 141–42, 146–47; Benicewicz, "Rod Bernard and Swamp Pop," 6; Broven, *South to Louisiana,* 288.

12. Ancelet, *Cajun Music,* 46–47, 50; Ancelet et al., *Cajun Country,* 161–63; Benny Graeff, interview by author, 24 June 1991, Lafayette, La., tape recording; Victor Palmer, telephone interview by author, 2 May 1994, Baton Rouge, La., to Lafayette, La., interview notes; Todd Mouton, "Return of 'Da Beans,'" *Lafayette (La.) Times of Acadiana,* 19 April 1995, 53–54.

13. Charles interview; Allan and Webb, *Born to Be a Loser,* 321; Benicewicz, "Poet of the Bayou," 2; Benicewicz, "Warren and Tommy," 3; Broven, *Rhythm and Blues in New Orleans,* 78–79, 231–32; Broven, *South to Louisiana,* 182–3, 185.

14. Broven, *Rhythm and Blues in New Orleans,* 78–79, 233; Broven, *South to Louisiana,* 76–79, 182–3, 185; Hannusch, *I Hear You Knockin',* 361, 362, 363; Ford "Snooks" Eaglin, "Irene," on Various Artists, *Black Top Blues-A-Rama, Vol. 6—Live at Tipitina's,* compact disc CD-BT-1073, Black Top, 1992; Joe Hudson and His Rockin' Dukes, "Baby Give Me a Chance," Silas Hogan, "Everybody Needs Somebody," and Slim Harpo, "Rainin' in My Heart," on Various Artists, *Sound of the Swamp,* compact disc.

15. Broven, *South to Louisiana,* 183–84, 281–86; Gillett, *Sound of the City* (1972), 97; Pareles and Romanowski, *Rolling Stone Encyclopedia,* s.v. "Bobby Charles," "Freddy Fender," "Bill Haley," "The Osmonds," "Sir Douglas Quintet"; Partridge, *Dictionary of Slang,* s.v. "See you later—alligator!"; Elvis Presley, "Pledging My Love," *Moody Blue,* compact disc 2428-2-R, RCA, 1977; Rod Bernard, "Pledging My Love," *Night Lights and Love Songs,* long-playing record LP 9010, Jin, 1975; Allan interview, 12 June 1991; Allan, interview by Harris, part 2, 10–11; Benicewicz, "Johnnie Allan: Cajun Chronicler," n.p.; Mike Flood Page, "Were These Guys Robbed of Their Hit by This Man?" *Sounds,* 8 March 1975, 28; McLain interview; Anson Funderburgh and the Rockets, "This Should Go On Forever," *Talk to You by Hand,* compact disc CD-BT-1001, Black Top, 1984; Sam Myers and Anson Funderburgh, "Life Problem," *My Love is Here to Stay,* compact disc CD-BT-1032, Black Top, 1986; T. Graham Brown, "I Tell It Like It Used to Be," *Greatest Hits,* compact disc CDP 7-941662-2, Capitol, 1990; Mark Collie, "Shame Shame Shame Shame," *Mark Collie,* compact disc MCAD 10658, MCA, 1993; Billy Joe Royal, "Burned Like a Rocket," *Greatest*

Hits, compact disc 82199–2, Atlantic, 1991; *Guinness Encyclopedia of Popular Music,* 1st ed., s.v. "Dale and Grace."

16. Gillett, *Sound of the City* (1972), 97, 263; Pareles and Romanowski, *Rolling Stone Encyclopedia,* s.v. "Creedence Clearwater Revival," "Dale Hawkins," "Tony Joe White."

17. Chas and Dave, "Ain't No Pleasing You," 45 rpm single KOR 14, Rockney, 1982; Johnnie Allan, "Ain't No Pleasing You," *Thanks for the Memories,* long-playing record 9026, Jin, 1983; Broven, *South to Louisiana,* 294; Millar, "Sounds of the Swamp," 1455; The Rolling Stones, "Oh Baby (We Got a Good Thing Goin')," *The Rolling Stones, Now!,* compact disc CD 509, Abkco, 1986; Pareles and Romanowski, *Rolling Stone Encyclopedia,* s.v. "The Rolling Stones," "The Beatles"; Gillett, *Sound of the City* (1972), 190–91; The Beatles, "Oh! Darling," *Abbey Road,* compact disc CDP 7 46446 2, Parlophone, 1987; William J. Dowlding, *Beatlesongs* (New York: Fireside, 1989), 282; Mark Lewisohn, *The Beatles Recording Sessions* (New York: Harmony, 1990), 174, 180; Riley, *Tell Me Why,* 319–21; Floyd Soileau, interviewer unknown, *Gris-Gris* (Baton Rouge, La.), 26 February–4 March 1979, n.p.

18. Dowlding, *Beatlesongs,* 282; Allan, *Memories,* 183; Broven, *South to Louisiana,* 128–34; Fred interview.

19. Lee Lavergne, interview by author, 1 November 1991, Church Point, La., interview notes; Randall interview; Jay Randall and the Epics, "Oh! Darling," 45 rpm single 548, Lanor, 1970; Lanor label discography, original in the possession of Lee Lavergne, Church Point, La.; Ancelet et al., *Cajun Country,* 159; Warren Storm, telephone interview by author, 9 October 1991, Lafayette, La., interview notes; Peter Brown and Steven Gaines, *The Love You Make: An Insider's Story of the Beatles* (New York: Signet, 1984), 78.

20. The Honeydrippers, "Sea of Love," *The Honeydrippers: Volume One,* compact disc 90220–2, Es Paranza/Atlantic, 1984; Pareles and Romanowski, *Rolling Stone Encyclopedia,* s.v. "Del Shannon"; *Sea of Love,* 113 min., MCA Home Video, 1989, videocassette; *Bull Durham,* 108 min., Orion Home Video, 1989, videocassette; Los Lobos, "I Got Loaded," *How Will the Wolf Survive?* compact disc 25177, Slash/Warner Bros., 1984; *Scandal,* 105 min., HBO Video, 1989, videocassette; James Lee Burke, *Black Cherry Blues* (New York: Avon, 1990), 3.

21. Allan interview, 12 June 1991; Allan interview, 20 October 1992; Allan, interview by Harris, part 2, 10–11; Allan, "South Louisiana—The Promised Land: Johnnie Allan," interview by Paul Harris, part 3 (England, 1986), *Now Dig This,* May 1987, 7–8; Allan, comp., "Johnnie Allan Discography," ed. Shane K. Bernard (Lafayette, La.: Privately published), 1994, 1–9; Broven, *South to Louisiana,* 215–16; Jill Furmanovsky, "The 'Coon Ass' Guide to London," *Sounds,* 8 April 1978; Mann interview; Lil' Bob interview; Storm interview, 13 June 1991; Author's notes taken from 1991 Utrecht *Blues Estafette* program, original in the possession of Warren Storm, Lafayette, La.; Shane K. Bernard, comp. and ed., "Rod Bernard Discography" (Lafayette, La.: Privately published, 1994), 1–7; Berglind and Olofs-

son, "Rod Bernard," 11–15; Shane K. Bernard, comp. and ed., *Bernard's Swamp Pop Music Source Book: A Semi-Official and Highly Incomplete Bibliography and Compact Disc-ography of South Louisiana Swamp Pop Music*, no. 3 (January 1995), privately published, 20–28.

22. Various Artists, *Alligator Stomp: Cajun and Zydeco Classics*, vols. 1–3, compact discs R2 70946, R2 70740, R2 70312, Rhino, 1990; Various Artists, *Alligator Stomp, Vol. 4: Cajun Christmas*, compact disc R2 71058, Rhino, 1992; *Alligator Stomp, Vol. 5: Cajun and Zydeco— The Next Generation*, compact disc R2 71846, Rhino, 1995; Various Artists, *Sound of the Swamp*, compact disc; Various Artists, *New Orleans Party Classics*, compact disc R2 70587, Rhino, 1992; Various Artists, *Chess New Orleans*, compact disc CHD2–9355, MCA/Chess, 1995; Various Artists, *J'ai été au bal*, vol. 2, compact disc.

23. Ben Sandmel, "Floyd Soileau," *Louisiana Life*, Winter 1994/95, 32; Graeff interview, 24 June 1991.

24. Rico, "Putting the Fizz in Swamp Pop," 22; Allan, "With Johnnie Allan," 39; Broven, *South to Louisiana*, 292.

25. Broven, *South to Louisiana*, 216–17, 314; Sasfy, "Bayou Beat," 17; Allan, interview by Harris, part 3, 7; Program of the 1984 New Orleans Jazz and Heritage Festival, original in the possession of the author; Rico, "Putting the Fizz in Swamp Pop," 22; Ancelet interview.

26. "Acadian Museum Gets Senate OK," *Lafayette (La.) Daily Advertiser*, 5 April 1995, A-5; Herman Fuselier, "Acadian Music Heritage Museum Slated at Church Point," *Opelousas (La.) Daily World*, 22 June 1995, 1, 14; Louisiana Senate Concurrent Resolution No. 16 (recognizing the Acadian Music Heritage Museum in Church Point as the official music heritage museum for Cajun, zydeco, and swamp pop), ca. June 1995; "Swamp Pop Is Clarified," letter by Johnnie Allan, *Lafayette (La.) Daily Advertiser*, 12 April 1995, D-3; Louisiana House of Representatives Concurrent Resolution No. 187 (recognizing Ville Platte as the "Swamp Pop Capital of the World"), ca. June 1995.

27. Rico, "Putting the Fizz in Swamp Pop," 22; Allan, "With Johnnie Allan," 39; Broven, *South to Louisiana*, 292.

28. Ancelet, *Cajun Music*, 51; Broven, *South to Louisiana*, 101–2, 104–5, 108–10, 185–86; Ancelet, introduction to *Cajun Music and Zydeco*, x; Ancelet, "Zydeco/Zarico," 48; Savoy, *Cajun Music*, 305–6.

Case Study: Huey "Cookie" Thierry

1. Broven, *South to Louisiana*, 187–89; Allan, interview by Harris, part 4, 28–29; Thierry and Jacobs interview.

2. Thierry and Jacobs interview.

3. Ibid.

4. Ibid.

5. Ibid.

6. Ibid.; Contract between Goldband Records and the Boogie Ramblers; Leadbitter and Shuler, *From the Bayou,* 33–34; Leadbitter and Slaven, *Blues Records,* vol. 1, 278; Terry interview, 8 January 1992; Broven, *South to Louisiana,* 78, 188.

7. Thierry and Jacobs interview.

8. Ibid.; Khoury interview; Broven, *South to Louisiana,* 153, 187; Gillett, *Sound of the City* (1972), 110–11; Escott with Hawkins, *Good Rockin' Tonight,* 203, 221.

9. Thierry identifies the place where "Mathilda" was recorded as KOAK radio station in Lake Charles; however, the correct call letters, KAOK, are cited by Jacobs. Thierry and Jacobs interview.

10. Ibid.; Ernest Jacobs, telephone interview by author, 5 September 1995, Bryan, Tex., to Lake Charles, La., interview notes; Broven, *South to Louisiana,* 335; Leadbitter and Slaven, *Blues Records,* vol. 1, 367; Leadbitter, Leslie Fancourt and Paul Pelletier, comps., *Blues Records, 1943–1970,* vol. 2, L–Z (London: Record Information Services, 1994), 79; Little Alfred interview.

11. Thierry and Jacobs interview; Jacobs interview.

12. Thierry and Jacobs interview.

13. Ibid.

14. Ibid.; Program of the 1995 Louisiana Folklife Festival (Monroe, La.), original in the possession of the author.

Case Study: King Karl and Guitar Gable

1. Karl interview; Gable interview, 1 November 1991.

2. Broven, *South to Louisiana,* 154–55; Benicewicz, "Guitar Gable and King Karl," 4, 7; Benicewicz, "Clarence 'Jockey' Etienne," 6; Karl interview; Allan, *Memories,* 207.

3. Karl interview; Benicewicz, "Guitar Gable and King Karl," 7.

4. Karl interview.

5. Ibid.; Benicewicz, "Guitar Gable and King Karl," 7.

6. Karl interview; Benicewicz, "Guitar Gable and King Karl," 7–8; Post, *Cajun Sketches,* 76, 190.

7. Guitar Gable, telephone interview by author, 22 October 1995, Bryan Tex., to Bellevue, La., interview notes; Gable interview, 1 November 1991; Benicewicz, "Guitar Gable and King Karl," 5; Brasseaux, *Founding of New Acadia,* 99; Allan, *Memories,* 207; Broven, *South to Louisiana,* 325.

8. Gable interview, 1 November 1991; Guitar Gable, telephone interview by author, 24 April 1994, Baton Rouge, La., to Bellevue, La., interview notes; Broven, *South to Louisiana,* 155, 329, 330; Ancelet et al., *Cajun Country,* 166–67; Lil' Bob interview; Benicewicz, "Guitar Gable and King Karl," 5; Benicewicz, "Clarence 'Jockey' Etienne," 6.

9. Gable interview, 1 November 1991; Broven, *Rhythm and Blues in New Orleans,* 98; Hannusch, *I Hear You Knockin',* 365; Benicewicz, "Guitar Gable and King Karl," 5–6; Benicewicz, "Clarence 'Jockey' Etienne," 6.

10. Gable interview, 1 November 1991; Karl interview; Benicewicz, "Guitar Gable and King Karl," 7.

11. Gable interview, 1 November 1991; Karl interview; Lee Lavergne, interview by author, 30 January 1991, Church Point, La., tape recording; Broven, *South to Louisiana,* 154–55; Benicewicz, "Guitar Gable and King Karl," 6, 8.

12. Broven, *South to Louisiana,* 154; Karl interview.

13. Gable interview, 1 November 1991; Karl interview; Broven, *South to Louisiana,* 154–55; Benicewicz, "Guitar Gable and King Karl," 6; Benicewicz, "Clarence 'Jockey' Etienne," 4, 6.

14. Guitar Gable, interview by author, 27 November 1991, Bellevue, La., interview notes; Karl interview; Broven, *South to Louisiana,* 154, 155, 195, 198–99, 206; Benicewicz, "Guitar Gable and King Karl," 6, 8; Benicewicz, "Clarence 'Jockey' Etienne," 6; Benicewicz, "Rod Bernard and Swamp Pop," 4, 5; Rod Bernard interview, 18 October 1991; Huggs, "Thirty Years of 'Forever,'" 40; Millar, "Hot Rod from the Bayou," 37; Millar, "Rod Bernard: Hot Rod," 40, 43.

15. Karl interview; Rod Bernard interview, 18 October 1991; Rod Bernard, "(I Have a Vow) To Have and Hold"; Rod Bernard, "Gimme Back My Cadillac"; Rod Bernard, "My Life Is a Mystery"; Topping, "Rod Bernard Discography," 46; Berglind and Olofsson, "Rod Bernard," 9; Benicewicz, "Guitar Gable and King Karl," 6.

16. Gable interview, 27 November 1991; Karl interview; Broven, *South to Louisiana,* 154, 155, 195, 198–99, 206; Benicewicz, "Guitar Gable and King Karl," 6, 8; Benicewicz, "Clarence 'Jockey' Etienne," 6–7; Leadbitter and Slaven, *Blues Records,* vol. 1, 171.

17. Gable interview, 1 November 1991; Gable interview, 27 November 1991; Karl interview; Benicewicz, "Guitar Gable and King Karl," 6, 8–9; Benicewicz, "Clarence 'Jockey' Etienne," 6–7; La Louisianne and Tamm label discographies, originals in the possession of David Rachou, Lafayette, La.

18. Karl interview; Gable interview, 1 November 1991; Benicewicz, "Guitar Gable and King Karl," 9; Herman Fuselier, "Swamp Pop Duo Reunited," *Opelousas (La.) Daily World,* 19 October 1995, TV and Entertainment section, 1, 8.

Case Study: Bobby Charles

1. Broven, *Rhythm and Blues in New Orleans,* 79–80; Broven, *South to Louisiana,* 182–85; Charles interview; Katrinna Huggs, "See Ya' Now, Bobby Charles," *Lafayette (La.) Times of Acadiana,* 15 October 1986, 14.

2. Charles interview; Benicewicz, "Poet of the Bayou," 2; Broven, *Rhythm and Blues in New Orleans,* 79; Broven, *South to Louisiana,* 183, 325; Huggs, "See Ya' Now, Bobby Charles," 14.

3. Charles interview.

4. Perkins interview, 22 October 1991; Broven, *South to Louisiana,* 183; Storm interview, 13 June 1991.

5. Charles interview.

6. Ibid.; Benicewicz, "Poet of the Bayou," 2; Broven, *Rhythm and Blues in New Orleans,* 79; Broven, *South to Louisiana,* 183; Huggs, "See Ya' Now, Bobby Charles," 14.

7. Charles interview; Benicewicz, "Poet of the Bayou," 2; Broven, *South to Louisiana,* 183–84.

8. Broven, *Rhythm and Blues in New Orleans,* 79; Broven, *South to Louisiana,* 184; Charles interview; Huggs, "See Ya' Now, Bobby Charles," 14; author's notes taken from promotional press release about Bobby Charles, original in the possession of Bobby Charles, Holly Beach, La.

9. Charles interview; Benicewicz, "Poet of the Bayou," 2; Broven, *Rhythm and Blues in New Orleans,* 79, 231; Broven, *South to Louisiana,* 183, 185; Hannusch, *I Hear You Knockin',* 360; Leadbitter and Slaven, *Blues Records,* vol. 1, 357. South Louisiana performer Charles "C. C." Adcock was present during the author's interview with Bobby Charles.

10. Charles interview; Broven, *Rhythm and Blues in New Orleans,* 79, 80; Broven, *South to Louisiana,* 210, 215, 231, 264; Simoneaux interview.

11. Charles interview; Benicewicz, "Poet of the Bayou," 2–3; Broven, *Rhythm and Blues in New Orleans,* 80; Broven, *South to Louisiana,* 185; Huggs, "See Ya' Now, Bobby Charles," 15; Pareles and Romanowski, *Rolling Stone Encyclopedia,* s.v. "Bobby Charles."

12. Charles interview; Benicewicz, "Poet of the Bayou," 3; Broven, *South to Louisiana,* 185; Huggs, "See Ya' Now, Bobby Charles," 14–15, 16–17; author's notes taken from promotional press release about Bobby Charles.

13. Charles interview.

Case Study: Warren Storm

1. Benicewicz, "Allons à Lafayette," n.p.; Benicewicz, "Warren and Tommy," 4; Broven, *South to Louisiana,* 137, 248–49.

2. For more information on the name *Schexnider,* see William A. Read, *Louisiana-French* (Baton Rouge: Louisiana State University Press, 1931), 111–12. Allan, *Memories,* 161, 267; Benicewicz, "Warren and Tommy," 4; Broven, *South to Louisiana,* 246, 326; Storm interview, 13 June 1991; Storm interview, 5 October 1992.

3. Storm interview, 13 June 1991; Storm interview, 5 October 1992; Benicewicz, "Warren and Tommy," 4; Broven, *South to Louisiana,* 246–47.

4. Storm is quoted in Broven, *South to Louisiana,* 247. Storm interview, 13 June 1991; Storm interview, 5 October 1992; Benicewicz, "Warren and Tommy," 4.

5. Storm interview, 13 June 1991; Benicewicz, "Warren and Tommy," 4; Broven, *South to Louisiana,* 247–48; The Alley Boys of Abbeville, "Tu ma quité seul," ("Prisoner's Song"), on Various Artists, *Abbeville Breakdown,* compact disc; Malone, *Country Music, U.S.A.,* 61, 62, 64.

6. Storm interview, 13 June 1991; Broven, *South to Louisiana,* 248.

7. Storm interview, 13 June 1991; Storm interview, 5 October 1992; Benicewicz, "Warren and Tommy," 4; Broven, *South to Louisiana,* 187, 248, 335, 337; Malone, *Country Music, U.S.A.,* 104.

8. Storm interview, 13 June 1991; Storm interview, 5 October 1992; Benicewicz, "Warren and Tommy," 4–5; Broven, *South to Louisiana,* 249.

9. Storm interview, 13 June 1991; Broven, *South to Louisiana,* 250; Benicewicz, "Warren and Tommy," 4–5.

10. Storm interview, 13 June 1991; Storm interview, 5 October 1992; Benicewicz, "Warren and Tommy," 5; Broven, *South to Louisiana,* 250; promotional press release about Warren Storm, original in the possession of Warren Storm, Lafayette, La.

11. Storm interview, 13 June 1991; Storm interview, 5 October 1992; Benicewicz, "Warren and Tommy," 5; Broven, *South to Louisiana,* 250.

Case Study: Rod Bernard

1. Broven, *South to Louisiana,* 188, 196.

2. Rod Bernard interview, 9 September 1992; Rod Bernard interview, 18 October 1991; Allan, *Memories,* 160; Broven, *South to Louisiana,* 196–97, 325.

3. Rod Bernard interview, 18 October 1991; Benicewicz, "Rod Bernard and Swamp Pop," 4; Broven, *South to Louisiana,* 196–97; Millar, "Hot Rod from the Bayou," 37; Millar, "Rod Bernard," 40.

4. Rod Bernard interview, 18 October 1991; Benicewicz, "Rod Bernard and Swamp Pop," 4; Broven, *South to Louisiana,* 197; Millar, "Hot Rod from the Bayou," 37; Millar, "Rod Bernard," 40.

5. Rod Bernard interview, 18 October 1991; Benicewicz, "Rod Bernard and Swamp Pop," 4; Broven, *South to Louisiana,* 197; Millar, "Hot Rod from the Bayou," 37; Millar, "Rod Bernard," 40; Malone, *Country Music, U.S.A.,* 242.

6. Rod Bernard interview, 18 October 1991; Benicewicz, "Rod Bernard and Swamp Pop," 4; Broven, *South to Louisiana,* 197; Millar, "Hot Rod from the Bayou," 37; Millar, "Rod Bernard," 40; Sara Marsteller, "Rodney Bernard, 14, Plays Guitar, Sings 'Cajun' Tunes," *Beaumont (Tex.) Journal,* ca. 10 November 1954.

7. Rod Bernard interview, 18 October 1991; Benicewicz, "Rod Bernard and Swamp Pop," 4; Broven, *South to Louisiana,* 197–98; Millar, "Hot Rod from the Bayou," 37; Millar, "Rod Bernard," 40.

8. Rod Bernard interview, 18 October 1991; Benicewicz, "Rod Bernard and Swamp Pop," 4; Broven, *South to Louisiana,* 198; Millar, "Hot Rod from the Bayou," 37; Millar, "Rod Bernard," 40.

9. Rod Bernard interview, 18 October 1991; Benicewicz, "Rod Bernard and Swamp Pop," 4–5; Broven, *South to Louisiana,* 196, 200–207, 335; Millar, "Hot Rod from the Bayou," 37; Millar, "Rod Bernard," 43–44; Huggs, "Thirty Years of 'Forever,'" 39, 40; undated *Hit Parade* clipping [1959], original in the possession of Rod Bernard, Lafayette, La.; various undated *Cashbox* clippings [1959], originals in the possession of Rod Bernard, Lafayette, La. See also Bernard, "A Swamp Rock 'n' Roller Remembers" (1994), 5–8; Bernard, "A Swamp Rock 'n' Roller Remembers," (1995), 64, 66, 129, 132, 138.

10. Rod Bernard interview, 18 October 1991; Benicewicz, "Rod Bernard and Swamp Pop," 5; Huggs, "Thirty Years of 'Forever,'" 40; Millar, "Hot Rod from the Bayou," 37; Millar, "Rod Bernard," 44; Broven, *South to Louisiana,* 207–9.

11. Rod Bernard interview, 18 October 1991; Benicewicz, "Rod Bernard and Swamp Pop," 5–6; Broven, *South to Louisiana,* 209–10; Millar, "Hot Rod from the Bayou," 37, 42; Millar, "Rod Bernard," 44.

12. Rod Bernard interview, 9 September 1992; Benicewicz, "Rod Bernard and Swamp Pop," 6; Fuselier, "This Couldn't Go On Forever," 1, 26; Broven, *South to Louisiana,* 210; Huggs, "Thirty Years of 'Forever,'" 40; Millar, "Hot Rod from the Bayou," 42; Millar, "Rod Bernard," 44.

13. Rod Bernard interview, 18 October 1991; Benicewicz, "Rod Bernard and Swamp Pop," 6; Broven, *South to Louisiana,* 210; Huggs, "Thirty Years of 'Forever,'" 39, 40; Millar, "Hot Rod from the Bayou," 42; Millar, "Rod Bernard," 44, 46.

Case Study: Johnnie Allan

1. Broven, *South to Louisiana,* 216; Allan, *Memories,* back cover; Benicewicz, "Johnnie Allan: Cajun Chronicler," n.p.; Allan, interview by Paul Harris, part 3, 7; Allan, "With Johnnie Allan," 37–38; Allan interview, 12 June 1991.

2. Allan interview, 12 June 1991; Allan, interview by Harris, part 1, 10–11; Benicewicz, "Johnnie Allan: Cajun Chronicler," n.p.; Millar, "Cajun and Proud of It," 14; Millar, "Johnnie Allan," 15.

3. Allan, interview by Harris, part 1, 11; Millar, "Johnnie Allan," 15; Millar, "Cajun and Proud of It," 14; Allan interview, 12 June 1991; Malone, *Country Music, U.S.A.,* 33, 67, 98–100.

4. Benicewicz, "Johnnie Allan: Cajun Chronicler," n.p.; Broven, *South to Louisiana,* 214; Millar, "Cajun and Proud of It," 14; Millar, "Johnnie Allan," 15; Allan, interview by Harris, part 1, 11; Allan interview, 12 June 1991.

5. Millar, "Cajun and Proud of It," 14; Millar, "Johnnie Allan," 15; Johnnie Allan, "Johnnie Allan Discography," 1; Allan, interview by Harris, part 1, 11.

6. South Louisiana performer Charles "C. C." Adcock was present during the author's interview with Johnnie Allan. Millar, "Cajun and Proud of It," 14; Millar, "Johnnie Allan," 15; Allan, interview by Harris, part 1, 11–12; Allan interview, 12 June 1991.

7. Although at least one source states that Allan's first group initially was called the Rhythm Kings, Allan confirms it actually was called the Rhythm Rockers. Allan, interview by Harris, part 1, 11; Allan interview, 20 October 1992; Broven, *South to Louisiana,* 214; Benicewicz, "Johnnie Allan: Cajun Chronicler," n.p.; Millar, "Cajun and Proud of It," 14; Millar, "Johnnie Allan," 15.

8. Allan interview, 12 June 1991.

9. Millar, "Cajun and Proud of It," 14; Millar, "Johnnie Allan," 15; Broven, *South to Louisiana,* 214; Allan, interview by Harris, part 1, 11–12; Allan interview, 12 June 1991.

10. Benicewicz, "Johnnie Allan: Cajun Chronicler," n.p.; Broven, *South to Louisiana,* 214–15; Millar, "Cajun and Proud of It," 14; Millar, "Johnnie Allan," 15–16; Allan, interview by Harris, part 1, 12; Allan, interview by Harris, part 2, 9; Allan interview, 12 June 1991.

11. Allan interview, 12 June 1991; Allan, interview by Harris, part 2, 9–10; Benicewicz, "Johnnie Allan: Cajun Chronicler," n.p.; Broven, *South to Louisiana,* 215–16; Aycock, "Johnny Allen," 62; Millar, "Cajun and Proud of It," 14; Millar, "Johnnie Allan," 16.

12. Allan interview, 12 June 1991; Allan, interview by Harris, part 2, 9–11; Allan, interview by Harris, part 3, 7–8; Allan, "With Johnnie Allan," 37–38; Benicewicz, "Johnnie Allan: Cajun Chronicler," n.p.; Broven, *South to Louisiana,* 214, 216–17; Millar, "Cajun and Proud of It," 14; Millar, "Johnnie Allan," 16.

Case Study: Gene Terry

1. Terry interview, 8 January 1992; Benicewicz, "Johnnie Allan: Cajun Chronicler," n.p.; Broven, *South to Louisiana,* 78.

2. Terry interview, 8 January 1992; Allan, *Memories,* 161, 267.

3. The sequence of Terry's reply has been altered for clarity. Terry interview, 8 January 1992.

4. Ibid.; Terry interview, 20 October 1992.

5. Terry interview, 8 January 1992.

6. Ibid.; Broven, *South to Louisiana,* 201; Gene Terry and His Down Beats/Ronnie Dee and the Down Beats, "Fine—Fine"/"This Should Go On Forever," 45 rpm single 1559, Savoy, ca. 1959; Goldband label promotional discography; various undated *Billboard* clippings [1959], originals in the possession of Rod Bernard.

7. Ibid.

8. Terry interview, 8 January 1992.

9. Ibid.; Terry interview, 20 October 1992; Broven, *South to Louisiana*, 78.

10. Terry interview, 8 January 1992.

11. Ibid.; Terry interview, 20 October 1992.

Case Study: Joe Barry

1. Barry interview, 26 June 1991; Broven, *South to Louisiana*, 223–24.

2. Barry interview, 26 June 1991; Allan, *Memories*, 160, 263; Broven, *South to Louisiana*, 218, 325.

3. Barry interview, 26 June 1991; Barry interview, 3 July 1992; Broven, *South to Louisiana*, 218–19.

4. Barry interview, 26 June 1991; Broven, *South to Louisiana*, 219.

5. Barry is quoted in Broven, *South to Louisiana*, 219–20. Barry interview, 26 June 1991; Barry interview, 3 July 1992.

6. Barry interview, 26 June 1991; Broven, *South to Louisiana*, 220-21.

7. Ibid.

8. Barry interview, 26 June 1991; Broven, *South to Louisiana*, 217–18, 221–22, 301, 335; Ancelet et al., *Cajun Country*, 160.

9. Barry interview, 26 June 1991; Broven, *South to Louisiana*, 222.

10. Barry interview, 26 June 1991; Broven, *South to Louisiana*, 222, 223, 224, 335.

11. Barry interview, 26 June 1991.

12. Ibid.; Broven, *South to Louisiana*, 224.

13. Ibid.

14. Ibid.

15. Barry interview, 26 June 1991; "Joe Barry," *Lafayette (La.) Times of Acadiana*, 23 June 1993, 25.

Case Study: Benny Graeff

1. Broven, *South to Louisiana*, 232.

2. Graeff interview, 24 June 1991; Allan, *Memories*, 160.

3. Graeff interview, 24 June 1991; Benny Graeff, telephone interview by author, 23 October 1992, Lafayette, La., interview notes.

4. Graeff interview, 24 June 1991.

5. Ibid.; Graeff interview, 23 October 1992.

6. Ibid.

7. Ibid.

8. Graeff interview, 24 June 1991; Rufus (Jagneaux), "Opelousas Sostan," 45 rpm single 242, Jin, 1973.

9. Broven, *South to Louisiana,* 232; Fry, liner notes for *Swamp Gold,* vol. 1; Graeff interview, 24 June 1991.

10. Graeff interview, 24 June 1991; Soileau interview, 12 February 1991; Broven, *South to Louisiana,* 232.

11. Soileau is quoted in Broven's book. King confirms the KVOL story. Broven, *South to Louisiana,* 232; Graeff interview, 24 June 1991; King interview.

12. Graeff interview, 24 June 1991.

13. Ibid.; Graeff interview, 23 October 1992; Broven, *South to Louisiana,* 64, 233, 288; Allan, *Memories,* 71, 179, 192; Druann Domangue, "And the Music Goes Round and Round," *Lafayette (La.) Daily Advertiser,* 2 May 1991, B-1, B-3.

BIBLIOGRAPHY*

Interviews

Interviewees are listed according to the names by which they are best known. Thus, some appear under their real names, others under pseudonyms. Lesser-known real names appear in brackets, while lesser-known pseudonyms appear in parentheses.

Adcock, Charles "C. C." Interview by author, 15 September 1992, Lafayette, La. Interview notes.

Allan, Johnnie [John Allen Guillot]. Interview by author, 12 June 1991, Lafayette, La. Tape recording.

————. Telephone interview by author, 20 October 1992, Lafayette, La. Interview notes.

————. "South Louisiana—The Promised Land: Johnnie Allan." Interview by Paul Harris. Part 1. England, 1986. *Now Dig This* (UK), March 1987, 10–12.

————. "South Louisiana—The Promised Land: Johnnie Allan." Interview by Paul Harris. Part 2. England, 1986. *Now Dig This* (UK), April 1987, 9–11.

————. "South Louisiana—The Promised Land: Johnnie Allan." Interview by Paul Harris. Part 3. England, 1986. *Now Dig This* (UK), May 1987, 7–8.

————. "South Louisiana—The Promised Land: Johnnie Allan." Interview by Paul Harris. Part 4. England, 1986. *Now Dig This* (UK), June 1987, 28–30.

————. "With Johnnie Allan in the Promised Land." Interview by Ken Weir. Lafayette, La., March 1990. *Big Beat of the Fifties* (Australia), March 1991, 37–39.

*For a more extensive bibliography of swamp pop music, see Shane K. Bernard, comp. and ed., *Bernard's Swamp Pop Music Source Book: A Semi-Official and Highly Incomplete Bibliography and Compact Disc-ography of South Louisiana Swamp Pop Music*, no. 3 (January 1995), privately published, 28 pp., on file in the author's collection in the Southwestern Archives, University of Southwestern Louisiana, Lafayette, La.

Ancelet, Barry Jean. Interview by author, 29 October 1991, Lafayette, La. Interview notes.

Barry, Joe [Joe Barrios]. Interview by author, 26 June 1991, Lafayette, La. Tape recording.

———. Telephone interview by author, 3 July 1992, Lafayette, La., to Galliano, La. Interview notes.

Bernard, Oscar "Ric." Interview by author, 28 November 1991, Opelousas, La. Tape recording.

Bernard, Rod. Interview by author, 18 October 1991, Lafayette, La. Tape recording.

———. Interview by author, 9 September 1992, Lafayette, La. Interview notes.

———. Interview by Louis Coco, KLIL radio, Moreauville, La., 23 July 1994. Tape recording in the author's possession.

Brasseaux, Carl A. Interview by author, 13 July 1992, Lafayette, La. Interview notes.

Broussard, Grace. Telephone interview by author, 2 October 1991, Lafayette, La., to Prairieville, La. Tape recording.

Broussard, Van. Telephone interview by author, 8 January 1992, Lafayette, La., to Prairieville, La. Tape recording.

Broven, John. Interview by author, 1 May 1992, Lafayette, La. Tape recording.

Charles, Bobby [Robert Charles Guidry]. Interview by author, 3 August 1991, Abbeville, La. Tape recording.

Comeaux, Phillip. Interview by author, 22 January 1995, Lafayette, La. Tape Recording.

Conrad, Glenn R. Interview by author, 20 July 1992, Lafayette, La. Interview notes.

Darby, Huey. Telephone interview by author, 16 January 1992, Lafayette, La. Interview notes.

Fred, John [John Fred Gourrier]. Telephone interview by author, 18 September 1991, Lafayette, La., to Baton Rouge, La. Tape recording.

Graeff, Benny (Rufus Jagneaux). Interview by author, 24 June 1991, Lafayette, La. Tape recording.

———. Telephone interview by author, 23 October 1992, Lafayette, La. Interview notes.

Guidry, Oran "Doc," Sr. Interview by author, 2 November 1991, Lafayette, La. Tape recording.

Guitar Gable [Gabriel Perrodin]. Interview by author, 1 November 1991, Bellevue, La. Tape recording.

———. Interview by author, 27 November 1991, Bellevue, La. Interview notes.

———. Telephone interview by author, 24 April 1994, Baton Rouge, La., to Bellevue, La. Interview notes.

———. Telephone interview by author, 20 March 1995, Lafayette, La., to Bellevue, La. Interview notes.

———. Telephone interview by author, 22 October 1995, Bryan, Tex., to Bellevue, La. Interview notes

Houston, Dale. Telephone interview by author, 15 February 1995, Lafayette, La., to Knoxville, Tenn. Tape recording.

Jacobs, Ernest. Telephone interview by author, 5 September 1995, Bryan, Tex., to Lake Charles, La. Interview notes.

Jivin' Gene [Gene Bourgeois]. Telephone interview by author, 9 October 1991, Lafayette, La., to Texas City, Tex. Interview transcript.

Khoury, George. Telephone interview by author, 25 September 1991, Lafayette, La., to Lake Charles, La. Tape recording.

King, Buddy [pseudonym]. Interview by author, 22 July 1991, Lafayette, La. Tape recording.

King Karl [Bernard Jolivette]. Interview by author, 11 December 1991, Scott, La. Tape recording.

Lavergne, Lee. Interview by author, 30 January 1991, Church Point, La. Tape recording.
———. Interview by author, 1 November 1991, Church Point, La. Tape recording.

Lewis, Stan. Telephone interview by author, 25 September 1991, Lafayette, La., to Shreveport, La. Tape recording.

Lil' Bob [Camille Bob]. Interview by author, 9 July 1991, Opelousas, La. Tape recording.

Little Alfred [Alfred Babino]. Interview by author, 9 July 1991, Opelousas, La. Tape recording.

Lynn, Barbara [Barbara Lynn Ozen]. Interview by author, 31 August 1991, St. Martinville, La. Tape recording.

McLain, Tommy. Telephone interview by author, 18 September 1991, Lafayette, La., to Alexandria, La. Tape recording.
———. "Tommy McLain Interviewed." Telephone interview by author, 18 September 1991, Lafayette, La., to Alexandria, La. Transcribed by John Stafford. Now Dig This (UK), September 1993, 24–26.

Mann, Charles [Charles Domingue]. Telephone interview by author, 12 September 1991, Lafayette, La., to Lake Charles, La. Tape recording.

Menard, D. L. Telephone interview by author, 31 March 1994, Baton Rouge, La., to Erath, La. Interview notes.

Millar, Bill. Telephone interview by author, 24 February 1992, Lafayette, La., to London, England. Interview notes.

Miller, J. D. Interview by author, 21 February 1991, Crowley, La. Tape recording.

Montalbano, S. J. [Sam Montel]. Telephone interview by author, 2 October 1991, Lafayette, La., to Baton Rouge, La. Tape recording.

Page, Bobby [Elwood Dugas]. Interview by author, 12 December 1991, Lafayette, La. Tape recording.

Palmer, Victor. Telephone interview by author, 2 May 1994, Baton Rouge, La., to Lafayette, La. Interview notes.

Perkins, Roy [Ernie Suarez]. Interview by author, 22 October 1991, Lafayette, La. Tape recording.

————. Interview by author, 22 January 1995, Lafayette, La. Tape Recording.

Preston, Johnny [Johnny Preston Courville]. Telephone interview by author, 9 October 1991, Lafayette, La., to Nederland, Tex. Interview transcript.

Rachou, Carol. Interview by author, 24 October 1991, Lafayette, La. Tape recording.

Randall, Jay [Jay Noel]. Telephone interview by author, 8 January 1992, Lafayette, La., to Opelousas, La. Tape recording.

Robin, Roland "Rocky." Interview by author, 2 January 1992, Lafayette, La. Tape recording.

Shuler, Eddie. Telephone interview by author, 25 September 1991, Lafayette, La., to Lake Charles, La. Tape recording.

————. Telephone interview by author, 7 April 1993, Lafayette, La., to Lake Charles, La. Tape recording.

————. Telephone interview by author, 12 April 1993, Lafayette, La., to Lake Charles, La. Interview notes.

Simoneaux, Harry. Interview by author, 1 May 1992, Lafayette, La. Tape recording.

Soileau, Floyd. Interview by author, 12 February 1991, Ville Platte, La. Tape recording.

————. Unknown interviewer. *Baton Rouge (La.) Gris-Gris,* 26 February–4 March 1979, n.p.

Stewart, Skip (Skip Morris) [Maurice Guillory]. Interview by author, 4 August 1991, Opelousas, La. Tape recording.

Storm, Warren [Warren Schexnider]. Interview by author, 13 June 1991, Lafayette, La. Tape recording.

————. Telephone interview by author, 9 October 1991, Lafayette, La. Interview notes.

————. Telephone interview by author, 5 October 1992, Lafayette, La. Interview notes.

Terry, Gene [Terry Gene DeRouen]. Telephone interview by author, 8 January 1992, Lafayette, La., to Port Arthur, Tex. Tape recording.

————. Telephone interview by author, 20 October 1992, Lafayette, La., to Port Arthur, Tex. Interview notes.

Theall, Ned. Interview by author, 3 July 1991, Lafayette, La. Tape recording.

Thierry, Huey "Cookie," and Ernest Jacobs. Interview by author, 19 July 1995, Lake Charles, La. Tape recording.

Vidrine, Lionel "Chick." Interview by author, 5 February 1991, Opelousas, La. Tape recording.

West, Clint [Clinton Guillory]. Interview by author, 4 August 1991, Opelousas, La. Tape recording.

Books

Allan, Johnnie [John Allen Guillot], comp. and ed. *Memories: A Pictorial History of South Louisiana Music, 1920s–1980s.* Vol. 1, *South Louisiana and East Texas Musicians.* Lafayette, La.: Johnnie Allan/JADFEL, 1988.

Allan, Johnnie, and Bernice Larson Webb. *Born to Be a Loser: The Jimmy Donley Story.* Lafayette, La.: JADFEL, 1992.

Ancelet, Barry Jean. *Cajun Music: Its Origins and Development.* Louisiana Life Series, no. 2. Lafayette: Center for Louisiana Studies/University of Southwestern Louisiana, 1989.

———. Introduction to *Cajun Music and Zydeco,* by Philip Gould. Baton Rouge: Louisiana State University Press, 1992.

Ancelet, Barry Jean, Jay Edwards, Glen Pitre, Carl Brasseaux, Fred B. Kniffen, Maida Bergeron, Janet Shoemaker, and Mathe Allain. *Cajun Country.* Folklife in the South Series. Jackson: University Press of Mississippi, 1991.

Ancelet, Barry Jean, and Elemore Morgan Jr. *The Makers of Cajun Music (Musiciens cadiens et créoles).* Austin: University of Texas Press, 1984.

Angers, Trent. *The Truth about the Cajuns.* Lafayette, La.: Acadian House, 1989.

Brasseaux, Carl A. *The Founding of New Acadia: The Beginnings of Acadian Life in Louisiana, 1765–1803.* Baton Rouge: Louisiana State University Press, 1987.

———. *"Scattered to the Wind": Dispersal and Wanderings of the Acadians, 1755–1809.* Louisiana Life Series, no. 6. Lafayette: Center for Louisiana Studies/University of Southwestern Louisiana, 1991.

Broven, John. *Rhythm and Blues in New Orleans [Walking to New Orleans: The Story of New Orleans Rhythm and Blues (UK)].* Gretna, La.: Pelican, 1988.

———. *South to Louisiana: The Music of the Cajun Bayous.* Gretna, La.: Pelican, 1983.

Brown, Peter, and Steven Gaines. *The Love You Make: An Insider's Story of the Beatles.* New York: Signet, 1984.

Burke, James Lee. *Black Cherry Blues.* New York: Avon, 1990.

Calhoun, Milburn, ed. *Louisiana Almanac, 1988–89.* Gretna, La.: Pelican, 1988.

Courlander, Harold. *The Drum and the Hoe: Life and Lore of the Haitian People.* Berkeley: University of California Press, 1960.

———. *Haiti Singing.* Chapel Hill: University of North Carolina, 1939.

Cowley, John Houlston. "Music and Migration: Aspects of Black Music in the British Caribbean, the United States, and Britain before the Independence of Jamaica and Trinidad and Tobago." Ph.D. diss., University of Warwick, Coventry, England, 1992.

Dormon, James H. *The People Called Cajuns: An Introduction to an Ethnohistory*. Lafayette: Center for Louisiana Studies/University of Southwestern Louisiana, 1983.

Dowlding, William J. *Beatlesongs*. New York: Fireside, 1989.

Epstein, Dena J. *Sinful Tunes and Spirituals: Black Folk Music to the Civil War*. Urbana, Ill.: University of Illinois Press, 1977.

Escott, Colin, with Martin Hawkins. *Good Rockin' Tonight: Sun Records and the Birth of Rock 'n' Roll*. New York: St. Martin's Press, 1991.

François, Raymond E., comp. and annotator. *Yé Yaille, Chère!: Traditional Cajun Dance Music*. Lafayette, La.: Thunderstone, 1990.

Fry, Macon, and Julie Posner. *Cajun Country Guide*. Gretna, La.: Pelican, 1992.

Gillett, Charlie. *The Sound of the City: The Rise of Rock 'n' Roll*. New York: Dell, 1972.

———. *The Sound of the City: The Rise of Rock 'n' Roll*. Rev. and exp. New York: Pantheon, 1983.

Grun, Bernard, and Werner Stein. *The Timetables of History: A Horizontal Linkage of People and Events*. 3d rev. ed. New York: Simon Shuster/Touchstone, 1991.

Hannusch, Jeff [Almost Slim]. *I Hear You Knockin': The Sound of New Orleans*. Ville Platte, La.: Swallow, 1985.

Kocandrle, Mirek. *The History of Rock and Roll: A Selective Discography*. Boston: G. K. Hall, 1988.

Leadbitter, Mike. *Crowley, Louisiana, Blues*. Bexhill-on-Sea, England: Blues Unlimited, 1968.

———, ed. *Nothing but the Blues*. London: Hanover, 1971.

Leadbitter, Mike, Leslie Fancourt, and Paul Pelletier, comps. *Blues Records, 1943–1970*. Vol. 2, L–Z. London: Record Information Services, 1994.

Leadbitter, Mike, and Eddie Shuler. *From the Bayou (The Story of Goldband Records)*. Bexhill-on-Sea, England: Blues Unlimited, 1969.

Leadbitter, Mike, and Neil Slaven. *Blues Records, 1943–1970*. Vol. 1, A–K. 2d ed. London: Record Information Services, 1987.

Lewisohn, Mark. *The Beatles Recording Sessions*. New York: Harmony, 1990.

Malone, Bill C. *Country Music, U.S.A*. Rev. ed. Austin: University of Texas Press, 1991.

———. *Southern Music/American Music*. Lexington: University Press of Kentucky, 1979.

Monroe, Mina, comp. and ed. *Bayou Ballads: Twelve Folk-Songs from Louisiana*. Schirmer's American Folk-Songs Series. Set 2. New York: G. Schirmer, 1921.

Oster, Harry. *Living Country Blues*. Detroit: Folklore Associates, 1969.

Palmer, Robert. *A Tale of Two Cities: Memphis Rock and New Orleans Roll*. I.S.A.M.

Monographs, no. 12. New York: Institute for Studies in American Music/Brooklyn College of the City University of New York, 1979.

Post, Lauren C. *Cajun Sketches: From the Prairies of Southwest Louisiana.* Baton Rouge: Louisiana State University Press, 1990.

Read, William A. *Louisiana-French.* Baton Rouge: Louisiana State University Press, 1931.

Riley, Tim. *Tell Me Why: A Beatles Commentary.* New York: Vintage, 1989.

Sacré, Robert. *Musiques cajun, créole et zydeco.* Paris: Presses Universitaires de France, 1995.

Savoy, Ann Allen, comp. and ed. *Cajun Music: A Reflection of a People.* 3d ed. Vol. 1. Eunice, La.: Bluebird, 1988.

Theall, Ned. *Living Like a King: An Autobiography by Ned Theall.* [New Iberia, La.]: Privately published, 1993.

Warren, Lee. *The Dance of Africa: An Introduction.* Englewood Cliffs, N.J.: Prentice-Hall, 1972.

White, John I. *Git Along, Little Dogies: Songs and Songmakers of the American West.* Urbana: University Press of Illinois, 1975.

Whitfield, Irène Thérèse. *Louisiana French Folk Songs.* Baton Rouge: Louisiana State University Press, 1939.

Articles

Copies of several obscure articles listed below are on file in the author's collection in the Southwestern Archives, University of Southwestern Louisiana, Lafayette, La.

"Acadian Museum Gets Senate OK." *Lafayette (La.) Daily Advertiser,* 5 April 1995, A-5.

Allan, Johnnie, comp. "Johnnie Allan Discography." Ed. Shane K. Bernard. Lafayette, La.: Privately published, 1994, 9 pp.

Ancelet, Barry Jean. "Zydeco/Zarico: Beans, Blues and Beyond." *Black Music Research Journal* 8, no. 1 (1988): 33–49.

Aycock, Martha. "Johnny Allen [sic] Single English 'Pick Hit.'" *Lafayette (La.) Daily Advertiser,* 2 April 1978, 62.

Bastin, Bruce. Liner notes. Various Artists. *Louisiana "High School Hop."* The Legendary Jay Miller Sessions. Vol. 51. Long-playing record FLY 616, Flyright (UK), 1988.

Benicewicz, Larry. "Allons à Lafayette." *Newsletter of the Baltimore Blues Society,* April 1988, n.p.

———. "Clarence 'Jockey' Etienne and the Crowley Staff Musicians." *Newsletter of the Baltimore Blues Society,* January 1994, 4–8.

————. "Guitar Gable and King Karl: A New Brand of Blues." *Newsletter of the Baltimore Blues Society*, March 1994, 4–9.

————. "Johnnie Allan: Cajun Chronicler." *Newsletter of the Baltimore Blues Society*, February 1989, n.p.

————. "Poet of the Bayou: Bobby Charles." *Newsletter of the Baltimore Blues Society*, November 1988, 1–4.

————. "Rod Bernard and Swamp Pop." *Newsletter of the Baltimore Blues Society*, February 1992, 2–6.

————. "Warren and Tommy: Still Crazy after All These Years." *Newsletter of the Baltimore Blues Society*, January 1990, 2–4.

Berglind, Bo, and Claes-Håkan Olofsson. "Rod Bernard." *American Music Magazine* (Sweden), June 1995, 4–15.

Bernard, Shane K. "Creole Swamp Poppers: King Karl and Guitar Gable." *Now Dig This* (UK), January 1995, 27–29.

————. "J. D. Miller and Floyd Soileau: A Comparison of Two Small-Town Recordmen of Acadiana." *Louisiana Folklife* 15 (December 1991): 12–20.

————. "Joe Barry: Swamp Popper from Cut Off." *Now Dig This* (UK), March 1995, 10–12.

————. "A Swamp Pop–Rockabilly Collision: Gene Terry and the Down Beats." *Now Dig This* (UK), September 1994, 5–6.

————. "A Swamp Rock 'n' Roller Remembers: Rod Bernard and *American Bandstand*." *Goldmine*, 31 March 1995, 64, 66, 129, 132, 138.

————. "A Swamp Rock 'n' Roller Remembers: Rod Bernard and *American Bandstand*." *Now Dig This* (UK), June 1994, 5–8.

————. "Warren Storm: The Workhorse of Swamp Pop." *Now Dig This* (UK), July 1995, 29–31.

————, comp. and ed. *Bernard's Swamp Pop Music Source Book: A Semi-Official and Highly Incomplete Bibliography and Compact Disc-ography of South Louisiana Swamp Pop Music*. No. 3 (January 1995). Published by Shane K. Bernard, 28 pp.

————. "Rod Bernard Discography." Lafayette, La.: Privately published, 1994, 7 pp.

Bernard, Shane K., and Julia Girouard. "'Colinda': Mysterious Origins of a Cajun Folksong." *Journal of Folklore Research* 29 (January–April 1992): 37–52.

Blackburn, Dick. Liner notes. Various Artists. *Sound of the Swamp: The Best of Excello Records*. Vol. 1. Compact disc R2 70896. Rhino, 1990.

Boyat, Bernard. "Swamp Pop." *Musiques et collections* [France], November 1994, n.p.

Broven, John. Liner notes. Various Artists. *Lafayette Saturday Night*. Compact disc CD-CHD 371. Ace (UK), 1985.

————. Liner notes. Rod Bernard. *Rod Bernard.* Long-playing record CH 143. Ace (UK), 1985.

Cable, George Washington. "Creole Slave Songs." *Century Magazine* 31 (February 1886): 807–28.

————. "The Dance in Place Congo." *Century Magazine* 31 (February 1886): 517–32.

"Cajuns Get New Respect from [Census] Bureau." *Lafayette (La.) Daily Advertiser,* 1 August 1991, A-12.

"Colored Band Man Faces 'Indecency' Trial over White Evangeline Girl." *Ville Platte (La.) Gazette,* 7 February 1957, p. 1.

Domangue, Druann. "And the Music Goes Round and Round." *Lafayette (La.) Daily Advertiser,* 2 May 1991, B-1, B-3.

Dormon, James H. "Louisiana's 'Creoles of Color': Ethnicity, Marginality and Identity." *Social Science Quarterly* 73 (September 1992): 615–26.

Dr. John [Mac Rebennack]. Liner notes. Dr. John. *Dr. John's Gumbo.* Long-playing record SD 7006. Atco 1972.

Elder, J. D. "*Kalinda*—Song of the Battling Troubadours of Trinidad." *Journal of the Folklore Institute* 3 (August 1966): 192–201.

Estaville, Lawrence E., Jr. "Changeless Cajuns: Nineteenth-Century Reality or Myth?" *Louisiana History* 28 (Spring 1987): 117–40.

Fry, Macon. Liner notes. Various Artists. *Swamp Gold.* Vol. 1. Compact disc CD-106. Jin, 1991.

Fumar, Vincent. "A Blues Lover from Britain." *Dixie/The New Orleans Times-Picayune,* 20 November 1983, 12–20.

Furmanovsky, Jill. "The 'Coon Ass' Guide to London." *Sounds* (UK), 8 April 1978, 30, 47.

Fuselier, Herman. "Acadian Music Heritage Museum Slated at Church Point." *Opelousas (La.) Daily World,* 22 June 1995, 1, 14.

————. "Swamp Pop Duo Reunited." *Opelousas (La.) Daily World,* 19 October 1995, TV and Entertainment section, 1, 8.

————. "This Couldn't Go On Forever: Rod Bernard Recalls Roots of Swamp Pop." *Opelousas (La.) Daily World,* 7 April 1994, TV and Entertainment section, 1, 26.

Green, Judy. "Be There, Honey, or Be Square." *Opelousas (La.) Daily World,* 25 July 1991, 6.

Guralnick, Peter. Liner notes. Elvis Presley. *Elvis Presley: The Memphis Record.* Compact disc 6221-2-R. RCA, 1987.

Hannusch, Jeff. Liner notes. Various Artists. *Swamp Gold.* Vol. 2. Compact disc CD-107. Jin, 1991.

Huggs, Katrinna. "The Boogie Kings Are Back." *Lafayette (La.) Times of Acadiana,* 2 October 1991, 28–30.

———. "L.A. Ain't No La." *Lafayette (La.) Times of Acadiana,* 24 January 1990, 29–30.

———. "See Ya' Now, Bobby Charles." *Lafayette (La.) Times of Acadiana,* 15 October 1986, 14–17.

———. "Sweet Dreams." *Lafayette (La.) Times of Acadiana,* 17 April 1991, 12.

———. "Thirty Years of 'Forever.'" *Lafayette (La.) Times of Acadiana,* 23 November 1988, 39–40.

"Jail Sentence of Year Imposed on Colored Band Man for 'Indecent Act.'" *Ville Platte (La.) Gazette,* 14 March 1957, front and back pages.

"Joe Barry." *Lafayette (La.) Times of Acadiana,* 23 June 1993, 25.

Keating, Bern, Charles Harbutt, and Franke Keating. "Louisiana's French-speaking Cajunland." *National Geographic,* March 1966, 352–91.

Kurtz, David. "Devilish Politics in St. Landry Parish." *Lafayette (La.) Times of Acadiana,* 4 October 1995, 13–16, 18.

Loder, Kurt. "Sound of the Swamp." *Esquire,* November 1991, 64–67.

McClain, Mason. "The Reunion of Dale and Grace." *Gonzales (La.) Jambalaya,* January 1995, 33–35.

Marsteller, Sara. "Rodney Bernard, 14, Plays Guitar, Sings 'Cajun' Tunes." *Beaumont (Tex.) Journal,* ca. 10 November 1954, n.p.

Millar, Bill. "Cajun and Proud of It: Bill Millar Talks to Johnnie Allan, the Louisiana Swamp Fox." *Goldmine,* June 1982, 14.

———. "Hot Rod from the Bayou." *Melody Maker* (UK), 4 August 1979, 37, 42.

———. "Johnnie Allan: A Swamp Pop Special." *New Kommotion* (UK), Summer 1978, 15–19.

———. "Rockin' on the Bayou." *Melody Maker* (UK), 17 February 1979, 51, 55.

———. "Rod Bernard: Hot Rod." *Goldmine,* 6 July 1984, 40–46.

———. "Sounds of the Swamp: Local Heroes Who Rocked the Everglades." *The History of Rock* (UK) 7 (1983): 1454–55.

———. "Swamp Pop-Music [sic] from Cajun Country." *Record Mirror* (UK), 12 June 1971, n.p.

Miller, Dave. "Local Musicians Swing on the 45's" *Lafayette (La.) Daily Advertiser,* 30 January 1963, B-8.

Mouton, Todd. "Lafayette's C. C. Adcock Debuts." *The Lafayette (La.) Times of Acadiana,* 9 March 1994, 30–31.

———. "Return of 'Da Beans.'" *Lafayette (La.) Times of Acadiana,* 19 April 1995, 53–54.

Nettel, R. "Historical Introduction to 'La Calinda.'" *Music and Letters* 27 (January 1946): 59–62.

Page, Mike Flood. "Were These Guys Robbed of Their Hit by This Man?" *Sounds* (UK), 8 March 1975, 28.

Porter, Tissa. "Creole Trailrides . . . A Zydeco What?" *Creole Magazine,* September 1991, 5–8.

Redd, Lawrence N. "Rock! It's Still Rhythm and Blues." *Black Perspective in Music* 13 (Spring 1985): 31–47.

Rico [Rick Olivier]. "Putting the Fizz in Swamp Pop." *Wavelength,* April 1984, 22.

Sandmel, Ben. "Floyd Soileau." *Louisiana Life,* Winter 1994–95, 30–32.

Sasfy, Joe. "The Bayou Beat." *Washington, D.C., City Paper,* 15 June 1984, 17.

———. "Swamp Pop: This Should Go On Forever." *Washington, D.C., Unicorn Times,* August 1982, 12–13.

Strachwitz, Chris. "Cajun Country," *The American Folk Music Occasional* 2 (1970): 14.

Tate, Paul. "The Cajuns of Louisiana." *American Folk Music Occasional* 2 (1970): 8–12.

Topping, Ray. "Rod Bernard Discography." *Goldmine,* 6 July 1984, 46.

Tregle, Joseph G., Jr. "On That Word 'Creole' Again: A Note." *Louisiana History* 23 (Spring 1982): 193–98.

Correspondence

Broven, John, Newick, East Sussex, England, to the author, Lafayette, La., 18 November 1991. Typewritten letter signed, original in the possession of the author.

Hannusch, Jeff, New Orleans, La., to the author, Lafayette, La., 21? January 1992. Autograph letter signed, original in the possession of the author.

Millar, Bill, Dartford, Kent, England, to John Broven, Newick, East Sussex, England, 12 November 1991. Autograph letter signed, original in the possession of the author.

———, Dartford, Kent, England, to the author, Lafayette, La., 25 February 1992. Autograph letter signed, original in the possession of the author.

———, Dartford, Kent, England, to the author, Lafayette, La., 9 January 1995. Autograph letter signed, original in the possession of the author.

———, Dartford, Kent, England, to the author, Lafayette, La., 14 August 1995. Autograph letter signed, original in the possession of the author.

Shuler, Eddie, Lake Charles, La., to the author, Lafayette, La., 10 July 1993. Typewritten letter signed, original in the possession of the author.

Warner, Manny, New York, N.Y., to Eddie Shuler, Lake Charles, La., 26 March 1945. Typewritten letter, original in the possession of Eddie Shuler.

Audio Recordings

Adcock, C.C. "Cindy Lou." *C.C. Adcock*. Compact disc 314–518 840–2. Island, 1994.

———. "Done Most Everything." *C.C. Adcock*. Compact disc 314–518 840–2. Island, 1994.

Allan, Johnnie. "Ain't No Pleasing You." *Thanks for the Memories*. Long-playing record 9026. Jin, 1983.

———. "Before The Next Teardrop Falls." *Johnnie Allan's Greatest Hits*. Long-playing record LP 9017. Jin, 1977.

———. "Cajun Man." *Promised Land*. Compact disc CDCHD 380. Ace (UK), 1992.

———. "Lonely Days, Lonely Nights." 45 rpm single 111. Jin, 1958.

———. "Please Accept My Love." *Promised Land*. Compact disc CDCHD 380. Ace (UK), 1992.

———. "Promised Land." *Promised Land*. Compact disc CDCHD 380. Ace (UK), 1992.

———. "Promised Land." The Boogie Kings. *Swamp Boogie Blues*. Compact disc CD 9045. Jin, 1995.

———. "South to Louisiana." *Promised Land*. Compact disc CDCHD 380. Ace (UK), 1992.

Allan, Johnnie. "Today I Started Loving You Again." *Promised Land*. Compact disc CDCHD 380. Ace (UK), 1992.

———. "Your Picture." Various Artists. *Swamp Gold*. Vol. 2. Compact disc CD-107. Jin, 1991.

Alley Boys of Abbeville, The. "Tu ma quité seul" ("The Prisoner's Song"). Various Artists. *Cajun, Volume 1: Abbeville Breakdown, 1929–1939*. Roots N' Blues series. Compact disc CK 46220. Columbia, 1990.

Anderson, Elton. "Please Accept My Love." 45 rpm single 71778. Mercury, 1961.

Ardoin, Doug, and the Boogie Kings. "Lost Love." 45 rpm single 101. Jin, 1958.

Barrios, Josef (Joe Barry). "Je suis bêt pour t'aimer." 45 rpm single 150. Jin, 1961.

Beatles, The. "Oh! Darling." *Abbey Road*. Compact disc CDP 7 46446 2. Parlophone, 1987.

Bernard, Rod. "Colinda." *Rod Bernard: Swamp Rock 'n' Roller*. Compact disc CDCHD 488. Ace (UK), 1994.

————. "Diggy Liggy Lo." *Rod Bernard: Swamp Rock 'n' Roller.* Compact disc CDCHD 488.
Ace (UK), 1994.

————. "Fais Do Do." *Rod Bernard: Swamp Rock 'n' Roller.* Compact disc CDCHD 488.
Ace (UK), 1994.

————. "Fais Do Do (Fay Doe Doe)." 45 rpm single 1906. Hall-Way, 1962.

————. "Gimme Back My Cadillac." 45 rpm single 104. Arbee, 1965.

————. "(I Have a Vow) To Have and Hold." 45 rpm single 237. Jin, 1968.

————. "My Life Is a Mystery." 45 rpm single 5338. Argo, 1959.

————. "Pardon Mr. Gordon." *Rod Bernard: Swamp Rock 'n' Roller.* Compact disc CDCHD
488. Ace (UK), 1994.

————. "Pledging My Love." *Night Lights and Love Songs.* Long-playing record LP 9010. Jin,
1975.

————. "Recorded in England." *Rod Bernard: Swamp Rock 'n' Roller.* Compact disc CD-
CHD 488. Ace (UK), 1994.

————. "This Should Go On Forever." *Rod Bernard: Swamp Rock 'n' Roller.* Compact disc
CDCHD 488. Ace (UK), 1994.

Bernard, Rod, and Clifton Chenier. *Boogie in Black & White.* Long-playing record LP 9014.
Jin, 1976.

Boogie Kings, The. "I Love That Swamp Pop Music." *Louisiana Country Soul.* Compact disc
9038–2. Jin, 1993.

Breaux Frères. "T'as volé mon chapeau." Various Artists. *Cajun, Volume 1: Abbeville Breakdown, 1929–1939.* Roots N' Blues series. Compact disc CK 46220. Columbia, 1990.

Brown, T. Graham. "I Tell It Like It Used to Be." *Greatest Hits.* Compact disc CDP 7–
94166-2. Capitol, 1990.

Carl, Joe, and the Dukes of Rhythm. *Everybody's Rockin' with the Dukes of Rhythm featuring
Joe Carl and Harry Simoneaux.* Compact disc RUN CD 7. Rundell (Germany), 1994.

Chalvin, Godar. "Anons au bal Colinda." 1956, Abbeville, La. Field recording in the possession of Michael Doucet, Lafayette, La.

Charles, Bobby. "Later Alligator." Various Artists. *Rock & Roll Originators.* Compact disc
TSD-3706. Tel-Star, 1991.

————. "Later Alligator." *Wish You Were Here Right Now.* Compact disc 1203. Rice &
Gravy/Stoney Plain, 1995.

Charles, Doug, and the Boogie Kings. Various recordings. *Bayou Beat.* The Legendary Jay
Miller Sessions, vol. 26. Long-playing record FLY 581. Flyright (UK), 1981.

————. Various recordings. *Rockin' Fever.* The Legendary Jay Miller Sessions, vol. 15.
Long-playing record FLY 540. Flyright (UK), 1978.

Chas and Dave. "Ain't No Pleasing You." 45 rpm single KOR 14, Rockney (UK), 1982.

Chenier, Clifton. "Zydeco sont pas salés." Various Artists. *J'ai été au bal (I Went to the Dance): The Cajun and Zydeco Music of Louisiana.* Vol. 2. Compact disc CD-332. Arhoolie, 1990.

Clanton, Jimmy. "Another Sleepless Night." Various Artists. *The Best of Ace Records—The Pop Hits.* Compact disc 72392–75266-2. Rock 'n' Roll/Scotti Bros., 1992.

———. "Just a Dream." Various Artists. *The Best of Ace Records—The Pop Hits.* Compact disc 72392–75266-2. Rock 'n' Roll/Scotti Bros., 1992.

Collie, Mark. "Shame Shame Shame Shame." *Mark Collie.* Compact disc MCAD-10658. MCA, 1993.

Cookie and the Cupcakes. "Mathilda." Various Artists. *Louisiana Saturday Night.* Compact disc CDCHD 490. Ace (UK), 1993.

Cookie and His Cupcakes [sic]. "I'm Twisted." 45 rpm single 1003. Lyric, 1958.

Cypress City. "Cajun Rap Song." Various Artists. *Swamp Gold.* Vol. 2. Compact disc CD-107. Jin, 1991.

Dale and Grace. "I'm Leaving It Up to You." *Swamp Gold.* Vol. 1. Compact disc CD-106. Jin, 1991.

Davis, Jimmie. "Colinda." 78 rpm single 28748. Decca, 1953.

Douget, Darby. "Mathilda Finally Came Back Home." *Swamp Gold.* Vol. 3. Compact disc 9041–2. Jin, 1994.

Eaglin, Ford "Snooks." "Irene." Various Artists. *Black Top Blues-A-Rama, Vol. 6—Live at Tipitina's.* Compact disc CD-BT-1073. Black Top, 1992.

Falcon, Joseph, and Cléoma Breaux. "Allons à Lafayette." Various Artists. *J'ai été au bal (I Went to the Dance): The Cajun and Zydeco Music of Louisiana.* Vol. 1. Compact disc CD-331. Arhoolie, 1990.

Fender, Freddy. "Go On Go On." Demo recording in the possession of Rod Bernard, original in the possession of Huey Meaux. Ca. 1980.

Forestier, Blackie. "What's Her Name." Various Artists. *Lafayette Saturday Night.* Compact disc CDCHD 371. Ace (UK), 1992.

Funderburgh, Anson, and the Rockets. "This Should Go On Forever." *Talk to You by Hand.* Compact disc CD-BT-1001. Black Top, 1984.

Guidry, Doc. "Colinda." Various Artists. *The Best of La Louisianne Records.* Compact disc LLCD-1001. La Louisianne, 1990.

———. "La valse d'amitié." Various Artists. *The Best of La Louisianne Records.* Compact disc LLCD-1001. La Louisianne, 1990.

Guitar Gable and the Musical Kings. "Congo Mombo." Various Artists. *Sound of the Swamp: The Best of Excello Records.* Vol. 1. Compact disc R2 70896. Rhino, 1990.

Guitar Gable and the Musical Kings featuring King Karl. "Irene." *Guitar Gable with King Karl: Cool, Calm, Collected.* Long-playing album FLY 599. Flyright (UK), 1984.

Hogan, Silas. "Everybody Needs Somebody." Various Artists. *Sound of the Swamp: The Best of Excello Records*. Vol. I. Compact disc R2 70896. Rhino, 1990.

Honeydrippers, The. "Sea of Love." *Volume One*. Compact disc 90220–2. Es Paranza/ Atlantic, 1984.

Hudson, Joe, and His Rockin' Dukes. "Baby Give Me a Chance." Various Artists. *Sound of the Swamp: The Best of Excello Records*. Vol. I. Compact disc R2 70896. Rhino, 1990.

Hulin, T. K. "Alligator Bayou." 45 rpm single 1005. Booray, 1976.

Jivin' Gene. "Breaking Up Is Hard to Do." Various Artists. *Swamp Gold*. Vol. I. Compact disc CD-106. Jin, 1991.

King, Earl. "Those Lonely Lonely Nights." 45 rpm single 509. Ace (USA), 1955.

———. "There's Been Some Lonely Lonely Nights [Those Lonely Lonely Nights]." *Glazed*. Compact disc CD-BT-1035. Black Top, 1986.

King, Gene. "Little Cajun Girl." Various Artists. *Louisiana Saturday Night*. Compact disc CDCHD 490. Ace (UK), 1993.

Little Richard. "Can't Believe You Wanna Leave." *His Greatest Recordings*. Compact disc CDCH 109. Ace (UK), 1990.

———. "Send Me Some Lovin'." *His Greatest Recordings*. Compact disc CDCH 109. Ace (UK), 1990.

Los Lobos. "I Got Loaded." *How Will the Wolf Survive?* Compact disc 25177–2. Slash/ Warner Bros., 1984.

McGee, Dennis. "Happy One-Step." Various Artists. *J'ai été au bal (I Went to the Dance): The Cajun and Zydeco Music of Louisiana*. Vol. I. Compact disc CD-331. Arhoolie, 1990.

———. "Madame Young donnez moi votre plus jolie blonde." Various Artists. *Louisiana Cajun Music, Volume Five, The Early Years, 1928–1938*. Long-playing record 114. Old Timey Records, 1973.

———. "O malheureuse." Various Artists. *J'ai été au bal (I Went to the Dance): The Cajun and Zydeco Music of Louisiana*. Vol. I. Compact disc CD-331. Arhoolie, 1990.

McLain, Tommy. "Before I Grow Too Old." *Sweet Dreams*. Compact disc CDCH 285. Ace, 1990.

———. "Sweet Dreams." *Sweet Dreams*. Compact disc CDCH 285. Ace, 1990.

Mann, Charles. "Walk Of Life." *Walk of Life*. Compact disc 002. Gumbo/Cooking Vinyl (UK), 1990.

Myers, Sam, and Anson Funderburgh. "Life Problem." *My Love Is Here to Stay*. Compact disc CD-BT-1032. Black Top, 1986.

Newman, Jimmy "C." "Hippy Tai Yo." Various Artists. *Lafayette Saturday Night*. Compact disc CDCHD 371. Ace (UK), 1992.

Page, Bobby, and the Riff Raffs. "Hippy-Ti-Yo." 45 rpm single 1338. Ram, 1958.

Page, Bobby, [and the Riff Raffs]. "Hippy Ti Yo" ["Hippy-Ti-Yo"]. Various Artists. *Shreveport Stomp*. CDCHD 495. Ace (UK), 1994.

Presley, Elvis. "Pledging My Love." *Moody Blue*. Compact disc 2428–2-R. RCA, 1977.

Price, Lloyd. "Just Because." Various Artists. *The Best of New Orleans Rhythm & Blues*. Vol. 2. Compact disc R2 75766. Rhino, 1988.

Randall, Jay, and the Epics. "Oh! Darling." 45 rpm single 548. Lanor, 1970.

Randy and the Rockets. "Let's Do the Cajun Twist." Various Artists. *Swamp Gold*. Vol. I. Compact disc CD-106. Jin, 1991.

Raven Eddy. "Alligator Bayou." Various Artists. *The Best of La Louisianne Records*. Compact disc LLCD-1001. La Louisianne, 1990.

———. "Crawfish Festival Time." Various Artists. *The Best of La Louisianne Records*. Compact disc LLCD-1001. La Louisianne, 1990.

Richard, Belton. "Give Me Another Chance." *Belton Richard: Modern Sounds in Cajun Music*. Compact disc CDCHD 378. Ace (UK), 1993.

———. "I'm Not a Fool Anymore." *Belton Richard: Modern Sounds in Cajun Music*. Compact disc CDCHD 378. Ace (UK), 1993.

———. "J'ai pleurer pour toi." *Belton Richard: Modern Sounds in Cajun Music*. Compact disc CDCHD 378. Ace (UK), 1993.

———. "Lord I Need Somebody Bad Tonight." *Good n' Cajun*. Long-playing record 6021. Swallow, 1974.

———. "Un autre soir d'ennui (Another Sleepless Night)." *Belton Richard: Modern Sounds in Cajun Music*. Compact disc CDCHD 378. Ace (UK), 1993.

Rockin' Sidney, "You Ain't Nothin' but Fine." Various Artists. *Louisiana Saturday Night*. Compact disc CDCHD 490. Ace (UK), 1993.

Rolling Stones, The. "Oh Baby (We Got a Good Thing Goin')." *The Rolling Stones, Now!* Compact disc CD 509. Abkco, 1986.

Royal, Billie Joe. "Burned Like a Rocket." *Greatest Hits*. Compact disc 82199–2. Atlantic, 1991.

Rufus Jagneaux. "The Back Door." Various Artists. *Swamp Gold*. Vol. 3. Compact disc 9041–2. Jin, 1994.

———. "Opelousas Sostan." Various Artists. *Swamp Gold*. Vol. I. Compact disc CD-106. Jin, 1991.

Rufus (Jagneaux) [sic]. "Opelousas Sostan." 45 rpm single 242. Jin, 1971.

———. "Port Barre." 45 rpm single 242. Jin, 1971.

Shondells, The. "A-2-Fay." Various Artists. *Lafayette Saturday Night*. Compact disc CDCHD 371. Ace (UK), 1992. [Mistakenly listed in liner notes and on rear cover as "A-2-Fee" by Rod Bernard.]

Terry, Gene, and the Down Beats. "Cindy Lou." Various Artists. *Eddie's House of Hits: The Story of Goldband Records.* Compact disc CDCHD 424. Ace (UK), 1992.

Slim Harpo. "Rainin' in My Heart." Various Artists. *Sound of the Swamp: The Best of Excello Records.* Vol. 1. Compact disc R2 70896. Rhino, 1990.

Various Artists. *Alligator Stomp: Cajun and Zydeco Classics.* Vol. 1. Compact disc R2 70946. Rhino, 1990.

Various Artists. *Alligator Stomp: Cajun and Zydeco Classics.* Vol. 2. Compact disc R2 70740. Rhino, 1990.

Various Artists. *Alligator Stomp: Cajun and Zydeco Classics.* Vol. 3. Compact disc R2 70312. Rhino, 1990.

Various Artists. *Alligator Stomp, Vol. 4: Cajun Christmas.* Compact disc R2 71058. Rhino, 1992.

Various Artists. *Alligator Stomp, Vol. 5: Cajun and Zydeco—The Next Generation.* Compact disc R2 71846. Rhino, 1995.

Various Artists. *Chess New Orleans.* Compact disc CHD2–9355, MCA/Chess, 1995.

Various Artists. *New Orleans Party Classics.* Compact disc R2 70587. Rhino, 1992.

Various Artists. *Sound of the Swamp: The Best of Excello Records.* Vol. 1. Compact disc R2 70896. Rhino, 1990.

Walker, Lawrence. "Mamou Two-Step." Various Artists. *The Best of La Louisianne Records.* Compact disc LLCD-1001. La Louisianne, 1990.

West, Clint. "Big Blue Diamonds." *Swamp Gold.* Vol. 2. Compact disc CD-107. Jin, 1991.

Wilson, Jimmy. "Please Accept My Love." Various Artists. *Eddie's House of Hits: The Story of Goldband Records.* Compact disc CDCHD 424. Ace (UK), 1992.

Video Recordings

Blank, Les, and Chris Strachwitz, prods. *French Dance Tonight: The Cajun and Zydeco Music of Louisiana.* 53 min. Brazos Films, 1990. Videocassette.

———. *J'ai été au bal (I Went to the Dance): The Cajun and Zydeco Music of Louisiana.* 84 min. Brazos Films, 1990. Videocassette.

Bull Durham. 108 min. Orion Home Video, 1988. Videocassette.

Lomax, Alan, prod. and dir. *Cajun Country: Don't Drop the Potato.* American Patchwork: Songs and Stories about America. 60 min. Pacific Arts Video/PBS Home Video/ Association for Cultural Equity, Columbia University (Hunter College), 1990. Video-cassette.

Scandal. 105 min. HBO Video, 1989. Videocassette.

Sea of Love. 113 min. MCA Home Video, 1989. Videocassette.

Miscellaneous

"Area Talent Featured at Benefit." Unidentified newspaper clipping from an unidentified source, possibly the *Lafayette (La.) Daily Advertiser,* ca. 1960 [May 1961?], original in the possession of Johnnie Allan.

Author's notes taken from 1991 Utrecht *Blues Estafette* program, original in the possession of Warren Storm.

Contract between Goldband Records and the Boogie Ramblers, 19 July 1952, signed by Simon Lubin, Ernest Jacobs, Shelton Dunaway, and Marshall LeDee, original in the possession of Eddie Shuler, Lake Charles, La.

Goldband label promotional discography, original in the possession of Eddie Shuler, Lake Charles, La.

Jin and Swallow labels discographies, originals in the possession of Floyd Soileau, Ville Platte, La.

KLOU radio station (Lake Charles, La.) playlist dated 13 July 1968, original in the possession of Rod Bernard.

La Louisianne label discography, original in the possession of David Rachou, Lafayette, La.

Lanor label discography, original in the possession of Lee Lavergne, Church Point, La.

Letter from Gabriel King to his admirer, 13 September 1956, Ft. Bliss, Tex., to Ville Platte, La., original in the possession of the Evangeline Parish clerk of court's office, Ville Platte, La.

Letter regarding Chick Vidrine and the Southern Club. *Opelousas (La.) Daily World,* 21 July 1991, n.p.

Louisiana House of Representatives Concurrent Resolution No. 187 (recognizing Ville Platte as the "Swamp Pop Capital of the World"), ca. June 1995.

Louisiana Senate Concurrent Resolution No. 16 (recognizing the Acadian Music Heritage Museum in Church Point as the official music heritage museum for Cajun, zydeco and swamp pop), ca. June 1995.

Notarized document filed with the Calcasieu Parish clerk of court's office, Lake Charles, La., regarding the founding of Goldband Records, 18 May 1993, photocopy in the possession of the author.

Obituary of Gabriel King, *Opelousas (La.) Daily World,* 30 December 1988, 14.

Obituary of J. D. Miller, *Lafayette (La.) Daily Advertiser,* 24 March 1996, A-14.

Obituary of Lionel "Chick" Vidrine, *Opelousas (La.) Daily World,* 24 January 1994, 4.

Personal record collection of Butch Landry, Bayou Vista, La.

Personal record collection of Johnnie Allan, Lafayette, La.

Personal record collection of Larry Benicewicz, Baltimore, Md.

Personal record collection of Pat Strazza, New Iberia, La.

Personal record collection of Rod Bernard, Lafayette, La.

Program of the 1984 New Orleans Jazz and Heritage Festival, original in the possession of the author.

Program of the 1995 Louisiana Folklife Festival (Monroe, La.), original in the possession of the author.

Promotional press release about Bobby Charles, original in the possession of Bobby Charles.

Promotional press release about Warren Storm, original in the possession of Warren Storm.

"Swamp Pop Is Clarified." Letter by Johnnie Allan. *Lafayette (La.) Daily Advertiser,* 12 April 1995, D-3.

Swamp pop TV program listings. *Lafayette (La.) Daily Advertiser,* 23 October 1964, 20; 24 September 1965, 8; 22 April 1967, 6; 2 March 1968, 10; 16 November 1968, 10; 24 May 1969, 10; 20 December 1969, 8; 17 January 1970, 10.

Tamm label discography, original in the possession of David Rachou, Lafayette, La.

Various court documents regarding the arrest and trial of Gabriel King, December 1956–March 1957, originals in the possession of the Evangeline Parish clerk of court's office, Ville Platte, La.

Various undated [1959] clippings from *Billboard, Cashbox,* and *Hit Parade,* originals in the possession of Rod Bernard, Lafayette, La.

Warren Storm discography, original in the possession of Larry Benicewicz, Baltimore, Md.

SONG TITLE INDEX

SUBJECT INDEX

ABOUT THE AUTHOR

A Cajun from Lafayette, Louisiana, Shane K. Bernard is the son of swamp pop pioneer Rod Bernard. He obtained his master's degree in history with an emphasis on Cajun and Creole studies from the University of Southwestern Louisiana, where he worked for the Center for Louisiana Studies. He attends Texas A&M University and serves as historian and archivist to the McIlhenny Company of Avery Island, Louisiana, maker of world-famous Tabasco brand products. Shane has contributed to the journals *Louisiana History, Louisiana Folklife* and *The Journal of Folklore Research,* as well as to *Goldmine* magazine; he also writes regularly for the British magazine *Now Dig This* and has annotated several music anthologies on compact disc.